Victim Condemned

To order additional copies, please contact us.
BookSurge, LLC
www.booksurge.com
1-866-308-6235
orders@booksurge.com

Victim Condemned

Patti Lewis

2005

Victim Condemned

ACKNOWLEDGMENTS

Kathy Mazur gave up a large amount of her time to nurse me back to a normal life. She was with me when I threw fits, and she was with me when I was able to laugh. When I began writing this book, she kept all of my records in order. I will never know how she managed to keep my records and me in order, but I am sure she knows how much I appreciate her help.

My doctors, including, but not limited to, Dr. Frank Palmer Sweet, listened when I spoke to them and believed in me. With Kathy's help, they kept me alive.

Thank you to my sons, Jerry and Larry, who have given me more support and encouragement than any mother deserves from her children.

Thank you to my mother, Amelia Poppe, who cried when I cried, laughed when I laughed and listened.

Thank you to James Matuschka, Barry Doss, and Brian Carlson, who believed in my book and encouraged me to publish.

A special thanks needs to go to Marla Wilson, my documentary editor. She forced me to go to the garage, get the proof, and produce all of the dates and times of each event mentioned in my book. She made sure that all of the events I wrote about were documented. In working with Marla, I found a new friend. I truly believe that without Marla's encouragement, I would have abandoned this project.

To Jerry Lewis, Phil Fox, and Mike Mazur,
who each in his own way became a victim condemned.

PREFACE

This is a story of a portion of my journey through life that took me through unbelievable trials and tribulations. The story is based on true events and how those activities were seen through the eyes of a victim who felt condemned by the people chosen to protect and serve.

The names of many of the characters in this book have been changed because in writing my book, it was not my intention to hurt anyone. While facing some very stressful periods, my doctor suggested I write down what was happening to me. I found things easier to understand after I had the opportunity to see the events unfold on the written pages.

Some friends saw my notes and suggested I should share my experiences with others in the form of a book. As I wrote, I kept all of the letters and documents supporting my allegations in several file cabinets in my garage. When all of the file drawers got full, I decided it was time to end the book. Even though the current status of the final litigation is unsure, I will keep updating my website that can be found at victimcondemned.com.

I wrote this book to help people understand how a victim, when unsure of what's happening, what's going to happen next, why their lives are interrupted, and why relief cannot be granted can feel condemned by those chosen to protect and serve.

CHAPTER I

In June 1987, while living in Hobbs, New Mexico, I made my first trip to Arizona in my small single-engine plane—a Cherokee 180. I was determined to pick up my friend Patsy Lee Cline (not the singer Patsy Cline), who had always declined to fly with me in my small plane, but who was also my friend and angel.

It was a beautiful day for flying. The sky was clear and blue. At 11:00 a.m., I prepared to land at the airport in St. Johns, Arizona for fuel. The Unicom operator answered my radio communication with a slight drawl.

"Welcome. The wind direction is perfect for landing here today. The favored runway is two seven. Wind is six five degrees at four knots. The local townspeople are havin' a barbeque and y'all are welcome to join in if ya have the time."

I answered, "5319 Lima. Thank you. We'll be right there."

I landed the plane, placed my order for fuel, and introduced myself to at least 70 friendly people. By the time I grabbed a burger, the serviceman had fueled my plane and washed the bugs off the windows. He briefly visited with me, praising female pilots and their attention to readying a plane for flight. I did my flight check and updated my flight plan, and took off. As I looked back, I saw many hands waving goodbye.

By 2:00 p.m., I reached the Kingman Airport. The Unicom operator offered no welcome, wind direction, nor favored runway. There was no response to my call. My guide for landing came from the nylon sock that was flapping in the breeze. The winds were not high, and the runway was extremely clean. It appeared to be set up for jet traffic. I tied down the plane and went to pay the tie down fees. A large woman at the front desk said, "Just put your fees in the little brown box that is hanging on the front chain link fence."

Despite the absence of any sort of welcome I thought, "Wow! They trust everybody enough to hang a collection box on a fence and expect people to be honest enough to pay the right amount." Following the instructions posted on the fence, I dutifully paid my fees for the two days the plane would be tied down.

Patsy had been widowed for many years. Her magnetic personality often attracted men to her, including a ranch owner named Moran, whom she met in a poker room in Las Vegas where she played cards. It was love at first sight. Her smile and independence had won his attention as well. She had been visiting his ranch, which is about 28 miles from the airport. She called me to take her back to New Mexico where she had property of her own. Moran had arranged for a part-time ranch hand to drive me out to the ranch.

There I was, at a strange airport in a strange town waiting for a stranger to take me out to a strange place. He arrived at the airport on time, thankfully. He didn't smile much, but was nice enough, and it was a quiet trip.

We reached the ranch house, and Patsy introduced me to her new friend, Moran Chef. He showed me the way to a guest room and then asked, "I know you fly planes, but can you ride horses?"

"Yes, I can ride. Do you have a horse that is so well broken a two-year-old child could stay on its back?"

He laughed and admitted that his horses weren't that tame, but most of them were safe to ride. They knew their way around the place and wouldn't let me get lost. The ranch covered some 6,200 acres. "That's a lot of room to get lost in," he explained. "I do it on purpose now and again."

We went out to the stables where Moran introduced me to his friend, Chet, who had come to the ranch planning to ride horses that afternoon. He asked Chet if he would mind giving me a tour of the ranch.

"Of course not," Chet said. "Glad to have the company."

Chet decided I would see more of the ranch if we rode up the west side of the Hualapai mountain range. The horse Moran had chosen for me was a gray mare that turned out to be a well-trained, long legged, quiet horse. On the path, the horse came across two diamondback rattlesnakes traveling together. She bucked high, I held on, and she quickly calmed down while we gave the snakes their right of way.

Perhaps ignoring or being unaware of a warning from a higher being, I shook off the experience and proceeded to have a wonderful time checking out the landscape. It was beautiful—still very hot. There were no trees to speak of on the lower lands, but the ocotillo cacti were in bloom, with their beautiful orange blossoms capping their broomstick branches, whispering to me, "See, there are some pretty things about the desert." The saguaros stood stately as if protecting the smaller plants and wildlife.

Continuing up the side of the rocky, steep mountain, the air began to cool down as we reached the top. I began to see a few tall, stately pine trees. Needing to rest my sore legs and rear end that hadn't been on a horse in ages, I sat down on a log for a break.

Sitting there in the cool shelter of the trees was peaceful. We tied the horses to a tree, recouped our strength, and went for a walk. The view was endless. Chet took me to a narrow path that led around to the west side of the large mountain. I found myself on a steep cliff looking a long way down onto the desert. The wall of the cliff contained beautiful, pale green, hexagonal prism formations. They were beryl crystals, which looked like eyes watching the world from their private domain. There were so many of them, I became curious. Why, with all the electronic manufacturing and progress, had no one from the high tech industry mined them and made a bundle of money? Considering their location and the desert heat, mining them might not have been economically feasible. Imagining the destruction the mining would cause to that beautiful mountain, it was nice to see that it had remained intact.

I wasn't comfortable on that narrow ledge looking at crystals, so I suggested we get back on our horses and move along. When we reached the flat lands and my borrowed horse realized she was going home, she bolted back to the ranch with me holding on for dear life. I am petite, just shy of 5 ft. 3 in. tall, and I weigh 113 pounds fully clothed. Moran's saddle was the smallest one he owned, but it was still way too big for me, and they couldn't get the stirrups up short enough for them to be of any use. Bouncing up and down on my sore butt, I finally approached the ranch house. The ranch hands watched apprehensively as I clung desperately to the horse. But I was able to hang on and get home alive. That deserved some respect!

Moran Chef was a tall, thin, elderly man who wore a pair of eyeglasses held together by a piece of electrical tape. He was a particularly gracious host after my wild ride. He did not say a word; he just handed me a stiff drink.

After tending to the horses in the stifling heat, we all disappeared into the cool ranch house. I talked about the excursion to the mountain and about the crystals. I asked Moran if he knew why the crystals had not been mined. He explained that the ranch house had at one time been a stage stop and that the Santa Fe Railroad owned the house and every other section of land for miles. The remaining sections belonged to the Bureau of Land Management or the State of Arizona. He had leases with all three entities, but the actual privately owned land consisted of only 90 acres.

Moran laughed as he explained to me, "Getting those three together to approve of such a mining operation has proven to be an impossible task. They just don't speak the same language."

Hearing Moran talk about the Santa Fe Railroad brought back memories for me. My grandfather, H. R. Lake, had worked for the Santa Fe Railroad most of his life. I told Moran about how Grandpa Lake had traveled to Kingman after the war in 1946. Many of the government's surplus Douglas C-47 transport planes—referred to by the railroad personnel as "Skytrains"—were dry docked at the Kingman airport. A new division of the Santa Fe Railroad had been formed, named Santa Fe Skyways, Inc, with Grandpa Lake as the appointed president. Joined by a man named George Lupton Jr., they planned to start a new unheard-of venture for the railroad. Grandpa Lake and Mr. Lupton came to Kingman, purchased two of the C-47s, transported them to California, and converted them into refrigerated air cars. For a little while, the railroad was using the planes to transport all sorts of flowers, fresh fruits, vegetables, and swordfish from California to Chicago to be served in the Fred Harvey restaurants that serviced the trains.

It was a great money-making venture for the railroad until the U.S. Civil Aeronautics Board refused them a required common carrier permit in 1948, claiming the venture would constitute a monopoly. Grandpa's refrigeration designs were subsequently sold to TWA, and the Santa Fe Railroad returned to its position as a surface carrier.

Thinking of business possibilities in the area, I noticed that the construction industry was growing. Chet knew the railroad had mining operations in the county. With my connections to the railroad, I might be able to purchase decorative rock for landscaping projects. He suggested if we could get a lease on the mining pit, we could make good money landscaping. He assured me he would help. He had some heavy equipment to contribute to the venture.

That sounded like a great business opportunity. The growth rate was spectacular. I checked a local newspaper to get a sense of the town and its people. The papers had only some mention of theft, drug related arrests, and the same problems we had faced in New Mexico. Most everything printed in the paper implied a relatively friendly environment. There were people helping people, pictures of children playing safely in a new park, and recaps of town meetings.

Falling in love with Arizona had been easy. I went back to New Mexico, taking the newspapers with me. After showing the articles to my husband Jerry, I told him about my ideas for a new business venture and asked him if he would consider moving to Kingman Arizona.

Jerry stood about 6 ft. 2 in. tall, and because he was the tallest and oldest Jerry in our house (our son was also named Jerry), our family and friends always referred to him as "Big Jerry." In addition to our son Jerry, we had another son, Larry. By 1987, both were in the United States Air Force and had families of their own.

Jerry and I had been looking for a place to relocate since 1985, and I believed the area I found in Arizona would fit the bill nicely. Fishing and recreation spots could be found within a few miles of the town. The railroad had an abandoned mining pit that had produced ballast for the tracks. The pit was mined out, but the railroad had left large piles of processed rock that were too small for their intended use. The rock was pretty and hard, and I knew it would make good decorative landscaping material. It was worth a try to bridge the communication gaps with the railroad and acquire the decorative rock necessary to start a new landscaping business.

Jerry began to be discontented with his work as a lawyer in 1980. Our two sons were still in high school, and we were also caring for foster children. We both worked hard at our jobs, but the money we earned was spent on raising all the children. "I need to work at an honorable job," he said. "I hate being a lawyer. All the politics are destroying the judicial system."

"Together, we can make anything happen that we want to, Jerry. But tell me, you love the law and all that it stands for in this country. You have been a good attorney. Are you looking for a change at your age? How drastic? What has changed your mind?"

"Well, now that's an honest question that deserves an answer. All those jokes about lawyers hold too much truth today. I've been in court these past few days against a young lawyer who obviously doesn't believe he has any obligation to present only the truth to the court. He has me stumped. The judge is an alumnus of his fraternity, and I don't think the judge hears anything I present. When I went to law school, the courts handled cases differently. Legal fees were high, but at least a man could afford decent representation. The new lawyers are swamping the courts with unnecessary paper and charging clients for crap. How greedy can a man get?"

"I'll look around and see if we can find a business you feel is honorable. We'll have to work our asses off if we intend to stay alive financially, but I'm game if you are."

By August 1987, Jerry returned to Kingman with me. He liked what he could see, but he warned me, "When Route 66 was the highway of choice, my father stopped here for coffee and fuel, and when he got 20 miles out of town, the radiator overheated. Come to find out, the radiator hose had been cut. After paying an exorbitant fee to get the car towed to the repair shop, the shop owner had a whole room full of hoses of different sizes hanging from the ceiling. He whacked off the length of hose my pop needed, wired it in place, and charged Pop 60 bucks. That was big money in those days. No matter how bad we had to pee, he would never stop there again."

My father had the same problem when we went to Long Beach, California to see grandpa. He too, would not stop there. It didn't matter how bad we needed to pee either. He would tell us he knew of a big cactus down the road that we could go behind.

Chet proved very knowledgeable about the area. He showed Jerry and me a large piece of land located in the middle of the town that belonged to the railroad. It had once served as a feldspar mill, but the mill had closed down years before, and the owners had left quite a mess. The property needed a lot of cleanup, but the people working for the railroad had refused to respond to the city's correspondence.

Old tanks, tires, large pieces of useless abandoned equipment, wood, and various metals were strung all over the property. Not only was it an eyesore, it was very dangerous. The rusted tanks were about 8 ft. in diameter and 20 ft. high. They had been laid down on their sides, and the neighborhood children were using them as skateboard runs. The City had initiated legal proceedings against the railroad in an effort to force them to clean up the property. The work was going to be very expensive, but Chet said, "Don't worry. I'll help ya clean it up."

In the fall of 1988, we entered into a partnership. Chet was to help us communicate with the city, and we were to communicate with the railroad.

Because he had no money, Chet would supply the labor and some of his old equipment to clear the area, and Jerry would handle the legal matters. It was my job to see that somehow the bills were paid.

Jerry maintained his law practice in New Mexico. He worked many hours getting all the venture's legal problems solved. When his presence was required in Arizona or Wichita, Kansas where his parents were, I would get him in the plane and take him where he needed to be, when he needed to be there.

After successfully negotiating to halt the City's legal action in October 1988, we were able to lease the land from the railroad. Our lease stated that we were given ownership of everything on the land, but not the land itself. It was our intention to clean up the property and sell what we could to pay the expenses incurred while clearing the land.

As we began the project, some of the townspeople would wait until we had gone to dinner, then come steal anything they thought they could use. When we reported the thefts to the police and presented our lease showing we owned everything on the property, they insisted they could do nothing because the railroad owned the land. Only the railroad could file a police report.

The representatives of the railroad explained to me it was my lease, and they had no legal right to file a complaint with the police. The items stolen were transferred to me in the lease. A representative from the railroad made a call to the police and miraculously the thefts and trespassing stopped. We had lost many articles that were to fund our cleanup efforts, but arrests were never made.

Jerry had to stay in New Mexico most of the time because of his office obligations. He liked the idea that he might be able to drive a dump truck in the near future, but he still had unfinished work to do. As a Christmas present, he bought me an old used dump truck.

We decided I would operate the new landscaping business. When the business was running well enough to support us, he would join me in the venture. Jerry was still not convinced that the reputation the area had built for itself as a yellow (soured) spot on the map should be ignored.

As with all states, the laws in Arizona are somewhat different from those in New Mexico. The strict requirements for owning a business are sometimes hard to meet. Jerry studied Arizona laws and interpreted them for us. By early 1989, we managed to get past most of the barriers, and with the help of the railroad, my little business seemed to be doing fairly well. Eventually, in November 1991, under protests made by Chet, we bought out his share of the landscaping portion of the company because Chet and I could not agree on how the business should grow.

One morning in July 1989, Patsy Cline called me. Her voice was cracking, and she had been crying. She said, "I need your help. That damn rancher Moran is stealing my cattle and auctioning them off. Can you or Big Jerry help me?"

We moved fast, and Jerry made arrangements with the Department of Agriculture to be sure that any checks written by the auction companies for the sale of Patsy's cattle were sent directly to Patsy. She got the greater portion of her invested funds back, but the losses she incurred were not recovered. The attitude expressed by the sheriff's officer was "You should have known better." No investigations or arrests were ever made. Patsy had fallen victim to fraud. The authorities would do no more. It was now only a civil issue.

About six months later, the Farmers Home Mortgage foreclosed on the 90 acres that constituted the "ranch." I went to the auction of that land. Present at the auction was a representative from the railroad and the Bureau of Land Management. By chance, I sat down next to a cowboy who was interested in bidding on the property.

When the property's number was called and all questions from the public were to be answered, I spoke up and asked the Bureau of Land Management representative if he had just planted the endangered desert tortoise in the same location of the main water supply that a rancher would need for his cattle. He admitted that he placed the tortoise in that section because the land there was more acceptable for habitat building by the tortoise.

"Well, if I bid this sale, can my cattle still use that watering hole?" I asked.

"No. No cattle can use that section," he admitted.

The ranch did not sell at that auction.

The railroad representative did not know that the Bureau of Land Management had planted that tortoise at the watering hole, and he didn't look like a happy man. The railroad had been leasing every other section of the land to the rancher, and a "no sale" of the ranch meant a "no lease" of railroad land or The Bureau of Land Management land.

There was a lot to learn in a short time if the landscaping company was to succeed. The biggest problem I faced was qualified and reliable labor. No one wanted to work for his or her paycheck. It seemed that about 90 percent of the applicants seeking work as laborers had a history of drug abuse, and applicants were afraid of our random drug testing policy. It was hard to believe so much drug activity was going on in such a small town. It appeared the county had more than its share of drug problems.

I had been commuting back and forth from New Mexico to Arizona in my Cherokee. During my absences, there was no one to supervise the business. One day, in the spring of 1991, a man named Michael Garloni came into my office and said he was also from New Mexico. He was looking for employment. An associate of ours from my hometown had sent him to me hoping I would give him work and a new chance at life. His past was shaky. He had been in prison, but had done his time. He passed the drug screening. I hired him. My company was in desperate need of laborers.

With the cooperation of the local parole officers, I decided to give the man an opportunity to prove he could do the job. Persons hired on probation were supposed to be given regular drug tests through that department to prevent my exposure to "drugged up" labor. It seemed a good safety factor. With the officer constantly calling and checking on Michael and me, I had state-paid assistance.

Michael Garloni worked hard for quite awhile. He spent many hours of his off time working on an old International Scout I had parked out near the tool shed. He kept insisting that the old vehicle did not run right, but he seemed convinced he could repair everything on it. He would take a part off, wipe it with an old rag, inspect it, lay it down, come into the office, and wash his hands. He would then go back out, pick up the same part, and wipe it off again. Shortly, he would be back in the office to wash his hands again. I remember thinking, "He sure worries about keeping his hands clean."

On a Sunday in November, Michael left the yard for the day, and I needed a welding part. I could not find it. As I searched the tool shed, I noticed some of my equipment and tools were missing from their designated places on the shelves. After checking the inventory thoroughly, I discovered that over $4,000 worth of tools and equipment was missing from the work shed.

When questioned, Michael freely admitted he had taken the items and traded them for drugs. He was a drug addict, and he believed he would always be hooked on drugs.

"Your encouragement helped me for a long time, but I can't win," he said.

"Didn't your time in the slammer teach you anything?" I asked.

"The day I was released, I was so high I had to be led down the sidewalk," he replied. "This town is ripe."

Hoping I would be able to retrieve my belongings, he took me to the location where he had bought the drugs. It was an old, brown mobile home in a run down area called "Bird Land". All the streets in the area were named after birds, such as Lark, Robin, and Dove. The residences in the area were mostly mobile homes, and many of them were in desperate need of repair. Michael Garloni told me if I wanted my things back, the woman he dealt with might sell them back to me. He thanked me for giving him a chance to get straight, got out of the truck, and walked away.

I went back to the office and called the police. After signing a complaint, I told the responding officer that Michael Garloni had taken the items. I showed the officer Michael's employment records. I explained to him where the drug deals had taken place. He was aware of drug dealing on the property I indicated. He told me never to go there again because the area was not safe. "The lady is very unstable," he said.

While the investigating officer was in my office, the woman called. She told me Michael Garloni had "given" her my watch, and he had later explained to her how important the watch was to me. He had asked her to return it to me. She offered to sell me my watch if I wouldn't call the police. I motioned to the officer to pick up the extension phone, and he listened as the woman made me the offer. She wanted $200 for the return of my own property.

Jerry had given me that watch as a gift on our 15th anniversary. It was white gold, and the band contained 14 diamonds. It was flashy, and I wore it when I was going somewhere special. I had not even noticed it was missing. I always hid it. The officer and I went to my hiding place, and sure enough, the jewel box was there, but it was empty. He told me to wait and that perhaps the woman would call again and I could get her to bring me the watch. He said if that happened, I was to call him immediately, and I was not to pay her any money.

I didn't know what I would do if she called again. At least the officer had heard most of her conversation. He knew that she had my watch. He knew how she got it. She probably bought the rest of my equipment.

I showed the officer the tool shed and explained the missing items. We talked about the old Scout, and I told him that I thought Michael was trying to fix it. I explained to the officer that it seemed strange the way Michael was always washing his hands. He explained to me that when a person is under the influence of drugs, they see things on their hands or clothes that are not there. From that day on, if an employee washed their hands more than twice a day I became suspicious.

After the officer left the plant with a list of the missing equipment, I never saw him again.

Michael Garloni hung around in the Lewis Kingman Park across the street from my plant. When I saw him there, I called for the officer who had initially taken my information. He was not on duty. I explained to the secretary that I had seen Michael in the park. She said the reports showed that the police report was given to the county attorney and that an arrest warrant had not yet been issued. She instructed me to continue to call the office if I saw Michael again. Every time I called, the county attorney had still issued no warrant. After three days or so, I learned that Michael Garloni had left town. One of my employees said he had boarded a bus for New Mexico. I called Jerry and told him what had happened. He drove to Kingman immediately. He was visibly upset and suggested we close the company and return together to New Mexico. He wanted me to stay in New Mexico until he could come back to Arizona and be with me full time. He believed he could finish all his work in less than two years.

I argued that I had worked hard to build my landscaping business. It did not seem prudent to shut down and leave. There were new homeowners out there waiting for me to landscape their yards. There were contracts to complete and leaving would place my contractor's license in jeopardy.

Jerry handed me the handgun he had bought me years earlier. He said he had brought it to me because I might need it. I was to keep it close at hand for a while. He had spent many hours teaching me to use it properly.

I thanked Jerry for bringing the gun and assured him I would be fine. We put the gun in a closet in a locked cabinet. I still failed to understand how putting a gun in a locked cabinet was going to help me if it was needed in a hurry, but I followed his orders like a good wife. In my heart, I knew the gun would stay locked up.

In an effort to assure Jerry that I did not have to be alone and I would be all right while waiting for him, I contacted a friend, Robin Rue. She was a sweet person—about 35 years old—and she had the most beautiful head of hair I had ever seen. It was medium brown with red highlights, very full, and it had the natural wave every woman needs if they live in hot, dry country. Her heart was always open, and she was always getting into trouble over it. It seemed there was very little she wouldn't give to anyone who asked, and she seldom had anything left for herself. We thought it would be safer to live in numbers, so she moved into the night watchman's quarters with me. She had been living out in the desert with a man named Phil Fox. The mobile home we would share was a huge step up from the living conditions Phil provided. And I felt much safer having her company. As the weather began to turn cold in January 1992, Phil started showing up to visit Robin. Soon he began helping me "on a temporary basis" with my work in the landscaping department. Phil was extremely talented. He was an artist, and his landscape drawings were very detailed and accurate. He loved the projects I designed, and his landscaping talents became very popular. Our jobs were coming in so fast, we had trouble keeping up with the demand. What began as "temporary" employment turned out to be ten hours a day, six days a week, for four years.

Because Phil was working such long hours, Robin began to feel useless and abandoned. She and Phil began arguing constantly. I listened to Robin's complaints. She seemed dissatisfied with the direction her life was going. She wanted more. She wanted to be a nurse and was convinced she should go back to Colorado to fulfill her dreams. She made plans to live with her sister and go to nursing school. She did have a natural talent for taking care of people. I gave her enough money to hold her over for a while, and she moved to Colorado.

Next month, in February, a call came in from the Citizens Utility Company. They were trying to verify my presence in Texas. After explaining to the caller that I had not been in Texas for over a year, he said someone was using my calling card number in Dallas. "Do you have your card?" he asked.

The card was in my wallet so I read the numbers off to the man. He said, "Please don't use the card again. The numbers you have given me are correct and a thief is using them. I will issue you a new card today and you should receive it tomorrow. When you get your next phone bill, just take it to the local office, and deny the charges you have not made. They will refigure your bill. As the victim, we may need to secure an affidavit from you."

When the bill arrived, it was one long stream of connected computer pages; they hadn't even taken the pages apart. It was over 40 feet long! The charges totaled into the thousands of dollars. There were many calls to other countries and to New Mexico. Looking them over, I knew immediately who made those calls. It had to be my ex-employee Michael Garloni.

I called the Dallas Police Department and spoke with a detective. After telling him all about the theft that had taken place at my plant and the size of my phone bill, I asked if he could find out if Michael Garloni had stolen my telephone card number and made the calls. He asked me to copy some of the pages and fax them to him. Many of the calls originated from the same pay phone. I gave him that number and Michael Garloni's description. Michael would be easy to spot. He was so tall that he had to duck his head to clear a doorway and so skinny that he could walk between the pickets in a fence.

Within three days, I received a call from the same detective. They had located the caller, and they were holding him for questioning. The detective was unable to find a warrant issued by Mohave County for Michael Garloni on the burglary charge that I had mentioned. He asked me to go to the county attorney's office and tell them that Michael Garloni was in custody in Dallas. If the county attorney would issue a warrant, the Dallas police would secure his arrest. Time was of the essence because they could not hold him long. The detective confirmed Michael Garloni's social security number and description taken from my employment file, and we were sure it was the same person. The detective gave me his name and telephone number. He instructed me to give both to the county attorney.

Before I went to the county attorney's office, I called Jerry to let him know what had happened. He said that it was a good break for us and perhaps we would get some victim's restitution money. We might eventually replace some of the things that were missing, particularly the watch. I was excited. Not knowing previously about victim's rights and restitution, it was a well-accepted surprise. I didn't waste any time getting down to the county attorney's office to introduce myself. Being taken in to meet the county attorney himself was rather frightening. I explained to him about having hired Michael Garloni in my landscaping business, the thefts, the drug dealing, and the police report I had filed. I also reiterated what the Dallas Police Department wanted me to do to take this guy off the streets.

The excitement left me right away. The county attorney explained to me that the County would not issue a warrant for Michael Garloni. Extradition would be too expensive. The County would have to pick him up in Texas and return him to Arizona. Then they would have to prosecute him and house him in jail. He said that the County maintained a policy that if no bodily harm had been done in the commission of the crime, they would not pursue extradition! (What I was hearing was that they would wait and see if someone got killed before they would do their job.) The county attorney explained to me that it costs over $42,000 a year to house a prisoner in Arizona. The State does not like having to spend the money. He assured me that if Michael Garloni should enter Arizona, there would be a standing warrant for his arrest. "If he comes back into this state, we will arrest him," he said.

"How are you going to arrest him if you haven't even issued a warrant? What about my rights as a victim?" I asked

"You took a certain amount of risk when you hired the man. Restitution will be awarded if he should come back into the state and be tried," he said. He also explained I could not file charges for the telephone bill because the phone company had to do that.

I offered to take a deputy sheriff and go get Michael in my plane and bring him back. That offer was not only laughed at but also refused. End of story...

I left that office madder than hell. There was no need to give that county attorney the Dallas detective's name and number. It was doubtful that he would spend the money to make the call.

I went back to my office, called New Mexico, and vented my frustrations to Jerry. I felt so naive. Jerry had never placed a monetary value on the safety of our family. If money had to be spent to protect the family, Jerry spent it. The amount stolen from me was enough to charge a felony. The officers knew exactly who had stolen and sold my property. Because of my business, I was paying very high taxes to the City and the County. One would think that I had paid for protection. How many more unsuspecting citizens would become victims of this man?

When I questioned the laws or the judicial system, Jerry would patiently explain the processes to me. The law was his livelihood. He had always believed that the United State's legal system was well-designed and the best in the world. He was beginning to question his position.

"What kind of an attorney would tell you things like that?" Jerry said. "There has to be more to the story than that. Sure money and costs are relevant, but how many victims would we have in this country if we just let all the crooks move on to another state? I'm certainly not comfortable with that attorney's explanation. I can't believe that he is ignorant enough to think that we don't know the federal government supplies the prison system with all sorts of grants so that these issues don't surface."

"Are you telling me the federal government pays the states to house these prisoners?" I asked.

"Well it's not that easy. The State gets funding from the federal government through federal grants for their correctional system and the counties get funding to prosecute criminals," he said. "The grants are intended to prevent this sort of thing from happening. Prisoners produce a lot of money (millions of dollars) for the prisons in the labor they provide. The cost per inmate is more like $20K not $42K as the county attorney claims."

"Then why doesn't the Dallas detective arrest Michael for stealing my phone card?"

"Perhaps his hands are tied by state law. You see, it is not where a crime is committed that counts, it is where the crime is felt. You are the victim and you are in Arizona. The offense committed is not worthy of an FBI investigation at this point."

Michael Garloni was an admitted drug addict and he was going to be doing damage to people all over the United States. The county attorney had it in his power to stop Michael's criminal acts, and he chose to ignore a victim's rights in favor of the money it would save "his" state, county, and taxpayers. Somehow, my mind and heart could not relate to his logic.

Jerry immediately called the Dallas detective and explained Arizona's monetary concerns and the prosecutor's decision to let Michael Garloni go. "I don't know what the man was thinking when he spoke to my wife. She is a victim, and he as much as told her to get lost. I had encouraged her to go see him, and now I am sorry I did."

The detective was angered by the county attorney's unwillingness to enforce the laws, but those same laws forced him to let Michael loose. He told Jerry, "Many prosecutors throughout the United States are taking the same position. With all the new mandatory sentencing laws, the prison population has grown out of sight. The new victim's rights movement has become a joke. The movement has created extra work for prosecutors and their staff. They just don't seem to have time to take these crooks to court, and no place to put them if they do convict them."

CHAPTER 2

Several months went by without incident, but by October Michael Garloni managed to enter our lives again. Jerry and I had been taking turns going back and forth from Arizona to New Mexico. It was Jerry's turn to come to Arizona, and I went to Las Vegas to pick him up at McCarran Airport.

While we were traveling back to Kingman, Jerry said, "Michael returned to Hobbs and was arrested for stealing some guns from a local auctioneer. He had the audacity to call me from jail wanting me to get him out. I refused, and I was a bit rude because I laughed while I was talking to him. I would have told him to go to hell, but they monitor those calls. Could you imagine me defending him?"

I laughed. "What an ass," I said. "First time, shame on you, second time..."

Michael got angry when Jerry denied him. He told Jerry, "If you don't get me out, I will get out anyway and I will pay you and your little wife a visit."

Two weeks later, Jerry felt sure Michael had been released. Someone had broken into our home in New Mexico while Jerry was gone. The intruder stole a small television, a gun, and a VCR out of the master bedroom. With all the expensive items in the house left untouched, Jerry felt that Michael was sending him a warning. "It is an awful feeling, Patti. My privacy has been violated," he said.

"I know that feeling. It came to me when I opened the cabinet and found my watch missing," I replied.

"Watch your back. If you see Michael, go directly to the police. Ask the police to explain to the county attorney that it is time the son of a bitch does the job he should have done a long time ago. Tell him to issue the damn warrant." Jerry was angry. The more we talked about the situation, the more emotional he got. Jerry was generally a very quiet, easy-going sort, but that day I was seeing a side of him I had not witnessed in all the years we had been married.

Jerry chose to spend the entire four days he had allotted to help me, gambling in Laughlin, Nevada instead. The stress was getting to him. His appearance was changing. He was getting too heavy and he did not look healthy. He ordered a great big juicy hamburger, and I objected. He said, "Look the other way. You are going to have to live your life prepared to bury me. And in the meantime, I like hot dogs and hamburgers, and I intend to eat them. My mom and dad ate only what the doctor ordered. They hated the food, and they died very young anyway. It doesn't matter what a man eats. Such restrictions do not guarantee longevity, and I am not going to live that way. I want to enjoy what life I have left, and you should love me while I am enjoying my life. Don't nag me about my diet."

"I do love you, Jerry, but I'm not around every day to take care of you. I'm supposed to do that, you know. It's my job."

"And you do it well enough," he said.

We did not get the necessary work accomplished at the plant, but we did have a wonderful time. On Tuesday, Jerry went back to New Mexico with a nice chunk of the casino's money. He was happy about that. It did not happen often.

A year later, on Friday, October 22, 1993, I received a call from the nurse in our doctor's office in New Mexico. She suggested I should come right away. Jerry had a heart attack in the doctor's office. They had transported him to the Lovington Hospital.

My hands were shaking and my mind was spinning. I called a truck driver to drive me to the airport in Las Vegas. The last plane to Albuquerque was to leave in 1 hour and 45 minutes. The trip was 110 miles. When we reached the gate at the airport, I walked right onto the plane, and within a minute or two, the plane took off.

When the plane landed in Albuquerque, my family was there to meet me. There were no seats available on the last plane to Lea County, New Mexico. I tried to buy a seat from the other passengers, offering a price that was higher than the cost of five tickets. On the loud speaker, the ticket agent explained my emergency to the passengers. Of the 29 passengers, not one would sell me a ticket for any amount. Though the event was disheartening, it proved to be a blessing.

My dad had stopped at a pay phone and called the hospital in Lea County. He spoke with the doctor attending Jerry and learned that the doctor had transferred him by helicopter to Lubbock, Texas.

I wondered if there was divine intervention that prevented me from traveling to Lea County, New Mexico when I needed to be in Lubbock, Texas or just 29 selfish assholes all on one plane.

My father explained to me that Jerry was in the best of hands and that I would not be able to see him until his doctor arrived on the next shift. He suggested we should proceed by car to Lubbock. He assured me we could get there before the doctor came back to work. There were no flights to Texas until the next day, so we got into my sister Cathy's car and drove. Cathy has no fear of speeding. She managed to get us to Lubbock by four o'clock the next morning.

The nurse on duty told us to wait. "Please do not go into his room as they are working on him right now, and you might be in the way."

A doctor appeared and told me my husband was having another heart attack and that I would have to wait while he did his work. He quickly left.

By that time, most of our family members and many of Jerry's close friends had arrived at the hospital. The family room was getting crowded, and I needed a private moment with the physician, so I stayed in the hall in front of Jerry's room. I could hear snores, and after 20 years of sleeping next to that noise, I knew whose snores they were. I just knew that everything would be okay. No one snored like Jerry.

The cardiologist appeared and was visibly upset. "I hate this part of my job more than anything I am called to do. Would you like to sit down?"

"No thank you," I said. "I've been sitting for hours."

"Then let's move over here where it is more private," he said. We moved down the hall a short way. "In my opinion, your husband has passed, he said." He was near tears while he tried to explain to me that Jerry had not only one but actually four heart attacks and that the second attack was fatal. His body had experienced two additional attacks that he knew nothing about. Jerry's brain had been deprived of oxygen much too long to ever be able to function in any capacity again. He said he could easily repair Jerry's heart because the problem was in the lower portion of his heart, but his mind would not be strong enough to help with the healing process.

My first reaction to the cardiologist's report was inner panic, then disbelief. Jerry couldn't be dead! I could hear his snoring.

The doctor led me into Jerry's hospital room. Jerry was lying there with his arms strapped to each side of the bed. His right arm was swollen and appeared to be broken. His feet were uncovered, and he had that life support equipment he always dreaded sticking down his throat. The doctor approached the right side of Jerry's bed and opened one of his eyes. He put a light up to Jerry's eye and tried to get Jerry to focus on the light. Nothing happened. He started talking to Jerry but was receiving no response of any kind. I suggested the doctor move to the other side of the bed. All his life, Jerry had been deaf in his left ear, and he could not hear anything coming from the direction the doctor was standing.

I remembered Jerry laughing about it when he was drafted. The local doctor had told the draft board that Jerry was deaf in his left ear. They didn't believe the doctor so they called in two nice looking young girls. Each girl was given a line to simultaneously whisper to Jerry in his ear. Because Jerry was able to repeat exactly what the girl speaking in his right ear had said and knew nothing of the other girl's conversation that went into his left ear, they excused him from the draft.

The doctor did as I suggested, but it made no difference.

The doctor shook his head and quietly began to leave the room. He said, "I'll allow you some time alone with your husband."

It seemed as if I had invaded someone else's dream. This couldn't be happening. The dimly lit room resounded with the metallic intake and whooshing exhaust sounds of the ventilator that was pumping air in and out of Jerry's lungs. My best friend and lover lay motionless upon his back, bare feet protruding from the white linen sheets. Carefully, I touched Jerry's left foot. It was unnaturally cold and unyielding. His hands were unnaturally strapped to the sides of his bed. They were cold and unable to respond to my touch. I found my mind reeling backward in time, and I briefly found comfort in the past. I found myself walking, talking, fishing, gambling, and laughing in the rain with a man who had lived the past 20 years devoted to and caring for me. Then the whooshing ventilator sound returned me to the grasp of reality.

I looked into Jerry's face. "I love you," I whispered. Of course there was no audible reply, but Jerry's lips trembled as though he was trying to speak. I took a small blanket and covered his feet. I got as close to the only ear Jerry could hear in, and, as the equipment would allow, I tried to talk to him. I found it hard to speak. My throat choked up, and all the words I wanted to say were held back by my emotions and fears. I told Jerry I loved him again, and his lips moved as if to respond. "Jerry, open your eyes," I ordered.

His eyes snapped open, but they were transfixed, glassy, and staring, and the loud, horrible snoring went on, prompted by the whooshing ventilator, pumping, pumping, and pumping.

Much confusion and an unbearable sadness swelled up inside me. "Close your eyes, Jerry," I whispered, knowing the man I loved more than life itself slept a sleep near death. Jerry's eyelids closed obediently.

I quietly went out into the hall and got the male nurse. I didn't want the man to think I was nuts, but I wanted to show him why I thought Jerry was trying to respond to my words. The nurse explained that often a wife or loved one would get a small response from a patient when no one else could. He explained that Jerry's mind was used to hearing my words and that the response to me had been rather automatic for 20 years. The nurse continued to examine and talk to Jerry for a few minutes to see if perhaps he had missed something. Jerry could not perform the slightest task. He could not move his fingers, feet, legs, or toes on command. He would not open his eyes for the nurse. The man uncovered Jerry's feet, explaining that he needed to see the color of his feet to help monitor Jerry's circulation. Once life support has been initiated, Texas law requires hospitals to maintain the support for 48 hours.

Somehow I felt, with Jerry's last spark of life, he had recognized I was there. I did not know why this was happening, but I had a decision to make. It was the hardest decision of my life. I had made a promise to Jerry. I could hear his words over and over in my mind as if he were in my head talking to me. "If my condition is ever declared terminal, don't make my children suffer. Don't make me live as a vegetable. If I cannot be assured a normal, full life, please love me enough to let me go."

I explained to the doctor that Jerry had prepared a living will stating his wishes if such a situation should develop. I called his law office in New Mexico, and the Will and Power of Attorney were rushed to me. At the doctor's direction, I gave them to the hospital administrator, and I signed papers for the hospital's release that stated if Jerry should have another attack, his body would not be resuscitated. My hands shook as I signed the hospital's DNR (Do Not Resuscitate) papers. It was Jerry's will. It was my duty to honor his last command. The world fell on my shoulders.

The doctors, at my pleading, were kind enough to tell everyone concerned about Jerry's written will and what he wanted. He explained that Jerry's living will clearly stated what must be done. All the doctors agreed they would continue Jerry's medication and his life support, as required by Texas laws, but if his heart gave way again, they would honor his will and let him go. Because I had been without rest for almost three days, the doctors insisted that my parents take me to a motel to rest.

One of Jerry's two sisters asked the doctor, "If it were your father, what would you do?"

Very bluntly, he stated, "I would have never allowed my father to be moved to Texas from New Mexico. He was dead when they moved him. He should have been declared dead in the state he loved so much."

Our youngest son, Larry, agreed to stay with Jerry until I was able to return. I gave him his instructions. He was to be strong. He was to stay with his dad and keep the DNR order in effect at all times. If there were any changes in Jerry's condition, he was to call me immediately.

Larry called me at the motel. "Mom, help. What do I do? The nurse is asking me if I still want them to keep the DNR on Dad's chart. He's dying, Mom."

"Larry, do as your father ordered, please."

Larry did exactly as I instructed. When the fifth heart attack hit Jerry's body, Larry called me again. I explained to him God was calling, and Jerry had a duty to answer his call. Jerry was allowed to die with the dignity he cherished on October 24, 1993.

I knew in my heart that my best friend and lover was moving on to a better place, and his painful days were over. The bitterness stage of my mourning began immediately. I found myself blaming Jerry for his own death. I couldn't understand why he ignored his body's signs. I knew in my heart he felt death coming. I reflected back to our conversation at the casino, just four days prior to his first attack. I knew he told me to prepare to bury him, but he failed to say "this week." I was not prepared and furthermore, I was only 48 years old. That is too young to be a widow. The pain I was suffering would remain with me for a long time.

While I was making all the arrangements for Jerry's body to be transferred to New Mexico, Larry drove ahead of us to our home. My son had been through so much, and I worried that he was traveling alone. He assured me he was quite capable of making the trip, but his hands were sweating and shaking. That is not a good sign. His plans were to see that the house was made ready for all the family and friends. Since Jerry had been home alone, Larry knew there would be dishes to wash and a house to clean.

Jerry's doctor told me to wait for the eye bank, and then the coroner would bring the body home. I thought it was very strange that only the eye bank responded to Jerry's donations. He had written documents stating that the hospital could acquire any organ in his body that was needed to enhance the life of another individual. My signed acknowledgment and acceptance of his wishes was required by the hospital. I was concerned. Jerry had a damaged heart, but prior to the first heart attack, he also had a good liver and kidneys. When I approved the donations, his body was still on life support. The eye bank immediately contacted me: "We will be placing a bag of ice over Jerry's eyes. Please do not remove it. We must keep them cold, so we can operate."

When I went into the room to see Jerry's body, the sight of the ice pack on his face did not disturb me. I knew it was there for the right reason. Two people were the beneficiaries of Jerry's eyes. Both recipients later wrote and thanked me for Jerry's contribution that allowed them a new lease on life.

I could not believe that with the long waiting lists, none of the other organs were needed! No one ever bothered to explain the medical details to me. I carried questions in my heart about this issue for 13 years. Then I met a nurse who worked in a hospice unit. She explained donor requirements to me thoroughly. The body has to be kept alive, monitored in an ICU until a receiver is found. It can be very costly. Jerry's living will and the DNR order prohibited the hospital from keeping his body alive. If the body is not kept alive, the organs cannot be saved and re-used.

After Jerry's death, I immediately felt bitter, angry, and then neglected, all in the course of a few hours. After the medical staff made all the decisions and gave me my instructions, the rest of my family took me home.

When we arrived at the house that day around 4:30 p.m., I found guns in several places—seemingly everywhere. All of them were loaded with a bullet in the chamber and ready to fire. In our bedroom, I found a pistol under the pillow on my bed. It too was loaded and ready to fire. A second gun was found under the bed. After the burglary, Jerry had sent his favorite guns to Larry's house for safekeeping. "Where and why did he acquire all these guns?" I wondered. Something had obviously gone wrong. Something or someone had scared Jerry so much he felt the need to be prepared. With all my family and friends coming, I had to find out what had been going on in my own home.

A friend of Jerry's, a district judge, came to the house. He had been on vacation when his wife informed him of Jerry's passing. He flew to Hobbs immediately. When he came to the house, I explained to him that the funeral would be soon, but I could not set a definite date because the Red Cross was sending our son Jerry home from Germany on the way home from the Gulf—he was in Desert Storm at the time.

While the judge and I were visiting, I asked him if Michael Garloni had ever gotten out of jail. He asked me, "Why? Are you concerned about him?"

"No, but he threatened Jerry's life. And these heart attacks were so fast and unusual, I want to know where he is." I told him about the burglary of our home and about finding all the guns.

"I'll check on his location for you, and I'll contact you as soon as I find out where he is," he said. He left, and within a few hours, I received his promised call.

He told me Michael Garloni had been released on bond. He sent the sheriff's office to check on Michael's whereabouts. They found him all drugged up and in possession of more stolen property. They found a television with the same serial number as the one Jerry had reported stolen from our house.

"You will never have to worry about that man again," the judge said. He then assured me he would set no bond again. He said Michael Garloni was a three-time felon. If convicted on the current charges, he would not get out of prison for a long, long time. He also explained that criminals refer to the sentencing Michael Garloni would receive, if convicted, as "The Big Bitch." That term originated from the Habitual Criminal Act that includes lengthy, mandatory sentencing for three-time felons convicted in New Mexico courts.

I felt much safer knowing Michael Garloni was finally put away by a state that seemed to care about their victims. I had questions, questions, and more questions running through my mind. Why didn't Mohave County arrest Michael when the police had him in custody? My answer always led to "follow the money." I knew there was more to that thought to be considered, but my bitterness had already set in.

As far as I was concerned, the county attorney's inaction and indifference aided the criminal who caused my husband's premature death. Jerry had become a victim condemned by a system that cared more about money than life itself. By ignoring the needs and rights of victims, the County had saved money. Because he was and I am self-employed, the government, including federal, state, and county tax agencies was collecting more than 63 percent of our net earnings. I wonder, is this good government?

The Dallas Police Department had handed the Mohave County attorney an opportunity to convict a four-time convicted felon on a silver platter. Money kept the county attorney from caring about the lives of future victims. It will always tug at my heart. I will always wonder how many more years Jerry would have lived had he not been terrorized by the threats from that drug addict and habitual criminal.

In the cases involving Michael Garloni, both the Kingman and Dallas police officers believed they had plenty of evidence to send him to prison. They certainly had enough evidence to justify a warrant. It is my belief that given the circumstances that followed the decision not to arrest and prosecute Michael Garloni, Mohave County was negligent and abused the privilege afforded them by the absolute immunity laws. Absolute immunity laws give immunity to a prosecutor (including county attorneys) from legal action for *failure* to arrest or prosecute someone as well as immunity for prosecutorial misconduct. I believe the laws give too much power to one individual. It leaves too much room for negligence, error, favoritism, and dictatorship. The police wanted Michael arrested. The county attorney did not want to spend the money to arrest and prosecute him, even if it prevented future victims from being condemned by the criminal whims of a convicted felon.

Later in January 2001, I was visiting my parents in New Mexico. *The Albuquerque Journal* had an article on the front page. It stated that a man had been arrested in Santa Fe for allegedly raping and beating a 17-year-old girl and her 20-year-old sister. Both girls had been reluctant to report the incident because they feared for the lives and safety of their family. The man had told the girls that if they told anyone, including the police, he would kill their family.

The girl's attacker had been arrested twice in Santa Fe on warrants issued from Wisconsin for crimes he perpetrated there plus other smaller crimes he had committed in Santa Fe. Each time, after serving his New Mexico court-ordered sentence, he was released without extradition to Wisconsin because the State of Wisconsin refused to accept extradition of him on the outstanding felony warrants they had issued. Just like Arizona, the court officer of Wisconsin did not want him back. The man had a lengthy criminal record of sex offenses, weapons violations, aggravated assault, and battery. I asked myself, "What would the taxpayers of the State of Wisconsin have wanted?"

This report sounded so familiar to me. It brought tears to my eyes. The only comment the Wisconsin district attorney had to offer was, "In hindsight, it is unfortunate."

In hindsight, this officer of the court condemned these two female victims to rape and abuse. He allowed these women to live tied up, raped, tortured, and in fear for their family members' lives if they complained. The district attorney in Wisconsin believed the man was dangerous when he issued the state warrants. To save money, he failed every future victim when he refused to take the man into custody and to trial. In Wisconsin, the district attorney who made the decision to let a habitual criminal roam the streets of New Mexico is immune from prosecution for making that decision. Any future victims of the criminal remain unprotected by the laws and condemned by an authority entrusted by the public to do his job. The taxpayers of New Mexico are now paying the bill for this man's confinement and Wisconsin doesn't have to worry about him.

CHAPTER 3

Because I had spent six years building my business in Arizona, and I knew my financial support depended on the success of the company, in November 1993, I moved my residency to Arizona as well. I believed that by having a company to keep me busy and friends there to help, I would be all right.

I felt things would become easier for me if I purchased a home or found a good location for building one. I knew that living in the night watchman's quarters at the plant was not going to work for much longer. The quarters consisted of a 12 ft. x 65 ft. mobile home located about 200 feet from a railroad track. There was a railroad crossing within 300 feet of the mobile home. Every time a train went by, the engineer blew a whistle. There were over 70 trains passing by on any given day.

An attorney in New Mexico, who had been a friend and colleague of Jerry's, had suggested, "Take your money and get out of this town. It's probably the only chance you will get."

I agreed. If I chose to stay in Hobbs, I would never get on with my life. I would probably turn into a miserable old widow living in a town that was as depressed as I was. Hobbs was built on oil money. The value of American oil had dropped so drastically in 1985 that people left the area by the thousands, leaving vacant stores, homes, and streets.

In January 1994, I began looking for both investment property and a new home. First I purchased a small two-bedroom rental house. Things seemed to be falling into place. It was not in the best shape, so I fixed it up. It took me a month, but I got it repaired and rented by February.

The first renters to move in were a married couple with no children. Three weeks after they moved in, the family grew to seven people. No one paid the rent. After the neighbors began complaining about the noise and filth, I moved the renters out and repaired all the damage they had done. They had lived in the house three months, and it took me a month to repair the damage they caused.

All the time I was painting walls, repairing windows, and replacing doors, I was angry with Jerry for not being there to lend a hand. The physical labor support he could have provided wasn't there, but thankfully, because of Jerry's previous financial planning, the money for the repairs was always available when I needed it.

I rented the property to another couple. All their children were grown. Two months after the couple had taken possession of the house, their daughter and her husband and four children had moved in with the couple. The couple could not afford to pay the rent, and after their court ordered eviction, I had to rebuild the house again. This couple had paid only two months rent and lived rent-free for four months. The house was such a mess that I called the authorities. The renters had stolen the double-wide refrigerator/freezer I had in the house and left a trail of filth and damage. There was also marijuana growing in the backyard!

The officer who came to the house was obviously not a rookie. He was in his forties and he seemed to have all the answers. He took the marijuana plant we had uprooted and advised me of my landlord rights. It appeared I had few.

"You know, when a landlord supplies a rental with furniture or appliances, they automatically agree to leave those items in the custody of the renter. If the renter sells the items, Mohave County does not consider that criminal theft. It is a civil issue. If your loss is under $4-5,000, I don't remember which, you can file a complaint in the justice court," he advised. "Good thing the refrigerator is all you lost. If you had lost more, you would have to pay a lawyer and sue in superior court for the damages."

The second renter's damages and "civil issues" cost me over $4600. The marijuana was never mentioned again. They lived in the house six months. This time, it took me two months to repair the damages.

The third and last renter paid the first month's rent and did not pay rent for 11 months. It was necessary to file suit, just to get him out of the house. When I went to court in February 1996 to have him evicted, he filed a countersuit against me for being a bad landlord. Thankfully, the judge did not buy his act. Ten days after his eviction, he hung dead animals in plastic bags from the light fixtures before he moved out. One of the varmints looked like a prairie dog, but the others were so decomposed that you couldn't tell what they were. None of them appeared to be rats or anything that the tenant might find invading the house.

In the summer that year, a meeting was held at the senior center for people who owned rental property. A representative of the county attorney's office explained to everyone that we were not allowed to post the names of renters who had caused us harm. Verbal references have similar legal implications, making their accuracy rather unreliable. Even though the posting or negative references might prevent financial harm to our friends, we would be violating the renter's civil rights. I gave up the rental business and sold the house.

There was certainly no point in seeking damages through litigation from any of the renters. None of them would have been able to pay the judgment. Taxes and insurance were so costly and general labor so poorly paid in Mohave County that the common laborer could not feed and clothe a family and pay the rent as well.

In January 1994, while looking for investment property, I also found an interesting piece of property in a new development away from the mainstream of traffic. I could build a new house there that I could call home. The advertising flyer said there was going to be a guarded gate for security, a lake for pleasure boating and fishing (bass, catfish, and trout), private paved roads, jogging trails designed and maintained for easy walking, underground utilities, cable TV, garbage services, and a tennis court. Also included was a homeowners association with voting rights to assure that everyone stayed happy. As I drove up to the closed front gate, a young, dark haired, petite lady greeted me.

"Hello. May I help you?" she inquired.

"I would like to look at the lots you have for sale."

"I will help you find the developer. Go through the gates and make the first left. He is screening material right now, but he will see you coming." I thanked her and drove over to a large front-end loader where a man wearing slacks, a sports shirt, and a very black toupee climbed down from the machine to greet me.

I realized we had briefly met before. My ex-partner had introduced us, explaining to me that this man came from a very old, reputable Mohave County family.

"My name is Toup LaPrix. Ya couldn't pick a safer purchase than buying out here. The improvements fell a bit behind on getting finished, but I have been working on this dam. The bureaucrats just won't let up. Gettin' approval on that dam was like gettin' approval to build the Hoover Dam. The rules are all the same. No difference at all. The subdivision improvements are bonded by the County. I put up a lot of money for the bond. Many of the lots are already sold, but I'll show you the ones that aren't. The improvements on the south side of the subdivision will be completed by November of this year, so ya should begin lookin' on that side if ya wanna build right away."

"Okay, just show me where to drive," I said.

As we drove around the south side of the subdivision, Mr. LaPrix gave me a short history of the site and a few do's and don'ts about buying into the subdivision.

"If ya go to build and ya remove trees, ya have to replace um. I have aerial photographs of this place, and I know where every tree is. I'll help ya move um if I can. Your house must have at least 2,000 sq. ft. of living area. I don't want anything cheap built out here. Gotta keep things high class. There are CCRs for this subdivision, and ya have ta read them before ya buy a lot. Ya gotta read my state report, too," he said.

"What's a state report?" I asked.

"Well, I don't have one handy right now 'cause my copier is broken, but I will get ya one if ya decide ya want to buy."

Before buying anything, I visited the mapping department for Mohave County and reviewed the final plan. I questioned planning and zoning and was told the subdivision would be a very quiet, private place to live, and they said there were assurances posted with the County that ensured the completion of the subdivision, should something happen to the developer. There was only one real estate saleswoman in the area that did not trust the project; and she did not trust the LaPrix family. All the others said it was going to fly.

I wanted to buy a lot in the area but I couldn't decide which lot I wanted. There was a corner lot I favored. Across the front portion of the lot was an old dirt road that had once been the main road used by miners many years ago. It provided a perfect place for a driveway area to the front of the house. The stately mountains surrounding the subdivision provided protection to the area from most of the heavy winds normally found in the desert. The summer temperatures are often 15 degrees lower than those in the surrounding areas. The views from all the lots were gorgeous. Each of the lots listed for sale were large—exceeded one-half acre, most averaging two-thirds—with a thick covering of trees, such as juniper and palo verde. Other native plant life included yuccas, barrel and cholla cacti sharing the shade afforded by the juniper trees. During my daylight visits to the area, I saw deer, rabbits, skunks, lizards, western geckos, quail, blue birds, cactus wrens, robins, and beautiful yellow and black birds. In the evenings, the skies are so clear that satellites passing over the area resemble shooting stars. The lights of the distant town add an array of color to the peaceful atmosphere.

A few days after my visit to the subdivision, Toup LaPrix came to my office and handed me a written list of all the lots he had for sale. Compared to the lots I had seen in other developments, all his lots were much more expensive. Considering the scenery and the trees, I felt they were worth the prices shown on his list. He had marked off the ones he had already sold. I noticed that the corner lot I preferred was marked "Sold."

"Did you sell my lot?" I asked.

"Nah," he said. "I kinda thought ya were favorin' that piece. I marked it off as sold so that no one else would look at it until ya had a chance to make up yer mind."

The number of lots Toup LaPrix had already sold impressed me, as did his concern that the lot I admired would be mine. The paper he gave me showed he had completed over $600,000 in sales. That one paper convinced me he had or would have plenty of money to finish his dream development. Very few subdivisions could offer what nature had afforded this area.

I explained to Toup LaPrix that my concerns about buying the property were with some of the rules in the Covenants, Conditions, and Restrictions (CCRs) and the water quality. I had read an article on the Internet about the problems the people of Lake Havasu City, Arizona were having with their water supply.

We went through my questions very carefully. He said, "Lake Juniper has six wells, and the water quality is the best in the county. There's plenty of water. It's got better minerals and qualities than most. It's good for ya. I've had the water tested many times. It's always proved to be of excellent quality."

"It says no home businesses. I do accounting in my home. I've done accounting in my home for 28 years. My clients mail me their work and I mail it back when I am finished. Would that be allowed?" I asked.

"This will be a gated community with 24-hour security. The gates will be guarded and ya won't be able to have strange traffic coming in and out all the time. Ya can't advertise or have a sign in the yard, but I won't stop a person from having an office in their home."

"Is the electricity stable enough for my computers?" I asked.

"I've got an office right in my living room. My computers have never gone down because of the electric supply. It's pretty stable stuff," he replied.

I bought the lot on February 17, 1994. I wrote a check to Toup LaPrix for the full amount due, less a credit he gave me for paying cash. With the help of several builders, I managed to draw suitable plans for the house. It was my dream house and I wanted it perfect. I placed every window in the house to reflect beautiful mountains or trees. I knew if I never hung a picture on the wall, I wouldn't be without all the pretty pictures I needed.

In anticipation of my need for a telephone and at Toup's request, I called the telephone company to obtain a line for my house. They assigned me a telephone number to use when the house was built and the lines were in.

The house I wanted had very simple lines and with help of the contractor's draftsman, we submitted the plans to Toup LaPrix in March for architectural review. They were professionally prepared and were immediately approved by Toup.

"The plans don't have any landscaping yet, but I'll show you what I have in mind. I can submit references to you that will prove the quality of my work, if you like. I really want to do the work myself," I said.

"No need. I'm sure ya know what you'll need later on. I've seen your work around town," he said. "Your guys know what they're doin'."

"I plan to build the retaining walls one rock at a time. I'll use the large native rocks, and because they're so big, the walls will go up in a hurry. I will have the rock hauled in."

"I've got all the rock ya need," he said.

Within a month when they began to build my house, the need for water was discussed, and Toup hooked up a one-inch PVC pipe to a water valve located on my lot next to an electric transformer. "Don't worry about the cost right now. I have to put down the pavement then I will know where to put the meters. In the meantime, don't worry. It's my company. I'll get the easements in." He explained he needed to get the work done and submit the "as-builts" for the water company lines and the wells to the ADEQ (Arizona Department of Environmental Quality) for inspection and approval.

Because he was "Mr. LaPrix" (tied to one of the county's original,

wealthy, families), the County made exceptions to the regulated requirements within his subdivision. The County had not required him to establish easements for the Lake Juniper Water Company prior to selling any of
the lots. His word was good; he'd get it finished.

The house was built in seven months. I learned that there were no
building permits required in the area because the County called it "in the
overlay." With proper applications, septic permits are issued in three days
or less. I began creating the landscaping. I spoke with Toup LaPrix about
my planting a vegetable garden, and I asked if they would grow well in the
area. He said they would do fine. The only thing he required was if he was
supplying the water for the garden, he should get half of what I grew.

Toup had not installed any water meters. I was not paying for water
usage. He was still paying the electric bill for the well pumps, so I didn't
question his comment. Besides, I was sure that by the time I started planting the garden, I would be paying for my own metered water.

Since I was the first outsider to build in the project, Toup LaPrix
seemed more excited about the building than I was. He tried to help in
every way he could. He brought a huge, eight-yard bucket loader full of
natural stones from the empty lake area to my driveway for the men to use
in building my walls.

By June more people started building homes in the subdivision. Martin Coole built a lovely dual level home to the north and across the street
from my lot. The garage was built underneath his living quarters. The results were lovely. He was a single man who owned a mining and excavating
business. He built a house every year or two, lived in the house for a year
or so, then sold it. That was his way of investing and earning a little extra
money. Mike and Kathy Mazur built a pueblo style home on the south side
of my lot. It reminded me of New Mexico. The Mazurs built the house to
sell it; they never intended to live in it.

When my house was finished in October and I was ready to move in,
I had called the telephone company and told them that I was ready to have
the line installed. They refused to follow through with the order.

I asked the engineer, "What is taking so long?"

"Take it up with Toup LaPrix," he said.

I did, and Toup connected a phone line and gave me a number to use.
He explained that the utility company was not equipped with enough lines
yet, but when the lines came in, I would have to change numbers.

Land value notices are mailed to home and lot owners in March each year. By March 15, 1995, I had not received my notice. I called the county tax department and was told the lot number I gave was incorrect. Their records showed it to be a vacant lot owned by Toup LaPrix. I explained they were in error, as I had a home on that lot.

I asked why the county assessor's office had not, in their field inspections, discovered the problem. I was told, "Unless there are complaints filed, the assessor doesn't do field inspections. The inspector does not have time to look at every subdivision in the county. Just call the title company and ask why the lot was not transferred to you."

The clerk at the title company told me that they knew the lot was mine, but the company had been unable to transfer the title properly because Mr. LaPrix had not paid the delinquent taxes on the land. I bought the house through a trusted title company, and I paid them pro-rated taxes for 1994. No property taxes had been paid on the lot since 1991. She could see where I had paid my portion of the taxes and would contact Toup LaPrix and ask him to come into the title company and pay his portion.

"Does he pay taxes?" I inquired.

"Not like he should," she replied.

The lady knew I was upset. When I get upset, my voice raises an octave or two. She explained that Mr. LaPrix had a "thing" about paying taxes. She said, "I'll convince him to come in today and pay his taxes."

CHAPTER 4

At the end of the next month, on April 30th, my foreman Phil Fox called my home late in the evening. He said I needed to come to the office right away. There had been a robbery. His voice wavered as he explained that he was scared and I should hurry. "Jack Tattoo stole my guns," he said.

From the time I started building the house in 1994 to January 1996, Phil was handling the company's heavy labor needs. I was able to see profits coming in from Phil's efforts. Phil managed the business and turned a profit, even though I was unable to show up for work on a daily basis. I continued to do the company's bookkeeping from my house and respond to the company's problems.

Phil had a drinking problem. Everyone close to Phil knew he had dependency problems. I overlooked his drinking because he was a very nice person most of the time. He had a history of drug use, but he had gone through drug rehabilitation and had not used hard drugs for over eight years. He always passed his drug tests. I suppose that made it easier for me to accept the alcohol problem. For six years I had tried to get him off the booze, but I wasn't very successful. He cared a lot for my company and he was extremely talented. I ignored any shortcomings he still had. At least the beer was legal.

Jack Tattoo had worked for our firm for a short time in the spring of 1994. He had come into my office one day with another young man. The labor laws do not allow a previous employer to say anything derogatory about a previous employee unless there is a court record proving the employer had just cause for terminating the employee. This law was enacted because employers would badmouth an employee they didn't like and ultimately blackball the employee from obtaining employment. The states had to support too many unemployed men. I, or someone from my company, always call. We get, "Well, he's healthy enough to do your type of work."

Both men were so young, it didn't really matter anyway, because the only employment references they had would be obtained from their folks. I hired them both. They appeared to be clean cut, had on clean clothes, and seemed willing to work. They sounded sincere. Their eyes were not bloodshot from booze or dilated from drugs. Both men were polite and very quick to respond, so I thought I should at least give them a chance. Phil agreed.

After my experience with Mike, I tried to hire "clean" people. But I always found myself stuck with men who would not work, did not know how to work, could not do the heavy work, or were dependant on alcohol or drugs.

Phil terminated both men's employment at the same time. The crews started at 6:00 a.m. These two men thought six o'clock only happened once a day—in the evening. They were good workers while they were on the job, but when they were late, the rest of their crew would sit and wait around for them. They were costing the firm a fortune in lost labor hours. I insisted the men go out on jobs together. That way, if anyone should get hurt, the others were there to help.

Jack decided to take advantage of Phil's drinking problem and the knowledge he had learned of Phil's guns.

When I got to the plant 20 minutes after he called, Phil described the events of the evening to me.

With a friend, Jack had come to the company's yard. He had beer for Phil, and they all began to drink. Because Phil was good at repairing equipment, Jack asked Phil if he would look at his truck. He said it had a mechanical problem.

Phil said, "Sure."

While Phil and Jack's friend had their heads under the hood of the truck, Jack went around to the back of the building. He said he was going to look in the service truck for a tool he thought Phil might need.

When he returned, he was bleeding profusely. Phil asked him what happened. Jack said he had cut himself on the utility truck that was parked behind the shop. Phil took him inside to the kitchen sink to clean up the wounds.

Jack excused himself and went into the bathroom. Phil went back outside with the other man. After spending quite a long time in the bathroom, Jack returned to the porch. He and his friend got into their truck and appeared to have left. Phil thought he had heard them hit one of the other vehicles, but it was dark and he did not see any damage from where he stood. He sat down on the porch to finish his beer.

Phil had recently moved into the night watchman's quarters where I had lived before I moved to the new house. The City had given me a permit to allow someone to live at the yard because of all the unsolved robberies.

Shortly after, Phil heard a noise inside the office. The night watchman's quarters shared the same unit as the office. He went inside to see where the noise was coming from. When he walked back to his quarters, he noticed blood on the door and his closet was open. Looking around, he also saw his bedroom window open and his guns were missing. He looked out the back window and saw Jack Tattoo and his friend putting the rifles in their truck. Phil grabbed his pistol from behind the bed and went out the back door. His words to me later about this were, "No matter what they were taking, I couldn't shoot."

Jack Tattoo saw Phil with the gun in his hand, and he jumped on Phil like a wildcat. He shoved Phil back into the building and managed to take the gun out of Phil's hand. He put the gun to Phil's head. At that point, he told Phil, "I could kill you right now. Don't ever point a gun at a man unless you plan to use it. Sorry man, I need the money bad. If you call the cops, I will come back and kill you." As he ran out through the front of the office unit, he shot a hole in the kitchen ceiling. The two men ignored the rest of the loot Jack had thrown out the back of the building. They jumped in the truck and sped off. Two hours later, Phil called me.

It had taken me about 20 minutes to drive the distance from my house to the yard. When I arrived, Phil was still visibly shaken. After he told me what had happened, I asked if he had called the police yet. He said he hadn't called them, and he wasn't going to. He was afraid Jack Tattoo would come after him and perhaps put everyone who worked for the company in danger. Considering what he knew of Jack's past criminal history, Jack would indeed kill him or anyone else who called the police.

"It has been over two hours. Why did you take so long to call me?" I asked.

He said, very quietly, "I had to take a shower because when Jack turned the gun on me, I shit my pants."

It was one of those situations where I wanted to laugh. I fought the feeling because the situation was not really a laughing matter. Phil was still in shock. It was easy to see that changing his mind about calling the authorities wouldn't be easy.

"We won't call the police then. We will go to them. I'll bet you they are right down there at the bottom of the hill. They sit there most of the time. Let's go see," I suggested.

We got into my truck and went to the location on Andy Devine Avenue where the police stop and visit with each other in the evenings. Sure enough, there were two police cars right where I was expecting them to be. I got out of the truck, interrupting their break, and told a female officer we had been robbed. She asked, "Where did this happen?"

"Right up this street," I explained. There were no more questions.

"We will meet you there," she said.

As we drove back to the scene of the robbery, Phil sat very straight in his seat. He was still scared. His eyes were searching everywhere. I asked him what he was looking for. He said, "What if Jack sees us with the police? If he does, I am a dead man, and you will be dead, too. We shouldn't have involved the cops."

I explained, "The police will be with us for a long time. Those druggies won't hang around. They are long gone. I can give the police everything they need to find Jack. They'll catch him."

When we entered my office with the police, the questions started flying. I sat quietly while Phil related the events of the evening. His report seemed honest. He did not hide the fact that they had all been drinking. He admitted he had brandished the pistol and that he was too much of a softy to shoot the gun. Hearing everything Phil told the officer in detail, I wondered how Phil had come out of the incident alive.

When the female officer began asking Phil questions, I got up and went to inspect the hole in the kitchen ceiling. I was hoping that my absence would make his story easier to relate to the woman. When she asked Phil why he hadn't called them sooner, he explained the accident he had had with his bowels without a flinch. He also admitted he was afraid to call the police because of Jack's threat.

The officer then followed me into the kitchen area and inspected the hole in the ceiling. She went outside for a few minutes and came back into the main office with two of Phil's rifles that she had found outside Phil's bedroom window. He identified them as being his and told her they were not loaded.

The officer looked at him scornfully and said, "I know that." She knew Phil was in a state of shock, but for him to insult her intelligence was going a bit too far. "How many guns did you have in your closet?" she asked.

"Four rifles and a handgun," he replied. He gave her the descriptions of the two missing rifles and his pistol. She asked me to follow her outside. I went with her. She showed me a broken window on a travel trailer we kept in the back area of the yard. The trailer was used at our mines (rock quarries for our landscaping materials) as quarters when we needed it. Because the mines were 50 miles or more from our yard, we often spent many days and nights preparing the rock for sale in the mining areas. No one had used the trailer for a long time. The officer asked if the window on the trailer door had been broken before the incident, as there was glass everywhere.

I told her no. She asked if she could go into the trailer, and I said, "Sure."

She went into the trailer and called for me to follow her inside. She warned me not to touch anything. As I entered the trailer, I looked around. Blood was everywhere. Without a DNA test, nobody could be sure where the blood came from, but Jack Tattoo was the only person with a cut. The trailer had the capacity to bed eight men. Every bed had been upturned. The mattresses were all bloody. The cabinets, bathroom door, and closets were all ransacked. Blood was on the inside of each of them. Everything was a mess. Again, she told me not to touch anything. She explained the department would be back early the next morning to investigate the trailer more thoroughly. With all the glass and blood, hunting around in there in the dark could be pretty risky. She suggested I warn all my employees against touching anything because the blood could be carrying the AIDS virus.

I hadn't thought of that. I didn't know much about AIDS, and I wasn't ready to learn about it by becoming infected. We went back into the office, and I sat back down in my chair. My eyes had witnessed more than my stomach wanted me to see. I was feeling pretty weak, and I was anxious about all the damages. There was no way to estimate how long it would take to clean up the bloody mess.

The officers explained to us what chemicals we should use to clean up the blood. They explained that no one should come into contact with it and that we should wear thick rubber gloves while cleaning it up. I had begun to notice the blood drops all over the office. This cleanup was going to be a real chore.

I got up from my chair to go to the files and search for the employment records for Jack Tattoo. "What are you doing?" The male officer asked.

"I was going to give you Jack's employment records," I replied.

"Phil. While she is doing that will you step outside with me, please?" he said.

"Sure," Phil replied.

I heard the officer ask Phil, "This was really a drug deal gone bad, now wasn't it?"

Phil said, "No sir. You are wrong. I can tell you Jack Tattoo was either drunk or on drugs or both, but he didn't get anything from me."

I don't know why the officer bothered to take Phil outside. Phil was so mad and talking so loudly that I could hear everything they said. After the officers left, I told Phil that it would be better if he came out to my house. Jack did not know where I lived. It would be safer. I did not want Phil Fox sitting in that office looking at all that blood, nor did I want that officer hassling Phil anymore that night. By now it was 3:15 a.m.

Phil agreed and he grabbed the beer he had left in the refrigerator. We locked up and put his dog Chogie in my truck. On the way to the house, I explained the condition of the travel trailer and the broken window to Phil. He said, "That must have been where Jack cut his arm. I didn't hear anything break. He probably waited until a train went by so I couldn't hear what was going on."

Phil was convinced that Jack was on drugs at the time of the robbery and that Jack was very desperate for more. He explained to me, "Even a drunk would not have broken the window with their hand. They would have realized the window in the trailer door was double-paned and chosen one of the other windows. There were some two-by-fours stored right next to the trailer. I put them there last week. A person who was just high on alcohol would have used the wood to break the window." He insisted, "Jack was on drugs."

Because he was now thinking a little straighter, I was sure he was going to be all right. How wrong I was! By the time we got to the house, the early morning hours were fast approaching. I turned on the television. There was an old time Western movie on, and Phil loved to watch those films. He sat down on the sofa and opened one of his beers. I went into the kitchen, and I could hear him talking. He was mumbling to himself. I handed him some extra strength, non-aspirin pain reliever and a cup of hot tea. He put the beer down, thanked me, took the pill, and drank the tea. I threw the beer out and I sent him off to the spare bedroom and begged him to try to rest.

At 4:30 a.m., Phil was up and making coffee. It had been a long night. But if he didn't start early, the weather would get too hot before he could finish his work. With just an hour of sleep, the time came very early for me. I got up, got dressed, and went to the kitchen.

As I entered the room, I saw Phil pouring coffee for both of us. He walked over to the table carrying two full cups. His hands were shaking so badly, he was spilling coffee all over the floor. He apologized, grabbed a towel, and wiped up the mess. I could see tears in his eyes. I asked if I could help, and he said, "Just sit there and let's talk a minute."

Phil explained to me how much it had hurt him when that male officer accused him of doing drugs. He said that the drug officers had always stayed right on his back before he came to work for me. He thought that after working for me for six years, they would give him credit for being clean. He knew the police were aware of our company's random drug testing policy. He was convinced the hospital lab informed the police of those things.

I told Phil that the police officer was probably a rookie and did not even know of his background of drug use. My words were soft as I explained his hurt was from past feelings of guilt. I reminded him of how proud his parents were of him and how hard he had worked to achieve his goal to be drug-free.

"I'm scared. I know that bastard Jack will cause us a lot of trouble. If he goes to jail, he will come after us when he gets out. We need to stay together until this is over. Either you move back to the yard, or I'll come here in the evenings after work," he said.

"Well, that shouldn't take long. I gave the officers everything but his fingerprints. They are all over the trailer, along with his blood samples. I will pick you up in the evenings and we will stay out here. We will be safer here. Do you feel like going to the yard? I am afraid the crew might get into the blood. We need to be there when they arrive," I said.

"Yeah. Let me get cleaned up," he said. His hands had stopped shaking, but his breath smelled of liquor.

We were the first to arrive at the yard. I suggested Phil stay at the plant for the day. We could get the chemicals and gloves we needed and ask Jeff and Janette to help clean up all the blood. It was too early for the stores to be open for business. The police were coming early, so to pass some time, I made a pot of coffee.

While the coffee was brewing, Phil and I began taking an inventory of the damages. Being careful not to touch anything, we started looking outside first. Phil noticed his bedroll and some other personal items sitting just outside the back door. They should have been in his closet. The travel trailer looked even worse in the daylight. It had been trashed. In his hurry to escape, Jack Tattoo had backed into the side of the pickup I used for traveling. I knew that repair was going to cost me plenty.

Inside the office, we noticed the VCR was gone from the closet in the TV room. The TV room was dark, and no one had entered that room the night before. There was blood all around the cabinet where it had been stored. We used the VCR to show prospective clients our work. I could see why Phil had thought Jack Tattoo might have passed out in the bathroom. Jack was losing a lot of blood fast. Phil said that Jack had spent a long time in the bathroom after he washed off his arm. What Phil didn't know was that Jack Tattoo had raided every room in the unit.

Phil went to put the things we had found outside back in his closet and noticed even more blood there. He asked me to come and look. I wondered how deep Jack's wounds were and if a doctor had been called.

At 8:30 a.m., a police car drove into the yard, and Phil met the officer at the front door. He told the officer that we had discovered that a lot more items were missing. He showed the officer the storage cabinet where we kept the missing VCR. Phil next showed the officer my truck and explained where Jack's truck had been when Phil was working on it. He showed him the things he had found in the backyard and the blood in his bedroom closet. The police officer made a note of the missing VCR and the truck damage. He asked if he could examine the travel trailer.

I said, "Sure," and he went out back to the trailer.

He did not stay long in that mess. He came back to the office and told us that Jack had been arrested. The officer was sure Jack would be released on bond that very day. He knew Jack Tattoo had made threats, but he also knew how the county system worked. He apologized and explained there was nothing the police could do to keep Jack confined in jail. He advised Phil to watch his back, while assuring him that the police force would be watching Jack. They believed he was very dangerous. He suggested we be very careful and stay together or with the rest of our employees as much as possible. Jack's accomplice had not been identified or arrested. The police had found Jack in possession of many newspaper racks that belonged to the local newspaper company. The officer said he would face several charges if he were brought to trial. The detectives had found marijuana growing in pots in Jack's closet. The officer hoped that if he were tried, he would be put away for a long time. Phil would not have to worry about him anymore. Advising us to "hang in there," he left.

Phil was shaking again. He said, "If it had been me they arrested, they would have locked me up and thrown away the key." He went to the refrigerator and looked for a beer, forgetting that he had taken them to my house. He opened a kitchen cabinet, pulled out a bottle of hard liquor that he had stored, and poured a drink.

The employees and I managed to get the trailer cleaned up and the hole in the ceiling repaired. It took the better part of two full days. The chemical we used to clean up the blood up was so powerful it took the paint off the walls. It left bleached spots on every piece of cloth it touched.

I called the insurance company the next day and explained the damage to the truck and how it happened. I delivered the truck for repairs. We shopped for a window to replace the one in the travel trailer.

Phil spent most of his time drinking.

Shortly after Jerry's death, Phil's mother had died, and he had spent a few weeks staying drunk. I had somehow convinced him to slow down on the booze, and he had been on the right track for over a year. The heavy drinking was starting again. I hoped I was strong enough to help him quit again, but he had a very dependent personality. With all the emotional pain he had suffered, and the fear he was experiencing, it was easier for him to stay drunk. I prayed that God would help Phil and make things better for him. Sometimes you have to be careful what you ask God for because the answer you get may not be what you expected—or wanted.

Jack Tattoo was released on bond the morning after he was arrested, on May 2nd. For the next three months, Phil complained that Jack was stalking him. He said Jack was following him everywhere he went, laughing and waving.

CHAPTER 5

May brought other problems—this time at the subdivision. My new neighbor, Kathy Mazur, was the first homeowner to complain about living conditions in the subdivision. She and her husband Mike had begun building their house a year earlier in June 1994 and moved in April 1995. By May 1995, they could not get a telephone line installed because there were no lines available. Mike Mazur had become very ill, and Kathy had been running back and forth from the hospital. Because the telephone company refused to install a telephone at her home, the Mazur's cellular phone bill was enormous. It took the telephone company about two months to install a line to their house. The lines we had were not very good. They had been poorly installed and no boxes had been placed over them to protect them from the elements. On one occasion, a stray dog chewed them up and the neighborhood was without telephone service while the company searched for the problem then corrected it.

Many times I would pick up the phone to call out, and I could hear people having conversations along with the dial tone. I was curious about what was going on with the phone, so I went out and bought a Tap Zapper. My zapper was a tiny little white box that plugged into the phone line. If someone was listening in on any calls, a red light came on in the box. There was a black button on the box and, according to the instructions, if I saw the red light come on, I was supposed to push the black button. Well, the red light came on and I pushed the black button. That activity knocked out everyone's telephone service for a mile or more. The entire area was reduced to cellular phones for a few days until the phone company could figure out what I had done. They suggested I quit using the box immediately and assured me they would install fiber optic lines in the near future.

For television service, Toup installed an antenna on my house. He said it was against the CCRs, but since there was no cable yet, the antenna would have to do. He said, "When I get the cable installed, you'll have to take this antenna down. In the meantime, I think this is the best TV reception ya can get out here. It's better than mine. I'll get the cable in soon. If I install the antenna, it's okay."

He connected a little silver box that had a black button on it to my television set. When he finished, I had access to three stations. Not knowing what that black button was for, I never pushed it. I'd been in enough trouble over black buttons!

I read the CCRs and they said anything the declarant (Toup LaPrix) installed was acceptable. He had installed an enormous, ugly dish in his front yard, and he had several antennas on his roof. He explained that the things he installed on his property were necessary for the installation of cable to our houses. We had no cable.

In May I received a call from the telephone company. The man calling asked, "Are you Patricia Lewis?"

"Yes, I am," I replied.

"Do you have a home in the Lake Juniper Subdivision?" he asked.

"Yes, I do. I'm standing in it," I said.

"The line number I called belongs to Toup LaPrix. Do you know how long you have had this phone number and who installed it in your home?" he asked.

"I have had this number for several months; it was installed in October. I called your company in February of last year and you gave me a reservation number to be installed in October, when my construction was finished," I replied. "I was at work when the line was installed. Mr. LaPrix called me. He said the phone company was very busy and they had not been able to install the number they assigned to me last February, so I would have to use this number until they got their work finished. Mr. LaPrix knew I had to have a phone. I live alone, own my own company in town, and without communication lines, I would be in big trouble. I have been paying the bill every month. Is there a problem?"

"Like I said, Ma'am, the phone number belongs to Toup LaPrix. It has not been legally installed on your property. I am going to place an installation order and you will be receiving a new number. I feel confident you did not know what was going on, but I am afraid you cannot keep that phone number," he explained.

"Well, you do what you have to do. Just as long as I have something here that rings and I can call out, I'll be fine. I am truly sorry if I caused your company any trouble," I said.

"Oh no, Ma'am. You have not caused any trouble. We just have a few problems we need to get ironed out in that subdivision. We will do our job. Please be patient with us," he said. He then assigned me a new number. The next day he called to let me know that my new number was active.

A man named Mr. Flarm was building a steel framed house across the empty lake from my house. He had started construction of a house for resale. Toup LaPrix had promised underground utilities to all lot lines, and he continued to refuse to supply the legally installed utilities that Mr. Flarm required. Toup LaPrix had hot electric wires and PVC pipe strung above ground and under trees to the construction site. The inspectors shut the project down, and Mr. Flarm took all the loan money he had received from the bank and fled the area. The bank lost money and wrote the note off as a bad debt. The citizens of the country lost $138,000 in tax money to a bad debt.

Because of the connection, every lot and home in the wooded sub-division was unnecessarily exposed to fire risks. When the public electric utility supplier noticed what was going on with the illegal connections, it took many months and a court order to force the sheriff and the County to see that the electrical wires were disconnected. The electric company could not just cut off the electric supply, because it was running the wells that supplied water to existing homes.

According to the deputy sheriff, there was no way to determine who was responsible for the crimes committed against the utility company or the residents of the subdivision. Without a video or pictures showing who actually connected the utilities to the house, no criminal charges could be filed. In a subdivision without fire protection of any kind, things were getting dangerous.

When I was first considering buying a lot in the subdivision, Toup had told me that he planned a guarded and gated community that would be secured by November 1994. After that date came and went, I realized that the subdivision was not going to get the promised guarded gates. Being concerned about security issues, I thought I should at least beef up my outdoor lighting, so I installed light sensors. In early November, Toup LaPrix decided he did not approve of what I had done.

"All those lights are gonna scare off the deer," Toup LaPrix explained. "The lights are against the rules in the CCRs. The idea of the rule is to preserve the beauty of the stars at night. Since yours are the only outside lights in the area, and they don't come on often, ya can keep um for a while. When more homeowners move in and the association has collected enough dues, there will be enough money to man the guard gates. Then you'll have to replace the lights or get covers. Don't worry about it right now. I'll get you the information on the covers."

Soon after, on October 16th at about 10:00 p.m., an intruder came into my house through a back door that is near my bathroom. The man just stepped into the house as I was getting out of the bathtub. My tub has a button I can push and the water swirls around. It is noisy, but it feels good when I have had a long day. I didn't hear him enter the house and I was buck-naked. I guess it scared him thoroughly. He looked me in the eyes, his eyes got real big, and he took flight out the same back door.

I could feel my face getting flushed and my heart pounding heavily. It seemed as if my body was going to split open at the seams. All the neighbors were gone for the weekend, except Toup LaPrix.

I called his number and got a busy signal. Getting his attention seemed most important at the time. The lights were on in his house, and I just knew he had to be home.

I took out my trusty revolver and fired a shot, aiming the gun towards the empty lake and being very careful that no animals would be hit. It was so quiet in the area, and the shot sounded like a cannon going off. There was no response. After making several attempts to telephone and continuing to get a busy signal, I asked the operator if she would cut into the conversation for me and explained my emergency. She said the phone number I was dialing was off the hook and asked for permission to connect me with the sheriff.

I explained to her that the man had gone next door and that it was a long way out to my house. "The local newspaper said the sheriff is short-staffed, and I'm sure they have more pressing problems than mine."

"What will you do if the guy comes back?" she asked.

In my frightened condition, the fact that he might come back had never occurred to me. I let her make the call. I explained the incident to the dispatcher, and that I had used my gun. I had fired a shot to get Toup LaPrix's attention. His truck was in his drive and it looked like he was at home. He had not responded to the gunshot. I suggested they might want to check on him. I was concerned. What if that man had visited Toup LaPrix and he wasn't as fortunate as I had been?

My house is about four miles outside of town, and the Mohave County Sheriff's Department sent two officers. I grabbed a robe and started putting curlers in my wet hair.

One of the officers was a woman and the other a young man. The woman officer stayed outside looking around with her flashlight while the male officer came into the house to talk with me. Considering the time of night and my state of mind and dress, I would have preferred to have the female officer ask me questions while the male officer checked the grounds outside, but my comfort was not of concern, obviously.

The deputy asked if he could look around. I consented and explained that the bathroom was the only place in the house I believed the man had been. All the rest of the lights in the house had been turned off. The officer looked all around anyway. As he looked around, he said, "This is going to be a nice area. The homes being built out here show real class."

He checked my bedroom, closet, and bathroom. When he saw the chandelier hanging over the bathtub, he smiled. Electrical light fixtures placed over a tub are against the Uniform Building Code. As we walked to the sliding door, I showed him where the man had been standing when I saw him. I showed him the direction and route the man had taken. As we walked out onto the porch, the sensor lights came back on. There is a landscaped terrace with a 7 ft. high solid stone wall three to six inches thick. I was thinking about the bruises that young man received to his butt when he tried to get down that terrace wall, and I started laughing. By the glare I got from the officer, I knew I had better explain myself. I did.

The officer asked, "How tall was this guy?"

I asked, "How tall are you?"

"Well, I'm about 5 ft. 11."

I said, "Well considering that, the man was about 5 ft. 8."

"How much do you think he weighed?" he asked.

"I don't know. He was built like you. How do I know what he weighs? All I know is he had pretty, wavy, brown shoulder length hair and big, beautiful, brown eyes. His eyes sure got big when he noticed me standing in front of him nude."

The officer laughed. He laughed and giggled over many things I said. I must have really been in shock.

I kept remembering how Jerry had explained to me the feelings he had when he knew someone had been in our home. He had said he felt "so violated." I was wondering if he was watching the events of the evening.

The officer asked me if I had any medical problems. I thought that was a strange question to be asking. This man was a cop, not a doctor.

Dutifully, I explained to him, "Lately, I have been having a problem with high blood pressure. Why do you ask?"

"I ask 'cause you are white as a sheet. Will you allow me to call a paramedic?"

"Okay, but I'm not going to the hospital. My neighbor is a nurse and she says the hospital will kill you," I said.

"Well then, she ought to know," he said.

While we were waiting for the paramedics to arrive, the officer asked me where I kept my gun. I got it and gave it to him. He jumped up and took it out to his vehicle. He returned without the gun.

"What did you do with my gun? Give it back to me," I demanded.

"I've got to take it in," he explained. "The dispatcher said a gun had been fired at the suspect. If you hit him, we will need the gun. The gun will then be evidence."

"Make her read back the tape. Then when you find out that's not what the tape says, and before I will agree to you confiscating my gun, we'll go into the computer room and I will write two statements. One of the statements will explain, in simple words, that you are taking the gun, knowing that no one in the neighborhood is available if I need help. You will state that you are aware I live out in the middle of nowhere, and if anything happens to me, you will accept full responsibility. On the second statement, I will place the complete description of the gun and its serial number so you can return it to me when everyone has completed their investigation and finds no one with a bullet hole in them. Would you mind signing both statements before you leave?" I asked. As a victim, I wasn't going to allow this officer to take my gun without explaining his actions on paper. He couldn't charge me with anything because it is not illegal to fire a gun in the county. In the city, there are different rules.

After thinking over the situation, he went back to his vehicle. He was gone for a while, probably having the dispatcher re-read the tape. Then he returned with my gun. He unloaded it and laid both the gun and the bullets on my jewelry box.

I asked him, jokingly, "Ya think I'm gonna shoot ya?"

He patiently explained, "If I did, I wouldn't be giving it back to you. It is procedure to unload guns before returning them to anyone. Let's go, the paramedics are here."

I walked outside to the fire department's medical unit, and the medic took my blood pressure. It registered high. Both men felt I needed to go to the hospital, but I declined their offer. If I could settle down, everything would be okay.

The next day I called a security system company and had a system installed. I bought a new back door. In the advertised "gated" community, security was nonexistent. I went on the Internet while the night alarm system was hooked up. Much to my surprise, my computer called the cops! When I purchased the security system, I was told I would be able to use the system whether I was in the house or not, but I wasn't told I couldn't use the computer if the system was activated. Apparently I needed a second dedicated line for the security system.

I called the telephone company and they said they were sorry, but I couldn't have another line. They knew I needed that second line, but they were not obligated legally or morally to bring me another line until Toup LaPrix paid his debt to them. I asked how much Toup LaPrix owed them, thinking that my life was worth some investment.

I guess I pushed too far because the man got rude. "Look lady I can't divulge that information. It was a contract between Toup LaPrix and our company. Ask the director of the Planning and Zoning Department or the Planning and Zoning Commission. If those people want you to have the answer to that question, they will give it to you."

Three times, I asked the County how much Toup LaPrix owed the telephone company, and I never received an answer. Whatever amount was owed, Toup had refused to pay them. He constantly told the commissioners he was still negotiating with the utility company. What it really boiled down to was he couldn't—or wouldn't—pay the amount necessary to see that the subdivision had proper utilities.

Toup had been negotiating for at least five years, and he was still unable to make a deal. The residents of the subdivision were lucky to have one phone line. The people who owned vacant lots couldn't get utilities of any kind.

CHAPTER 6

My foreman, Phil Fox, continued to drink, and by the beginning of January 1996—eight months after the incident with Jack Tattoo—he became useless as an employee, but he was still my friend. The other crewmembers were trying to fill in to keep the work up to par, but the company was suffering badly. The men were getting behind in their work, and Phil was always too drunk to help.

After awhile, he got so sick that he didn't want to drink. He was coughing a lot, so I had him come out to the house where I knew it would be warmer and safer. It was late January and the trailer had very little insulation, and it always seemed cold. Phil stayed at my house for about five days. He then decided he had become too much of a burden for me. He wanted me to take him back to the office and see if he could be of any help to the crews. He had been sober for several days. He was still coughing, and he knew he couldn't work outside in the cold. January 1996 seemed to be the coldest month we had experienced in two years. Phil insisted he could at least answer the phones and give directions to the crews.

I said, "You need to see a doctor before you go back to that cold trailer." Phil refused to go to a doctor. When he got to the plant, he called back to the house and asked me to come into town. He admitted he needed to go to the doctor. I knew he had to be getting worse. I left the house immediately and went to the plant.

When I got to the office on January 30th at 8:30 a.m., I called to Phil, and he answered from the bathroom in his quarters. He called for me to come to him. When I went in, he was sitting on the toilet, naked, and shaking all over. He had taken a shower, and his hair was wet. I asked him if he had a hair dryer. He said he didn't. I ran and got a blue blanket off his bed and covered him up. I told him, "I'll call the doctor. As soon you are able, get dressed."

"Okay," he said.

The receptionist said the doctor did not have an opening for Phil right then, but he could see him the next day. I explained that I felt this was an emergency. She advised, "In that case, you should immediately take him to the hospital emergency room."

I went into the bathroom and told Phil what we had to do. He said, "Okay, I'll be there in a minute."

I went back to the desk to wait for him to get some clothes on. I heard him flush the toilet, and move to his bedroom, so I waited. The noise stopped. I was afraid something might be wrong. I called out to him. I got no answer. I went into his room. The door was open. He was sitting on the side of his bed, naked, with his head on his knees. I spoke to him, but again he didn't answer. I touched him and his body was cold. There was blood coming from his nose. I called 9-1-1 and explained to the dispatcher that I needed help. I told her Phil was either dead or dying. I needed help quickly. She said help was right across the street and that while they were getting there, I might want to start CPR on Phil. I laid him back on the bed and began CPR.

I wiped the blood from his face, and I stuck my fingers in his mouth to be sure I had clear passage. I found a breath mint. Phil had been drinking. After searching for another mint and not finding one, I started CPR. After a few minutes, Phil grunted. That grunt gave me some encouragement. I learned much later that the "grunt" was probably a death grunt. When I had my CPR training, no one told me about a death grunt. Many of my friends had heard that grunt, but it was my first experience at facing death head on. People were supposed to die in hospitals, not while I was there alone with them and watching.

The Fire Department was located just across the street from our plant, and the firefighter arrived in minutes. I hollered out to him so he would know where we were. A paramedic came running into the bedroom. He said we needed to get Phil onto the floor so he could do his work. I do not know where my strength came from. The paramedic took position at the upper portion of Phil's body, and I put my arms under Phil's limp form. We lifted his 6 ft. 160 pound body right up over the bedposts and laid him carefully on the floor.

The man seemed shocked by my sudden strength and thanked me for my assistance. Another firefighter entered the small room. Realizing the room was too small for my presence, I jumped back onto the bed to make room for him. I left the bedroom and went into the office. I knew there was no more I could do for Phil, and the firefighters did not need my help. I was just in their way.

By 9:15 a.m., my body was shaking, my heart was broken, and there was nothing more I could do. I phoned my friend, Norv Elkins. He was a big friendly guy of about 65. He always seemed to know what to do and when to do it. Somehow, through the tears and fears, I was able to cry for his help. I told him I knew Phil Fox had just died, and I had tried hard to save him, but I knew I had failed. I hung up the phone and went outside on the porch to wait. Norv Elkins' business was close to mine, so he got there right away. I was so grateful when he arrived. I felt alone and very scared.

The firefighters managed to get Phil's body into an ambulance. One firefighter sprayed the room with a disinfectant. The second firefighter came out on the porch. He told me they were transporting Phil to the hospital. He seemed more concerned about my condition than Phil's. I assured him that I would be fine, and he left.

Norv suggested I go into the office and get cleaned up. "After you clean up, I will take you to the hospital."

I went in and quickly washed Phil Fox's blood off my hands. When I went back to Norv, he said, "Are you ready now?"

I said yes, believing I would survive the trauma. Norv's eyebrows raised, but he didn't say anything. He ushered me to his car, and we left for the hospital.

As we left the yard, Phil's right hand man, Jeff Brawer, was in the rock yard at the plant. Norv Elkins drove me over to the rock pile where Jeff was gathering rock for a landscaping project. Jeff was on a tractor. As we came up, he got down and asked me what was going on. I told him I didn't think Phil had a chance. The situation looked real bad. Jeff and Phil had worked, played, and drank beer together for many years. When they worked on jobs together, my landscaping designs were followed closely. Together they brought my pictures to life. Tears were streaming from Jeff Brawer's eyes. He said he would go to the job site and get the rest of the crew. He didn't think they would get much more accomplished that day.

We got to the hospital within minutes and waited for Phil's doctor. After what seemed like hours, the doctor came to talk to us. He had already verified the information on the hospital's records. Phil had been in the hospital before, and the doctor seemed to know some of his medical history. Phil had instructed the hospital to contact me in case of an emergency. The doctor learned I was Phil's employer, so he proceeded to tell me that Phil had passed away on the ambulance ride to the hospital. He told me that a neighbor had revived Phil from a first heart attack by using

CPR. When he had the second attack in the ambulance, the medics could not save him. Knowing I was the "neighbor," I left the hospital believing I had done all I could do to save my friend.

When we got to the house, Norv told me to go get cleaned up. I went into the bathroom, and for the first time since I left the house that morning, I looked into a mirror. I had blood all over me. No wonder the doctor had looked at me so strangely. I took a bath and put on some clean clothes. I took the clothes I had been wearing and put them in the laundry to soak. I knew I could never wear them again without reliving the events of that day.

I telephoned Phil's family first and then Norv took over the phone duties. He called his office and explained what had happened. He called the hospital and got all the details concerning the death and funeral arrangements. Phil's body was to be taken to California where he was born. He would be buried next to his mother. Norv waited until someone came to be with me, then he went down and locked up my office.

Jack had threatened and stalked Phil just as Michael Garloni had threatened and stalked my husband. The stalking of Phil Fox, or what Phil believed was stalking, had turned out to be more than his heart could handle, just as my husband couldn't take the stress of Michael's actions. I knew Phil had his weaknesses. Regardless, I felt that he, at age 41, had died prematurely of a heart attack, just like Jerry.

The officer's report showed that the county prosecutors ignored the officer's pleas when he wrote that Jack was too dangerous to be on the streets.

In a very short time, I had witnessed the deaths of two men who had become victims condemned because of inaction and indifference to their plight.

CHAPTER 7

What had started as an occasional problem at the subdivision was starting to become a major problem. The water, which came into my home from Toup LaPrix's water company, had shut down several times since I moved into my home, but Toup was always around to try to repair it within hours. When he got it turned back on, the air in the lines made a terrible racket. The thumps and bangs made by my water pipes were scary. I thought the walls in my house would collapse from the vibrations. When I complained to Toup, he would say, "I'll show ya how to turn it off and restart the system again. I'll fix it just as soon as I can. The parts are on order."

I never saw county inspectors come to the subdivision to inspect its progress. It had been three years since anyone had seen Toup LaPrix do any constructive work towards completing the subdivision. The County kept giving him extensions for a completion date and things just did not look promising for the land investors or the homeowners.

Toup LaPrix had received five years of Extensions of Time to Complete when, by January 1996, the land investors began to get angry. They had money tied up in the land and their lots had no utilities. The roads were not paved and many required four-wheel-drive vehicles. There was no lake, no water system. Few new homes were being built. As a homeowner, I had much more to lose than a lot owner. The lot owners paid for only vacant lots. My home and those of my neighbors were losing value.

The lot owners began to complain to the Arizona Department of Real Estate (ADRE). They wanted to know why the subdivision was not finished as promised. They also wanted to know what that department was going to do about the problem.

In Arizona, state law says the counties shall require all sub-dividers (any person who offers for sale or lease six or more lots) to pave roads and install utilities to each lot before selling lots to the public. This law can be found in the Arizona Revised Statutes, Title 11 § 806. 01 (G). "Boards of supervisors of counties shall prepare specifications and make orders, inspections, examinations and certificates as may be necessary to protect and complete the provisions and make them effective. The regulations shall require the posting of performance bonds, assurances or such other security as may be appropriate and necessary to assure the installation of required street, sewer, electric and water utilities, drainage, flood control and improvements meeting established minimum standards of design and construction."

Without adequate provisions by the counties, subdividers are not allowed a subdivision permit. Subdividers are also required to generate a State Real Estate Public Report, which must be made available to each prospective customer and furnished to each buyer or lessee with a copy before they sign any offer to purchase or lease.

A State Real Estate Public Report is not issued until the improvements are accomplished or the sub-divider has posted a bond or assurances covering the entire costs of completing the project. If a subdivision has not been completed, a State Public Report must include the projected completion date and who the bonding agent is. State Public Reports in Arizona are something akin to an owner's manual for the property, including such information as the location of the property relative to town and emergency services, in addition to current taxes, status of offsite improvements (water, electric and telephone hookups), and projected assessments.

The State Public Report for Toup's subdivision was based on what he had written and was supposed to have been approved by the Planning and Zoning Commission (an advisory board of volunteer citizens), the Mohave County Board of Supervisors (the executive branch of county government), and the county departments involved in issuing the necessary subdivision permits. The planning and zoning department director (who works under the supervision of the Planning and Zoning Commission) submitted the approved report directly to the ADRE for publication in March 1991, thereby sidestepping much of the approval process. At that time, the County Board of Supervisors had declared to the Arizona Department of Real Estate that Toup LaPrix had posted proper assurances for completion of all improvements in the subdivision and such assurances were approved by the county attorney and accepted by the Board of Supervisors.

In 1996, the director of the ADRE was Jerry Hotman. Back in 1989-1991, when Toup LaPrix received his permits to begin his sub-division and sell his land, Mr. Hotman had been on the Board of Supervisors of Mohave County. When we found out that he had, previous to that, been involved in a very questionable subdivision development outside of Yucca, Arizona that was never completed, we were even more discouraged.

In January, when the lot owners complained to the ADRE, they quickly learned that the ADRE could not stand behind the report, nor could they assist us in seeing that all the listed items were completed. The ADRE's speedy reply to everyone explained how there was nothing the ADRE could do for my neighbors or me. They regretted they had no authority to help or force the completion of the subdivision.

The State Real Estate Public Report I received from Toup had allowed for extensions of time for the completion of improvements, but the deadlines set by the State were November 1994. Prior to the purchase of my property, the County Planning and Zoning Department told me, and it was written in the state public report Toup gave me that completion of the subdivision was assured by Mohave County. The improvements would be in place by November 1994. In Toup LaPrix's case, the rules were changed. The completion of the roads and utilities had not taken place, and the County had failed to provide the subdivision with the paved roads and utilities, as agreed in the original contracts with the sub-divider.

Rather than calling in the required assurances and finishing the project for him in 1994, the County had chosen to extend the completion dates over and over again. They truly did not want to be forced to perform the fiduciary duties required by the law and approved by a previous board. It appeared that Toup LaPrix's securities demanded by the County would not cover the cost of completing the subdivision. The County employees believed the promissory note he had presented to the County was not collectable. The County did not want a legal conflict with him over the land assurances that accompanied the promissory note. If they foreclosed on the land he used to assure his completion of the improvements, they would have to take that money and finish his subdivision for him. The biggest problem they were trying to avoid was the publicity. Once the story got out proving the favoritism they had shown Toup LaPrix, every developer in the county would expect the same privileges.

One developer did hear of the "land-as-assurance deal" that had been made. In April 1998, he applied to the County for a deal similar to the one they had given Toup LaPrix. They were already in trouble with Toup LaPrix's non-performance, and in June 1998 they refused to allow the other developer to put up land as an assurance. He filed a lawsuit against

Mohave County in April 1999. The bond the County required was so high, he could not afford the cost. He did own land, and he was willing to put up a smaller bond and use his land value for the difference. He based his lawsuit on the fact that Toup LaPrix had been afforded a similar privilege and the County was discriminating against him.

We learned through a deposition taken in that case that the Lake Juniper Subdivision was never approved by the Planning and Zoning Commission because it was never presented to them for final approval. The laws state that this independent commission must approve the subdivision. Favoritism had allowed the laws to be broken.

A settlement was reached with the developer who sued in April 2000, and the taxpayers became the victims who had to pay.

On April 12, 1996, Toup LaPrix asked if I would mind preparing some kind of financial statement for the Lake Juniper Property Owners Association because he needed something to present to the Corporation Commission. The report was due April 15th.

I am a tax preparer and I was just finishing tax season. I told him to bring me all the financial information he could gather. I explained I would call the county assessor's office and get the assessed values of the common areas that were owned by the homeowner's association. He showed me the legal descriptions of the common areas. He brought me 13 bank statements. I started posting the checks and deposit amounts supplied in the statements. The bank had subtracted hundreds of dollars from the account for overdraft fees. On the check stubs, I noticed that many of the checks were written for "cash" and that Toup LaPrix would put "utilities," "garbage," "electric," or "maintenance," but he was cashing all the checks himself. Many of the checks had no endorsement at all. I suggested he needed to produce the receipts for those expenses. He said he would if it ever came up. I never saw any receipts.

I noticed many checks written for $140 to the girl who handed out maps of the development from the guardhouse. She was certainly no security guard. When a car came to the gate looking for Kathy and Mike Mazur's house, she informed the driver that he would find Kathy Mazur at home, but Mike Mazur had just left for work!

I told Toup LaPrix if he was going to pay an employee, he should register the association with the proper tax and insurance departments and keep everything legal. I suggested the association would be better off if he would just save the money in an account until the development got up and running. The nest egg would be very helpful later.

My brains were telling me embezzlement, but my heart was hoping my brain was over-reacting. After a good review, my brain won the argument.

He said, "We can't save money in the association. We have to spend every cent. That account can't have a positive balance. Don't worry about the taxes. I don't have to pay taxes. I'm exempt."

He explained at length how he had entered into an irrevocable trust. He said many rich people do that to protect their assets. According to Toup LaPrix, everyone was always picking out a rich person to sue. An irrevocable trust was the only way to go. He said that was how all his assets had been converted. The trustees then hired him to manage the assets. The money Toup LaPrix was paid came from the trust in the form of wages. It was an expense of the trust and all his housing, food, car expenses, and anything he needed became tax-exempt. If someone sued him, he owned nothing. No one could ever take anything from him.

I knew there had to be more to that story. I began to wonder why Toup LaPrix would need such a trust. I asked him, but I did not get an answer.

When I returned my unaudited completed work to Toup LaPrix, he said the Homeowner's Association would be having a meeting within a couple of months and that he would ask them to pay me for my services. I agreed.

There was never an association meeting with anyone or any votes approving any expenditure. A check never came. The lot owners were getting upset because many had no utilities, no water, and no paved roads to their lots. Toup LaPrix had now decided it was time to bill them late charges for failing to pay their homeowner's association dues. The dues were to be collected to provide maintenance of improvements that did not exist.

The lot owners wanted some answers. Because I lived in the subdivision, I received many calls and letters. The investors were hurting. Some had borrowed money to purchase their lot, hoping to turn over a profit. Some wanted to build, but the improvements to their lots had not been made.

Nineteen people owned property in the subdivision. Some had purchased lots from Toup LaPrix and others had exchanged work for land. It seemed every one of those owners were angry. Many knew that they had become victims of land fraud and many were prepared to sue to get their money back.

On April 20th, I received a letter from a man who lived in California and had purchased a lot in the subdivision. The road leading to the man's lot was not passable. It had a big 3 ft. deep wash that crossed the main road. Without a good horse, you could not get over it, under it, around it, or through it.

The man expressed concern over the lack of improvements in the subdivision. He informed me that in March 1995, Toup LaPrix had begun billing him for homeowner's dues. He wanted to know: "#1. Are the roads paved? #2. Are there any utilities to my lot line? #3. Does my lot have water service? #4. How many lots in the subdivision have the promised improvements? #5. Is the gate guarded 24-7? #6. When was the last homeowner's meeting? #7. Did you approve of the 100 percent per month late penalty being imposed by the homeowner's association?" He gave me a telephone number to call and the hours I could reach him.

For a year, I had been paying homeowner's dues because I knew Toup LaPrix was blading the roads on the south side of the development when it rained. I live on the south side. Since the dues were only $50 a month, with Toup LaPrix's permission, I paid them quarterly. I had never been charged 100 percent late fees or harassed about payments. I had never seen a bill for dues.

I called the man in response to his letter and I explained: "In March 1995, Toup LaPrix had invited Martin Coole and me to breakfast at his house. Since we were the only homeowners living in the subdivision at that time, we jokingly called the meeting to order and said the most important issue to discuss was if Toup LaPrix had made a good Bloody Mary. We formally closed the meeting, hitting our spoons on our glasses. We had our drink and meal. It was a good Bloody Mary, and Mr. LaPrix had proved he knew how to cook with class. No one took minutes. During the meeting, I noticed broken plumbing pipes had flooded Toup LaPrix's house. The ceilings in his den area were in desperate need of repair. I was careful not to walk under a piece of sheetrock that was hanging by a lone nail. I looked up and asked him what happened. He explained the plumber had done a real bad job at connecting his pipes and that he was having a battle getting the necessary repairs completed. I don't think he has any money."

(It was much later that I discovered what really happened to Toup's pipes. The failure of his water company to filter out the high TDS or supply reverse osmosis to correct the water problems and the inconsistent water pressure was raising havoc in the homes built with copper plumbing.)

"I can assure you, Toup LaPrix has done nothing noticeable towards improving the subdivision or the water company since 1993. He has been working on the dam and another subdivision down the road," I said. "Your lot does not have water, utilities, roads, drainage, or access at this time."

"Thank you for being so honest. May I contact you again?" he said.

"Anytime," I replied.

In early June 1996, the same man sent me a copy of a letter he had written to Toup LaPrix. The letter called for a formal meeting of the association. I had no problem with that request. My dues were paid. By this time the man's bills for dues and late fees amounted to over $1600, and Toup LaPrix was threatening to file liens against his lot. The dues were low enough, but the late charges were killing everyone who was questioning what right Toup had to collect the dues when the lots in the subdivision had no services of any kind.

A man named Olson called me long distance several times, and another man named Don Hamilton phoned from Golden Valley, Arizona. All the men were upset over the possibility of losing their investments. No pressure from anyone could convince Toup LaPrix to call a homeowners association meeting or to complete any of the improvements in the subdivision. The lot owners refused to pay dues for maintenance of things that did not exist. They could not start construction on their lots because the banks would not finance a project without water connections to the lots and they could not sell.

Because of the beautiful location, the investors from other states had been easily taken in by Toup LaPrix's false promises. It was not hard to visualize profits in such an area. By this time, all the lot owners were convinced that they had become the victims of land fraud. When the men complained to the county attorney, they were told, "You took a certain amount of risk when you purchased lots in an unfinished subdivision."

Six of the lot owners got together two months later, in August, and decided to file a class action civil lawsuit against Toup LaPrix in the Arizona Superior Court.

Fraud in Mohave County is usually considered a civil issue. When approaching most anyone of authority in the county, I found the words land and fraud are never used together in a sentence by the officials and ultimately do not appear to constitute a criminal act. Land fraud causes so much heartache and destruction for the victims that it should have a special criminal law in Arizona, with large fines, penalties, and mandatory victim's restitution, plus about ten years in the slammer.

There were several files in the courthouse with Toup LaPrix's name on them. A large hamburger chain had a federal case going. The Internal Revenue Service had placed a levy on the rent the hamburger chain was paying Toup LaPrix. When the hamburger chain stopped sending the rent money to Toup and sent the money to Uncle Sam, Toup LaPrix sued them. An electric sign company had recently won a $160,000 judgment against him. A mortgage company and a trust had a judgment against him, and a single land investor had won a suit against him. A foreclosure on his home was in progress and Toup LaPrix had not paid anything to anybody.

Everyone who owned property in the Lake Juniper Subdivision was frustrated, and they all believed the County should call the assurances (bond) and finish the subdivision, as agreed. We knew Toup LaPrix did not intend to do any more with the lands.

Toup warned me to quit talking to the lot owners about the subdivision. He said, "You are just getting everyone all stirred up over nothing. It may take me a few more years to complete this project, but if the County gets involved, it will be a disaster. Those bureaucrats will destroy this subdivision." Even though I too was a victim of his fraud, I had immediately become the cause of his problems!

Toup LaPrix told me he was not at all worried about the completion dates set for him by the bureaucrats. He would complete everything when he damn well pleased. He stated he would continue to receive extensions for the rest of his life because his power was absolute. He said there was nothing that either the State or the County could do to prevent him from getting those extensions. He told me he had one inspector thrown in jail for trespassing on his private land when the state inspector entered the subdivision to inspect his progress. He claimed that in a period prior to my arrival in the subdivision, he held the inspector at gunpoint, called the sheriff, accused the inspector of trespassing on his private land, and had the inspector thrown in jail. The sheriff dutifully took the inspector to jail! When I asked officials for a copy of that police report, I learned it was a legal issue, and I could not have the report without first obtaining permission from the Arizona attorney general. The attorney general's office ignored my request. I felt sure there would be no further inspections of the subdivision by state employees. In learning it was a legal issue, I began to believe Toup's story was true. I wondered, "What kind of power does this man have? Will all of the authorities ignore my requests for information?"

That inspector was obviously not from Mohave County. For six years, the County had not received even an "as-built" progress report from an inspector. (An as-built progress report documents the state of the project at a particular time.) It was well known to all the residents of the subdivision that county employees had not been on the grounds of the Lake Juniper Subdivision for many years. When the lot owners met at a local restaurant in August 1996, they discussed the lack of improvements to the subdivision. There was much talk about "the Good 'ol Boys" and how the long arm of the County reached into and squeezed the state agencies. An *Arizona Republic* newspaper article brought to the meeting said the governor believed no one should be taking a risk when purchasing land in Arizona.

The lot owners were not getting helpful responses from the County or the governor, and they felt sure there would be no help unless they got together and sued Toup LaPrix. One man was selected to find an attorney who would handle the case.

Explaining that I didn't know much about the laws but I could read, I volunteered to research land fraud and see what I could find about other cases that had been tried in Arizona.

There were several cases in the Arizona appellate courts that cited fraud as being a major issue in land sales. Searching the Arizona Revised Statutes for "land fraud" on the state's website returned a blank screen. In most counties, fraud appeared to be reviewed as a civil issue. In one court case, I found an appellate court judge's opinion that said, "...In earlier times the law gave no protection to the consumer. Land fraud was rampant in Arizona. The judgment creditor had to get his money out of the judgment debtor any way he could and at his own expense. Then the legislature wrote new laws in Title 11 in the 1970s. These laws were written to protect the consumer from land fraud."

It was a great thought and a good effort on the part of the legislature to provide Title 11, but the state laws were not reaching to rural counties. On a radio broadcast on K-AAA the County Attorney was answering questions as they were received at the Station. A man who lives in a less fortunate part of the county asked the attorney why the slumlord laws were not being enforced in Mohave County. He said his neighborhood was over run with trash and that the people who owned the property didn't even live in Arizona and could care less about their property or the safety of the neighborhood. The attorney's response given to the man's question was that many of the laws passed by the state legislature were not meant to apply to Mohave County. The county is such a remote, rural area, that the laws passed by the state legislature cannot possibly be enforced there. Many laws apply only to populated counties such as Maricopa County, which includes the city of Phoenix.

Also in August 1996, when I had lived in my home almost two years, another of Toup LaPrix's unfulfilled promises became an issue. "When are you going to get around to installing the cable?" I asked.

"Oh just get yourself one of those new receiving dishes and install it in your attic. They are a lot cheaper than what I would charge you to bring the cable to your lot."

I said, "Toup, I paid for cable to be brought to the lot line when I purchased the high-priced lot."

He responded with, "No, ya didn't, and I don't need to take your shit."

I said cautiously, "I'm sorry. I didn't mean to make you mad."

"Oh yes you did." He quickly went to his car and drove off at high speed, leaving a big trail of dirt on my new landscaping project. I knew he was upset over the actions being taken against him by the lot owners, so I didn't allow his reaction to bother me much.

CHAPTER 8

The month before, I got to see first-hand how the Superior Court of Mohave County operates. I had received a notice from the Victim Witness Program announcing a hearing the following week regarding Jack Tattoo. Apparently he had been "busy" since his release on bond on May 2, 1995 and had been arrested in California. Judge Blinders would be presiding over the State's case.

When I arrived at the courtroom door, it was locked. There was a man standing in the hall waiting for access to the same courtroom. Not knowing who the man was and considering the muscles he had under his shirt, I quietly sat down on a chair next to the courtroom door.

"You here for the Tattoo hearing?" he said.

"Yes. I am a one of his victims," I replied.

"No need for you to sit and wait. The only thing that will happen in there today is the court hearing my plea," he said.

"Your plea?"

"Yep. The son of a bitch jumped bail. I am the bonding agent. I found him in a prison in Riverside County, California, so I can't bring him back. I have to beg the judge to give me my 5,000 bucks back," he explained.

"Do you know why he is in prison in California? What did he do over there?" I asked.

"Misuse of firearms, a felony violation. They say he was scaring the people on the freeway with a loaded gun. Can't tell ya for sure, but whatever he did, it cost him a year in prison. He's been missing for a few months, but I only found out recently that they were planning on forfeiting the bond. I don't know why the probation office didn't tell me they had problems months ago. Once I found out he was missing, I found him. I can't bring him back here, though," he said.

After we were allowed into the courtroom, the judge made a deal with the bondsman. The County would be reimbursed for the cost of transporting Jack Tattoo from Riverside County, California back to Mohave County to stand trial out of the bond money. After the trial, Jack Tattoo would have to be taken back to finish his sentence in California. The bondsman would get the money the sheriff did not use. He had paid out $5,000; he would get back about $4,500.

To my knowledge, the other victims did not know Jack Tattoo was even missing! No one had informed *me* of the problem. I went directly to my office and started going through the office files. Phil had a file of his own there, and I wondered if the Victim Witness Program had sent him any information regarding the disappearance.

Phil had collected and hidden a stack of letters he had received from the Victim Witness Program. Not one of those letters explained to Phil that the court lost Jack, but they had enough information in them for Phil to figure that out for himself.

Jack Tattoo was arrested by MAGNET (the drug enforcement section of the county's law enforcement). There was a report written on November 8, 1995 to the court by the arresting officer. A Pre-sentence Investigation Report filed with the court by the Probation Department stated that the arresting officer felt Jack Tattoo was getting a light sentence, possibly too light. The officer was not pleased with the outcome of this case. The report stated they had interviewed Phil Fox, and he also did not agree with the outcome. He had asked the officer how someone could point a gun at another person and get probation. MAGNET had arrested Jack Tattoo and charged him with six offenses, five of which were felonies and one "undesignated." Listed in the order of the counts, the paper read: "I. Burglary, 2. Aggravated Assault, 3. Theft, 4. Theft, 5. Theft." The sixth charge, with count number 2 again written before it, read: "Possession of Drug Paraphernalia and Driving under the Influence of Intoxicating Liquor."

The next letter, written in December 1995, contained a Supplemental Pre-sentence Investigation Report under the heading Probation Evaluation. The officer wrote that on four occasions, Jack's girlfriend called the Probation Department and rescheduled his appointments for Intensive Probation Supervision (IPS) screening, using the excuse that Jack was ill. For quite some time, the probation officer had been unable to speak with him.

The Probation Department had no way of knowing Jack's whereabouts. In a final effort to speak with him personally, the officer telephoned Jack's residence. His girlfriend answered the call and explained to the officer that Jack was not home. The officer was also told that Jack was going to talk to his attorney before he came into the office for an IPS screening.

That excuse seemed strange to me. Since when does the defendant tell the court what he is going to do before he will comply with the court's order?

In the same envelope, the probation officer assigned to Jack's case submitted a probation evaluation to the court, also written in December 1995. She respectfully recommended in that report that Jack Tattoo *not* be granted Intensive Probation Supervision.

I was sure Phil hid those letters so I wouldn't worry about our safety. More letters began to arrive at the office addressed to Phil Fox sent from the Victim Witness Program. I called Phil's family and explained the letters. Phil's sister told me to open them, read them, and send her a copy.

One of the letters stated that the State and Jack Tattoo had successfully reached plea agreement on November 18, 1996. The county attorney's office had entered into an agreement with Jack's attorney that would allow Jack probation rather than spending time in the penitentiary. All but two of the counts filed against Jack Tattoo would be dismissed. If Phil did not agree to the terms of the agreement, he was to notify the prosecutor immediately.

The letters allowed that a victim of crime in Arizona has the right to let the court know what the crime had done to the victim's life. The victim can either appear in court in person or write the judge a "Victim's Impact Statement." Such a statement must be submitted to the prosecutor, in an open envelope, to be presented by the prosecutor to the judge.

I later decided to test the victims' rights laws. Writing to a judge would be hard on me emotionally, but what was there to lose? After long discussions with Phil's family, I sat down and wrote a long letter to Judge Blinders on December 1, 1996. Making sure it was sent, as directed, to the county attorney in charge of the case, the letter included a case number and a cover letter addressed to the attorney doing the bargaining, asking that my letter be given to the judge.

My letter simply stated that Jack Tattoo had threatened to return and kill the people who turned him in—namely Phil Fox and me. I could only tell the court what Phil Fox told me when I found him in a state of fear. The letter also explained to the judge Jack Tattoo's threats, Phil Fox's reaction to the threats, Jack Tattoo's stalking of Phil Fox, Phil's return to the bottle, and his ultimate death. My damaged possessions could be replaced, but the victim who stood to lose the most was Phil Fox's 14-year-old son. A sentence of probation was not acceptable.

It was my hope that having read such a letter, the judge would see that Jack's crimes had far-reaching consequences.

It would be another six months until the felony hearing for Jack would come around—20 months after his original arrest on April 30, 1995 (and release the next day).

CHAPTER 9

November 1996 was a busy month for the subdivision issues. In that month, Toup LaPrix filed for another extension of time to complete the subdivision. No one had witnessed any progress being made in the subdivision. All the property owners were against any more extensions. When the County posted a zoning notice in front of the subdivision stating there would be a meeting on November 13th involving our subdivision, my neighbors and I were of very curious as to what would go on at the meeting and, of course, planned to go.

One week before the meeting date, the homeowners sent a letter asking for an audience with the Mohave County Planning and Zoning Commission. The letter suggested we were in need of help and that we wanted the County to call in someone competent to complete the subdivision improvements, utilizing the bond that had been posted by the developer.

In that letter, we used the word "bond." Toup LaPrix had told us the subdivision was bonded. That word "bonded" was plastered on billboards advertising the subdivision. It was on all the advertising fliers. The real estate brokers believed the subdivision was bonded. The lot owners could not find that the county attorney had required Toup LaPrix to obtain a bond or any kind of insurance at all.

At the public meeting of the Zoning Commission November 13th, the approval of Toup LaPrix's time extensions was already on the consent agenda along with several other consent items, and it appeared our letter to that commission was misplaced. The consent agenda appears on the top of the formal agenda and all activity listed there is considered in one single vote at the beginning of every meeting, unless there is an objection.

We were never called to speak. The microphone was acting up, and the chairman cut it off because of the noise it was making. He then leaned over, lowered his head, and said something to the other members. The next thing we knew, the microphone had been miraculously repaired, and the extension of time had been recommended by staff and approved for the sixth year by the commissioners.

Toup LaPrix immediately left the room, and when we publicly questioned the previous events, the planning and zoning director, Director Mallard, called for a recess and met us outside. She listened to our complaints about not being heard, and she suggested we might be allowed to voice our complaints later in the meeting, but the decision could not be changed because Toup LaPrix was no longer present. No one had even read our letter or, if they did, they ignored it. She suggested we appear at the County Board of Supervisor's meeting next month and voice our opinions. The Board of Supervisors had to give the extension their approval as well.

I gave Director Mallard a handful of pictures I had taken in the development. They showed oil spills, illegal electric wiring, plumbing lines, and a lot of garbage piled up. I suggested she might want to check out the oil spills and some other violations that were present. I explained the violations could be found near the proposed lake area and eventually would cause great harm to someone.

It seemed more than a coincidence that Toup LaPrix dug holes and covered some of the offending areas within a week after I gave Director Mallard the pictures.

At a November Board of Supervisors meeting, we filled out the proper requests for a hearing, then sat all day waiting for our turn to speak. After hours of waiting, we were not allowed to speak. We were placed last on the agenda and when they got to us, the item was "Referred to Staff."

The Mohave County Board of Supervisors held a posted meeting on December 2nd, 1996 with regards to extensions of time reviewed by the Planning and Zoning Commission that had taken place in September. They knew it was the last time they could approve or disapprove of the Zoning Commission's findings. It was certainly the last meeting they would have to review our problems and face us. None of the sitting board members had chosen to run for a new term. All the people who had purchased lots at Lake Juniper showed up at that meeting, except Toup LaPrix.

We had all formally signed in asking to speak against the extension issue. The meeting started at 9:00 a.m., and we waited for our turn to speak. Our item had been placed close to last on the agenda. After most of the public had left the room, we were actually asked to speak. We explained to the supervisors the confusion we experienced in the commissioners' meeting, and they allowed us to express our views. They learned right away that none of us were happy campers and that suits were being prepared and/or filed against the developer for fraud.

Only then was the public advised by the planning and zoning director that the state's Real Estate Department, of which Supervisor Hotman's husband was the director, had pulled Toup LaPrix's public report from the active file on October 5th. Toup LaPrix had been asked to submit a letter to the State, voluntarily withdrawing his rights to sell any more lots in the subdivision until the completion of the roads and utilities were accomplished. It was December and For Sale signs were still on the lots as well as a billboard advertising the subdivision.

The chairman of the Board of Supervisors suggested that the board approve the extension of Toup LaPrix's phase one (our tract) until March 17, 1997. With that approval came limitations. Toup LaPrix would be given that extra time to pave all the roads in the subdivision and see that proper utilities were afforded every lot.

I asked to be heard, and I argued that Toup LaPrix could not achieve all the requirements the chair was requesting of him in such a short period. I suggested it was an unreasonable request.

One of the county employees put a map of our subdivision up on the wall, and the chair asked us where we lived. We showed him the lots we owned on the map. He asked if I thought it would be fair for the board to request a portion of the roads to be completed. The portion he had in mind covered the main gate area and one-half of the distance of the road leading to our homes.

I agreed that was fair and stated that I also believed the utilities most needed were the telephone lines. I didn't want to financially strap Toup LaPrix, and we were all willing to work with him to succeed in a fine development. Toup LaPrix's shoes kept telling me he needed help. They were old, polished loafers, but they were telling me he was broke. My suggestion was made in an effort to give him some sort of a financial break.

After the meeting, Director Mallard returned my photos. She told me she had the oil spills checked by the Health Department and they were not dangerous. She admitted they were not pretty, but she insisted they were not harmful. In her opinion, there was nothing dangerous in the subdivision.

When I questioned the female representative of the Mohave County Health Department, Sally Mander, she told me she was never asked to check out any oil spills in the subdivision. She claimed her department never knew of nor had seen my pictures of the oil spills. She said perhaps

OSHA (Occupational Safety and Health Administration) had been called, but I laughed at that suggestion.

If I had spilled that much oil at my rock plant, I would have been in big trouble with the environmental people. Anyone who came from such an influential family in Mohave County would, of course, be exempt from being held liable for spilling a "little bit of old oil." For the next three years, we lived with the fear of fire that the illegal electrical wiring exposed us to, as well as the oil spills that could take out the whole area.

When the December 2nd resolution came in print from the board, it stated exactly what portion of the roads had to be completed. It stated that two telephone lines had to be available for each existing residence in the development. The second and third phases of the development were not allowed any further extensions of time and those permits were withdrawn. (That one small statement saved 159 people and their families from becoming additional victims of Toup LaPrix.) If the work was not accomplished timely, the assurance property would be sold and the subdivision permits withdrawn. Toup LaPrix was not to sell, trade, or in any way dispose of any more lots in the subdivision until the subdivision was completed. Our fears of fire were not addressed.

That same day as the Board of Supervisors meeting on December 2nd, Toup LaPrix was busy changing his trusts around. He added his friend Cowboy Joe to all his deeds as a trustee of the lands as well as a company called The Brats Consulting Group. When they did that and recorded the transaction, the county assessor doubled the assessed values of every lot in the subdivision. The lands had no water, power, sewer, roads, or fire protection, and many could not be reached without four-wheel drive vehicles, but the assessor couldn't have cared less. The people who were paying the abnormally high taxes were investors who had purchased a Certificate of Purchase (CP) at tax sale hoping to make a buck or two on the interest. They were not allowed by law to protest the assessment increase because they did not own the property. The County made a swift $256,000 on that deal, and the victims were the CP holders, not Toup LaPrix. He did not pay taxes. Not only was the assessor failing to punish Toup LaPrix and Cowboy Joe by increasing their tax obligations, she was succeeding in punishing everyone else who owned lots in the subdivision and, at the same time, successfully increasing the County's income. She needed a paycheck and that was the deal. All the defrauded lot owners now became the victims of the county assessor.

Toup LaPrix had deeded land over to the County as assurances for completion of the subdivision in 1990. He had changed the deed to the property that the County was holding for assurance and recorded his new deed, thus causing a clouded title.

Cowboy Joe and Toup LaPrix mistakenly believed that by changing the trustee, Cowboy Joe would then be able to sell the lots in the subdivision. Since Toup LaPrix had made the voluntary agreement with the State of Arizona to discontinue the sale of lots until the development improvements were completed, Cowboy Joe took over the sale of lots.

CHAPTER 10

January 1997 brought the felony hearing for Jack Tattoo. Watching what went on in that courtroom turned my stomach sour.

Entering the courtroom, not knowing who was related to whom and which one had a gun, was scary. I was petrified. Even though the courtroom seemed quite large, there were only two rows of seating for the spectators. Phil's brother-in-law, Gary Van Ness, sat next to me, and we both made sure we had our backs to a wall.

The courthouse had no protective devices in use that screened people for weapons before they entered. I understood they owned such equipment, but at that time, it was stored in the basement of the courthouse. (The courts had not been given the funding by the Board of Supervisors to pay for guards, installation, and operation of the equipment.)

An officer brought in two men dressed in bright orange. Both men were shackled. The deputy seated the men in the empty jury box. There was no need for a jury that day. Plea bargains had been reached. One convict was Jack Tattoo. Mohave County finally "borrowed" him from California for his hearing here. Seeing him there in chains reminded me of what my late husband Jerry had said about his responsibilities as a lawyer, and how he was spending too much of his life seeing all the bad sides of life.

Until a person becomes a victim, it is difficult to realize what really goes on in the courtrooms. I had previously shut out all the surrounding crime, believing, "It will never happen to or affect me." Well for me, it was happening. Much worse, I was facing the "New American Judicial System" that my late husband had hated.

Attorney Bargain, the prosecutor, would never bring peace to his victims, and in my opinion and those of the arresting officers, his agreement fell a long way short of justice. The police, probation officers, Phil, and the victims didn't approve of the bargain. Would the judge stop it?

As the judge entered the courtroom, everyone was instructed by the clerk to rise. He moved quickly to his position on the bench and instructed everyone to be seated.

I looked at that judge, wiped my eyes, and looked at him again. He was the same man that Phil had helped after the wind blew down his climbing rose bush. Phil and the crew went to this judge's house, trimmed all his bushes, and reset his trellis. The men had worked a couple of days sprucing up the landscaping. When it came time for me to bill the judge for the work the men had done, Phil asked me not to send the bill. He explained that the young judge had a lot of children, had not been on the bench long, and said he could not afford the landscape plumbing work that the yard desperately needed. He thought the least he could do to help was to secure his trellis and trim his bushes. "Forget the cost of the labor, and we will catch the judge the next time around," he had said.

The first case called did not involve Jack. I listened to that case but it didn't mean a lot to me, except for the fact that this prisoner stuttered often, and he obviously needed a considerable amount of counseling and attitude adjustments. The prisoner knew he had done something wrong. After the judge allowed him to speak, I was not so sure the prisoner knew exactly what was illegal. His actions had produced a victim, but I did not see his victim in the courtroom. The judge ruled that the defendant needed some mental help.

When the case number for Jack Tattoo was called, Jack rose from his chair and moved toward the defense table. The shackles made it difficult for him to walk. He, like the criminal before him, was wearing a carrot-colored outfit that resembled a pair of short-sleeved pajamas. His footwear resembled house slippers. For the first time, I could see that Jack's upper body, arms, and neck were full of massive tattoos. He did not have much skin showing that was not colored by ink. It was a bit shocking to learn that the long sleeved shirts Jack wore to work were hiding all those tattoos.

"This Court understands a plea agreement has been reached. Is that correct?" the judge asked.

"Yes, Your Honor," Attorney Bargain, the prosecutor, replied.

The judge scanned the pages in his file and he said, "I do not see the plea agreement in the court's file."

"Oh, excuse me, Your Honor," Attorney Bargain said, as he stood up and took a copy of the agreement to the judge.

It made me feel rather insecure knowing that the judge did not have the plea agreement in the court's file to review as he read my victim's letter. He began reading the papers given to him, then he said, "I recall reading somewhere that the Probation Department did not feel Mr. Tattoo was a candidate for probation. Is my recollection correct?"

"Yes, Your Honor, that was the first report, but they have changed their position on that," both attorneys replied in unison.

Now why would the probation officers change their position, when they had to get this defendant out of prison in another state before he could appear in this courtroom? His actions had proved their original reports were correct.

"Are there any victims present who would like to speak to the Court?" the judge asked.

"Yes, Your Honor. Gary Van Ness, the brother of Phil Fox, would like to speak," Attorney Bargain responded.

"If you will make it brief, the court's time is running short," the judge advised.

Gary stated that his family firmly believed Phil's early demise was caused partially by the fear instilled in Phil's mind by Jack and his actions. Jack did not know Phil had a weak heart, but his lack of knowledge could not excuse his stalking of Phil while Phil was working. The family found it hard to believe that Jack was being allowed probation, no matter how strict the probation was to be. Gary lived in California, close to where Jack was currently serving a year in prison. Jack had been sent to prison for one year just for wielding a gun in that state. He had three felony convictions when he committed the two felonies bargained and brought before the court.

Gary's pleas on behalf of his family fell on deaf ears. The deal was done. It saved the court money and time. There could be no changes in the pre-planned decision.

As Gary spoke, there appeared to be boredom in Judge Blinders' eyes. He left the impression of, "So sit down, shut up, and quit wasting the court's time." Gary Van Ness' trip was just a waste of time and money. A lot of money! The county doesn't have a major airport, so the airline tickets were extremely costly.

When Gary sat down, the judge said," I believe there was a letter from a Mrs. Lewis sent to the court. Did both counsels read her letter before reaching an agreement?"

The prosecutor (the same man I sent the open letter to for forwarding to the judge), told the judge the letter was not in his file. He did not believe he had seen it! The defendant's counsel said he had not seen the letter either. Jack Tattoo and his father stated in that courtroom, they had read it. Who gave it to them? Why would the prosecutor ignore something that might help prosecute a firearm-enhanced, drug-related crime? How could the prosecutor lose a victim's statement?

The judge ordered the court clerk to make a copy of the letter and to see that both attorneys received copies of the document for their files.

I put my fingers to my lips and started quietly patting my mouth. Gary leaned over and whispered, "Are you okay?"

"I really prefer to be kissed while I am getting screwed," I answered.

The judge glared in our direction as if to say, "Be quiet," then turned his attentions to the defendant's counsel. He asked the lawyer if his client understood and agreed to the plea agreement. Jack's lawyer assured the court that Jack was willing to accept the agreement. Jack was asked to confirm his lawyer's statement, which he did without any hesitation.

As Jack sat straight in his chair, he was sentenced to probation, as per the final agreement. This was the first time in my life I had witnessed the "Let's Make A Deal" portion of our judicial system. It was obvious to me as a victim that no consideration was given to what really happened the day Jack went on his crime spree. The State was indifferent to the arresting officer's reports, the Probation Department's reports, Jack's past criminal record, and to the future victims of Jack Tattoo.

Everyone in that courtroom was silent. I was so angry that my heart began pounding. I placed my hand on my chest, hoping to quiet my heart's reaction and hide that reaction from the people in that courtroom.

It appeared the laws of the State of Arizona were set aside.

I began questioning whether I lived in the U.S.A. or in another world. I had gone to all the trouble to write to the judge and tell him how badly Jack Tattoo affected my company and me. The response Gary and I felt in that courtroom was "Big deal! Quit whining! Die if you must, but shut up about it."

Judge Blinders set a date for the restitution hearing for six months later, on June 27th, so the attorneys could consider the impact Jack Tattoo's actions had on me and on Phil Fox's family. He explained to Jack the probation conditions. If Jack Tattoo accepted the terms, he would not be able to appeal the court's decision.

After it was explained what Jack Tattoo's punishment was to be, the judge told Jack he was lucky to be receiving such a plea agreement. He said the court would be watching his every move. The judge then concluded the hearing.

The restitution Jack should have paid to his victims was about 15 years in prison. No money awarded the victims would satisfy. The taxpayers pay through the nose to educate our children against crime, and we can't even afford to successfully prosecute the criminals that are ruining our children's safety. Gary had pled for some sort of security for Phil Fox's son. The court denied that security. A deal had been made and it seemed to the victims that the laws of Arizona had no enforceable meaning.

The deputy county prosecuting attorney, Attorney Bargain, came over to where Gary and I were getting up from our seats. Perhaps he felt that if Gary was related to a dead victim, he should spend a small amount of the County's time and money to offer his condolences. He introduced himself and said he would answer any questions Gary might have regarding the proceedings. He assured us that we would be kept updated on Jack Tattoo's progress with regards to his probation. He said he understood our concerns and we would be hearing from the Victim Witness Program regularly. He never apologized to us for being a political pawn, and his promises never happened.

Our conversation was interrupted by the appearance of Jack Tattoo's father. He was very angry with me for the letter I had written. After listening to his complaint, I realized that he was in denial about what his son had done. Jack's father's inability to accept the fact that his son was a habitual criminal and had destroyed the lives of many people easily placed him in the category of being a victim of his own son's criminal acts. I wondered how many years he would suffer because of a father's love for his son.

I stood quietly listening to the distraught man until Attorney Bargain intervened and told him that he should move along. He told Mr. Tattoo that if he wanted to sue me for what I had said in the letter, to just do it and quit threatening.

Gary Van Ness asked many questions of the prosecutor about the plea-bargaining and the sentencing. I listened to the questions, and they were very straightforward. The responses, however, were not very acceptable.

Attorney Bargain explained to Gary that there had been no real need for Gary to spend the hundreds of dollars necessary to appear in the courtroom that day. The agreement had been reached, and everything was cut and dried. Nothing the victims had to offer made any difference.

He tried to explain how difficult it would be to convict Jack Tattoo before a jury because Phil had died and would not be available to testify. He never tried to explain Jack's side of the story about what happened. If there was one, it was ignored.

All we, as victims, heard was a convenient excuse! The other victim died, so the suspect walks and the prosecutor saves the time and cost of an investigation and a trial. Could a criminal imply from this that it is better to kill their victim than to "let them off the hook?" It was strange that the suspect had marijuana growing in his closet, had the stolen newspaper racks in the bed of his truck, and had left his own blood all over my property, but the State could not find enough evidence to convict.

Attorney Bargain said that if we wanted to file a civil suit against Jack Tattoo for the damages we felt his actions caused, we should contact his clerk. She would get us the papers and instructions for filing such a suit. He also requested we get the forms from his office that would allow his and any other agency involved to keep us informed of any post-conviction rulings on the case. He explained it would allow us to learn of Jack's progress and whereabouts until his probation period was completed.

What we were facing was a civil lawsuit against a life-long criminal who had nothing of value to his name. We could file a civil suit, pay the lawyers thousands of dollars, and get a useless judgment in return. We were just victims condemned by the system.

Because we filed the necessary forms, the Victim Witness Program was supposed to keep us advised of what was going on. Actually, we learned very little. There were no reports as to this criminal's progress. I had occasionally received *very* small checks from the court clerks who were monitoring the restitution ordered by the court.

January 1997 was also the month when my body began acting up. It seemed no matter what I wanted to do, my body told me, "not today." I was passing out and hitting the floor for no reason at all. My blood felt like it was burning inside my body, and I was having severe pains behind my breastbone. At times, my vision was so impaired that I'd just go back to bed. The whites of my eyes were often yellow; my pupils glittered; sometimes it felt as if I was looking at the world through the bottom of a brown beer bottle.

My neighbor, Kathy Mazur, had been monitoring my blood pressure as often as she could. My friend Norv Elkins would come to the house every morning at 9:00 a.m. and take me to the fire station. The firefighters were always happy to monitor my blood pressure. They said it gave them more experience. My pressure was running very high. The readings were often 200/110. I was very weak, and it felt like my white and red corpuscles were having a war inside my system.

I went to my family doctor, and he sent me to other medical facilities for tests. The tests were very expensive and the results did not explain anything. A cardiologist said I needed a full battery of tests and that it was going to cost tens of thousands of dollars. My insurance did not pay well unless I was hospitalized, so the doctor decided to put me in the hospital on February 16th to run the tests. His report said I looked much older than my given age. That comment did not make me feel any better, but it was true. The tests were something I could have gone through easily enough on a much less expensive outpatient basis, but the new insurance rules stated I had to be in a hospital room or they would not pay.

In the late morning on February 14th, I went to Laughlin, Nevada with some friends. We ate lunch, then ended up staying the whole day. By the time I ate again—at dinner—it was 10:20 p.m., and I was quite hungry. I got up to go through the buffet line and a burning sensation ran up my neck. It felt like I was going to spit fire. I asked my friend, Guido, to take me outside for air. As we were heading for the door, I collapsed. When I came to, I was looking up at two security guards hovering over me. I had been drinking bottled water all afternoon and evening. I had consumed two glasses of wine at lunch, but that had been ten hours earlier. I told the officers what had occurred and that I didn't know what was wrong. I didn't think the wine I drank at lunch would have caused such a reaction. They assured me I was sober. They kept an eye on heavy drinkers, and I surely was not one. One guard suggested that perhaps I just stood in line too long waiting for something to eat. They took me outside for fresh air and it helped for a minute, but as soon as I went back into the restaurant, I started to pass out again.

Guido got the guards and they called an ambulance. They took me to the Bullhead City Hospital, where I stayed for five days. The hospital ran a full battery of tests on my heart, my blood, and my head. There were cat-scans, blood tests, stress tests, and nothing could be accurately diagnosed. They called in heart specialists from Las Vegas, but my heart passed all his tests. The alcohol level in my blood remained constant for three of the five days. I knew nothing had been added to my bottled water. The waitress, as a courtesy, broke the seal on the bottles when she handed them to me. I watched her. There were no shenanigans performed by the casino employees. No one suggested that perhaps my liver was not functioning properly, but I was curious.

The next day, when I asked the doctor to explain the alcohol level, he said it was nothing to worry about. I worried anyway. I could picture myself having wine on Sunday and on Tuesday getting picked up for DUI. For someone who enjoys wine, that would present a real problem. I asked him to check my liver. He did and my liver was fine.

Kathy Mazur was a nurse as well as a good friend, so she and her husband Mike came to see me at the hospital. When I explained the alcohol retention problem to her, Mike spoke up and said, "Wow, a cheap date!" I guess that was one way to look at it, but I was pretty concerned.

Kathy questioned my doctor about my high blood pressure. It was 200/100, and she was worried about my heart. The doctor said it was nothing to worry about, but she was not convinced. She told me to get the hell out of that hospital and get to Las Vegas as soon as I could.

The doctor thought that perhaps I had an ulcer and that the pain from the ulcer was what made me black out. He ordered medication for the ulcer and sent me home. I was to return to the laboratory in two weeks so they could run tests. I went for the tests, and they proved negative. There was no ulcer. I was concerned that I had been taking medicine for an ulcer when no ulcer existed.

Fortunately, the United States Air Force had generously allowed my son, Jerry, to come to me immediately. It was a blessing to have him with me at a time like that. He suggested I should return to the service of a local physician. I was doing a landscape job for a doctor at the time. My work performance was the pits. If I had not owned my company, he would have fired me. I explained to him the trouble I was having, and he suggested I see Doctor Cooper.

I went to see Dr. Cooper. He read my records and ran a few more tests. He admitted he was stumped. He sent me to a neuropsychiatric physician. I knew of him because I had done some landscaping at his home. He was a nice person. I was wondering if Dr. Cooper thought I was imbalanced, but he assured me he did not think that. He just wanted some testing done to see why I was passing out. He felt I might be experiencing pressure on my brain.

The new doctor ran a series of tests on my head. What a mess! I went directly from the hairdresser to the doctor's office. The technician put gunk all over my head that looked like petroleum jelly. By the time the testing was finished, my hair looked like someone out of a science fiction comic book. That was embarrassing. The head tests all proved to be normal. When the doctor laid me down on a table and took my blood pressure, things were pretty good, but when he sat me up and took the pressures again, I failed. He ushered me into a small room and we talked. He asked me if I was depressed. Well, with all that I had been going through, who wouldn't be depressed? I knew that was not the main problem. He asked me to take some medicine for depression for a few days and see if it would help. I tried to take the medicine. I threw it up. He changed the dosage, but nothing was working.

The doctor suggested I go back to the cardiologist, but I knew I couldn't afford all the tests again. Furthermore, the cardiologist from Las Vegas who had charged me $600 per visit said there was nothing wrong with my heart. The medical profession was quickly depleting this widow's stash, and I was too sick to earn more money to cover the tests. The insurance company was continually refusing to pay a large portion of the medical bills I was accumulating. I pay $536 a month for medical insurance through my corporation. It covers only me. It gets higher every year, and there is no insurance I can obtain that is any better because of my past medical history. My insurance company claimed the fees charged by the laboratories and the doctors in my area grossly exceeded the national average, so instead of paying their 80 percent, they paid about 60 percent and I had to pay the rest.

The next month, in February, Toup LaPrix began writing demanding letters to everyone who owned property in the subdivision. I didn't feel like putting up with him. The lot owners were again told to pay their dues and late fees or receive liens on their properties. My neighbor was to remove his television disc from the roofline of his home and put it in his "addict." [sp] The Mazurs were to move their camper from the street. I was to remove my retaining walls, gazebo, television antenna, and get rid of my pets. I was not to improve anything else on my property until I had done these things.

The County was leaning on Toup to finish the subdivision, the lot owners were suing him, and he was being pressured by the bank. It was almost as if he was begging the residents to make their move.

Instead of working towards completing the subdivision's utilities and roads, he had decided, by now, that everyone needed an attitude adjustment. Many of the lot owners and residents had not paid their homeowners' dues. Toup began filing liens and writing nasty threatening letters again to everyone. Perhaps because I was the oldest of the group, everyone turned to me for help, and they sent me a copy of the threats they received. Upon the insistence of Supervisor Golf, I gave the threatening letters to a female deputy sheriff. She took copies of them to the county attorney, but he never said anything to us or did anything about them.

Martin Coole was very upset when he came to my house and showed me his letter with the past-due penalties for homeowner's dues. He asked if I was paying dues, and I said that I was. He asked, "Why?"

"I don't know. Because I agreed to pay them when I bought my lot, I guess."

"But Toup also agreed to install roads, utilities, and have a decent water company. The rules say the dues are for maintenance of the paved, private roads. Where are the roads, and where's the money going?" he asked Mike Mazur, who came to the house for coffee. He had a handful of nasty letters that Toup had placed in his mailbox.

I asked him, "Mike, are you paying your homeowner's dues?"

"We did in the beginning, but we quit. Kathy and I will pay dues when we have proper water and paved roads. The CCRs (Covenants, Conditions, and Restrictions) say the dues are to be used to maintain the paved roads. No roads, no dues," he explained.

"Well, Martin Coole asked me why I was paying dues, but I really didn't know how to answer him. I feel sure, after reviewing his records, that Toup is using the money for his own needs, but he could surprise us and come up with receipts for all those checks he has written for cash," I said.

"No he won't. Unless you believe he can produce a receipt for all the booze he's been drinking and explain the write off," he said.

"What are we going to do about all these letters?" I asked.

"That is one reason I came over today. Will you call the sheriff's office and see if they enforce the postal regulations? Tampering with my mailbox and mail is illegal. Just explain to them what we are getting in our mailboxes. He's not putting stamps on the letters. See if you can get that stopped. If he has to pay for all the stamps and he can't learn who I bank with, maybe he will stop writing the letters."

"I gave all the letters Martin and I received with and without postage to the supervisor. They didn't do anything. Do you know Toup told me to take down my retaining walls?" I cried.

"He can't make you take down those walls. Who does he think he is?" he asked.

"He signed the letter, "Cowboy Joe." Do you know who that is?" I asked.

"Yeah. That is the guy who is living over there with him. He claims to be the trustee of Toup's trust," he answered.

As Mike waited patiently, I called the sheriff.

The sergeant said, "We have nothing to do with the United State's mail. You have to call the post office. It would be very helpful to them if you would take a video of Toup while he is tampering with your mail box."

I thanked him for his time and I called the post office. Brian, the postmaster's assistant, told me, "You have to call the sheriff. Toup LaPrix is breaking the law."

"I just called the sheriff and the sergeant told me to call you."

"Well, the United States postal department delivers mail. We do not enforce the laws," he replied.

"Is there someone else I can call? Is there a postal inspector in this area?" I asked.

"Nope, you have to call Phoenix."

"Do you have that number?" I asked. He said he would look, and he left me waiting on a dead line for about five minutes. When he returned he said, "Nope. There aren't any numbers in these files for the Phoenix offices."

After a lot of human ping-pong and frustration, I got on the Internet and found out how to contact the postal inspector in Phoenix. I called and received voice mail. The woman who called me back from the Phoenix office said that putting anything in my box without proper handling was against postal regulations. She explained, "I will notify your county attorney and tell him to warn Mr. LaPrix to discontinue that practice. He has to receive no less than two written warnings before the postal service can file charges. The county attorney must issue a warning, and it will be served on Mr. LaPrix by the Sheriff's Department. I will get that process started and you keep all the original copies of the envelopes and the letters.

We might need them later. It would be a good idea to get a video of Toup with his hands in your mailbox."

To my knowledge, Toup LaPrix was never served or warned. Kathy Mazur went to check her mail one day, expecting a check, and someone had torn all her mail to shreds. I never caught Toup LaPrix tampering with mail in my mailbox, but he sure knew more about me than he should have known. I was afraid to leave my house. I just knew that if given the opportunity, Toup would destroy my property. He wanted everything at my residence torn down. I never knew what he would pull next. We all had American dreams that had turned into Arizona nightmares.

I suggested to both of my neighbors that we might find relief by contacting an attorney I had used in the past.

My husband had always preached that any legal issues had to be handled through an attorney. When I purchased my company's land, I had solicited the legal services of a nice man named Attorney Law. I had known him to be honest, and my husband had given me his seal of approval on the man. That month, February 1997, Martin, Kathy, and I went to see Attorney Law. We took all our files concerning our problems in the development. The files were getting quite thick.

As we understood him, he was paid by the hour. He said if we wanted to go into a lawsuit together, we needed to pay him $1,000 apiece as a retainer. He would then read our files and information and tell us what we might be able to do. He said a lawsuit against Toup could cost $30,000 or more, and with all the trusts Toup had, we may never get satisfaction on a suit. He joked about Toup LaPrix having owned and lost a McDonald's franchise, and that "nobody loses a McDonald franchise except Toup LaPrix."

He told us he was a friend of the county attorney, and he wanted to learn how legal the County's arrangement with Toup was and if it was indeed a secured position.

When we left his office, Martin and I felt perhaps this attorney could help because he was a friend of the county attorney. Kathy felt differently. She was the only one to realize that the friendship between the two attorneys was a real detriment to our cause. She stated there was a conspiracy in Mohave County, and if we were going to get any legal satisfaction on the fraud, we would have to seek an attorney in another county or even another state. She said she had previously seen the Mohave "Buddy System," and she wasn't going to be taken in by it. All the way home Kathy hollered and begged me not to trust "that fat fucker."

I admit Attorney Law was a bit overweight, but Kathy's first impression of the man seemed a bit harsh at the time.

When I received my mail, I was building the gazebo. Keeping a close watch out for their safety, I had my employees finish it, and I ignored Toup's blackmail.

By March 17th—the closing date set by the supervisors for completing the subdivision—no work of any kind had been done to improve the development. Not one shovel had been wielded. The Board of Supervisor's resolution made in December 1996 was totally ignored, and the extension of the time request was going back to the Planning and Zoning Commission. I asked the director of the Planning and Zoning Department, Director Mallard, why there was a reverse in procedure. She told me that the resolution, made in December 1996, had been made by the previous Board of Supervisors. They had all been unseated. The new Board of Supervisors would have to vote on the issue again.

That seemed strange to us. When a law or decision is made, we do not reverse the old ones and make new ones just because we had an election and our legislators were unseated. We reluctantly went along with the County's peculiar process. We had no choice.

We went to the March meeting of the Planning and Zoning Commission and learned that a new attorney from Scottsdale, Arizona, Attorney Whiner, had been hired to represent the County Planning and Zoning Department. After waiting all evening for the Lake Juniper issue that was near the bottom of the agenda, we learned the item had been "Continued to Staff."

In April Director Mallard sent some of her staff to the Lake Juniper Subdivision to see what improvements had or had not been completed, and to inspect the illegal water and electric connections on the properties. Toup got very angry when her officers started snooping around.

The county regulation manuals stated that the county engineer was required to inspect the project on a regular basis. Since there were no inspection reports, I could only assume by the County's actions that they interpreted "regular" as meaning at least once every seven or eight years.

Irene, the girl Toup LaPrix hired to hand out For Sale flyers at the front gates, told me Toup was extremely upset. She explained, "Toup is going to lock the gates so the county employees can't go snooping around anymore. He has given me permission to open the gates on weekends so I can show lots." Why would he show lots if he wasn't supposed to sell them?

Also in April Attorney Whiner began preparing a different completion contract for Toup LaPrix to sign. When finished, it would be sent to Toup, and they would allow him to negotiate the conditions in the contract. We sat in the April meeting for over six hours waiting for our turn to speak. Again, we had been placed last on the agenda. We were told the new attorney needed time to get all his paperwork done. The item was referred to staff for another month, and we went home.

On May 12th, all the landowners received notices in their mailboxes that the gates would be locked April 10, 1997 for construction. Considering the date he originally planned to lock the gates (April 10), it looked like he had gotten angry with the County for snooping around. It just took a month for him to decide to send the letter and actually do the dastardly deed.

On May 14th, the gates were locked and the homeowners were advised to use a "back road" named South Bay. This road resembled an abandoned alley. It was unpaved and poorly maintained, as were the roads leading to it. Rather than remove trees that lined South Bay, Toup had bladed around them leaving the road very narrow in many areas. There was no room for ingress and egress (entering and exiting), as required by law. The road was so poorly marked from the crossroad that even the sheriff's officers could not find it.

Toup had previously placed boulders across South Bay explaining that they were there to keep people from entering the subdivision from the back. At that time, he had cameras installed on the front gates, and he watched that entrance often. That gave him control. When he decided the residents were going to use the back road, he removed the boulders from South Bay and left large holes in the road.

My friend, Terry Augustine, and his son Jeff came to the house, and we made a video of the development on a timed and dated tape. The date on the tape was May 14, 1997. Our purpose in doing this was to show how long the gates remained locked and to reveal the illegal activities that were going on behind those gates.

Toup saw us making videotapes of his messes. I instantly became

"Public Enemy Number One." He drove by the three of us at a speed of about two miles per hour and gave us a menacing glare. After he passed us, he spun his tires on the dirt road and threw dirt all over us.

With no construction activity by May 21st, Mike Mazur and I called the county attorney's office. We were told by Deputy Attorney Nogut that if there was access of any kind to our properties, there was no crime committed, and the County could not interfere. He suggested we encourage Toup LaPrix to open the gates. "Yeah, right!" Mike exclaimed.

I expressed my concerns about the locked gates to our county supervisor's office that same day. The supervisor's aid suggested I contact Toup and request the gates be opened. "Haven't they learned yet that you do not tell or suggest to Toup what he should do?" Mike asked.

I dutifully wrote a letter the next day to Toup and asked him to open the gates. I explained I was worried about our health and safety with the unmanned gates being locked.

His written response was as follows:

"The front gates will remain closed tell [sic] further notice. As far as your health and well-being, I suggest you pay your homeowner fee of $50.00 and your late charges of $50.20 by May 31, 1997. Failure to do this will result in having your water disconnected sense [sic] part of your homeowner fees go to pay your water bill. If your water is disconnected there will be additional fees for hook up."

Sig.

The county supervisor affirmed Mike and Martin's views regarding the homeowner's dues. The homeowner's fees paid to Toup were designated for repairing and maintaining the paved roads (which didn't exist), and to maintain the common areas (which didn't exist), and I shouldn't pay for non-existent services. Mike Mazur said he had not paid dues for five months. It appeared Toup LaPrix was taking me for a ride.

I faxed a copy of my letter and Toup's reply to the offices of our supervisor. I was told not to worry about the water disconnect threat. I was assured Toup could not do that legally. The office sent another officer from the Sheriff's Department to my home to pick up a copy of all the current letters and threats. She assured me, as had the director of Planning and Zoning that Toup could not shut off my water. They both assured me that if he did, he would be breaking the law and would be arrested. The deputy asked if she could have copies of all the communications we had received to date, as the copies I had sent earlier had been misplaced. I gave her a big file, believing in my heart that the previous copies were sitting on the county prosecutor's desk. It appeared to me, he just did not have the guts to do anything with them.

When I questioned the planning and zoning director about the contents of the proposed contract Attorney Whiner was preparing for Toup LaPrix's signature, she said it would not be made public until all the interested parties had agreed to the conditions in the contract. I had, and my neighbors each had over $200,000 investments in the project. "Are we not interested parties?" I asked.

Director Mallard's answer to that question was, "No. Not exactly." She said she felt my request for knowledge of the contract's contents was a reasonable request. She told me she would ask the legal department if I could have a copy when it was finished.

CHAPTER 11

A few days earlier, a realty company posted a "for sale" sign on lot 155, in spite of the fact that he was forbidden to sell any more lots. Kathy Mazur asked me to call the tax department and see who owned that lot. She was concerned about the situation because the lot was directly behind her house. She had already expressed to Toup in 1995 the desire to purchase that lot for her mother. Kathy Mazur believed he could not sell lots in the subdivision after 1996 due to the lack of a current state public report.

I called the real estate company and inquired as to the ownership of lot 155. The agent said that Jane Waters owned the lot. She lived in Las Vegas and was supposedly unaware of the problems that existed in the subdivision. The warranty deed for lot 155 that she had presented to the realtor showed a purchase date of May 9, 1997.

I called the county tax department and was told that, according to their records, lot 155 was owned by Toup and a trust. The tax department also stated that the taxes had not been paid on that lot since 1991. There was a tax lien on the lot that would have to be paid by the developer before that lot could change ownership.

On May 20th, I called the planning and zoning director, Director Mallard, and explained that there was a lady by the name of Jane Waters who had listed lot 155 for sale, but that the tax office said that lot belonged to Toup LaPrix. I told her about the deed the real estate company had, and asked her to see if Toup LaPrix or Cowboy Joe was related to Jane Waters.

She said she would call me back, but she needed to get the records. Within the hour, she called and said that her examination of the records showed Toup LaPrix owned lot 155. She seemed confused as to how this lot could possibly have a for sale sign on it. She said she would look into it. She never called to ease my curiosity.

I was trying to explain to my hairdresser, Charlotte Wilda, about the lot that was for sale. I still wanted to know if there really was someone named Jane Waters. I always explained what was going on in the subdivision to Charlotte. I went to see her faithfully every week. She was a good psychologist and an excellent listener.

While I was there, a man came into the shop in need of a haircut. Charlotte had just put me under the hairdryer, and she had some free time to cut his hair and have a small chat.

The customer told Charlotte that his girlfriend was purchasing property in the area, and he seemed pleased with the lot she had just purchased at the new Lake Juniper Subdivision. He explained Jane Waters had traded a half-acre lot for a three-quarter acre lot because the developer could not supply water to the smaller lot. They were going to sell the newly acquired lot and make some bucks.

Charlotte asked him if his lot number happened to be 155, and he said it was. She suggested he might want to talk with her client who was sitting under the hair dryer.

The man came over to me and asked if I would mind talking to him about the subdivision. I said, "No problem." I had never met the man, but he looked friendly enough. He was dressed in blue jeans and sneakers.

He told me that Jane Waters had originally purchased lot 29, which was located much further into the subdivision, for $29,000 in 1995. She had cleared a pad on her lot and prepared it for construction. Toup had sold her leach rock for her septic system, then informed her that the lot would not have water or utilities for at least a year and a half. She was livid. To quiet her, Toup traded her lot 29 for lot 155 because lot 155 already had water connections, was much larger, and had a sale value of $34,500.

I explained to him that it appeared Toup LaPrix had given Jane Waters a warranty deed for lot 155 that was never recorded. Jane Waters had given Toup LaPrix a warranty deed for lot 29 that he immediately recorded. Because there was no recording of the deed to lot 155, Jane was never billed for taxes. As far as the assessor knew, Toup still owned both lots and had not paid the property taxes on either lot for many years. The tax bills were still being sent to Toup LaPrix.

I suggested he might want to check with the title company and find out why Jane Waters' trade of the lots had not been filed with the county recorder's office. When I asked the man what lot they were paying taxes on, he explained to me Toup LaPrix told them when they purchased lot 29 in 1995 that there would be no bills for taxes because the subdivision was exempt from taxation. I explained that the taxes had not been paid on either lot and that Certificates of Purchase (CPs) on both lots were sold at tax auction. If he didn't get the lot recorded and pay the past due taxes on her lot right away, Jane Waters would lose her $29,000 investment. (Certificates of Purchase are basically property tax liens.)

He jumped up from his chair and asked if he could come to my home for more information if he needed it. He explained, excitedly, he was on his way to the title company. Lot 155 remained listed for sale with the realty company for a long time.

Ultimately, tax deeds were issued to the CP holders, because Toup failed to pay his property taxes in the time frame afforded by the law. Jane Waters had become another victim condemned through Toup LaPrix's fraud.

On Saturday, May 31st I left my home about 10:30 a.m. to go with my son Jerry to help paint his newly purchased house. When I returned at 6:30 p.m., full of paint and sweat, I found my home had no water.

Jerry went to the main water connection to discover the water had been locked off. It was a small, cheap lock. He cut it off and restored the water supply. He inserted a lock on the valve that he thought would prevent Toup LaPrix from shutting the water off until we could get the sheriff. We immediately called the sheriff's office. After clearing the air that had built up in the lines, I took my much-needed bath. Little did I know that it would be the last bath I took in that tub for many, many months.

The sheriff's deputy, the board supervisor and the planning director had previously told us that Toup could not legally cut off the water for non-payment of homeowner dues. I felt they should come and inspect the fact that he had done just that.

By the time the deputy arrived at 7:10 p.m., the neighbors were all at my house. We showed him what we had done to get the water turned back on and keep it on. It was a Saturday, so we could not get legal help. We asked if he would see that Toup left the water alone until Monday when I could call the Corporation Commission Utilities Division and get the dues and water issue resolved.

The deputy agreed. He went to Toup's home and explained that the water to my house had been restored, and that the connection would be left alone until Monday, when the proper officials could be contacted.

The threat of learning I planned to call the proper authorities really made Toup angry, but telling him what "would be done" made him mad. He insisted that Deputy Ingress arrest me for stealing water.

The deputy explained he would contact the county attorney, Billy Willy, Jr., on Monday. He advised Toup to stay away from my property until that time. He came back to my home and gave us a full report.

The deputy was looking into the baggy eyes of a little frail woman who lived in a beautiful house and had her water disconnected on a weekend. He seemed nervous over his conflict with one of the county's Good 'ol Boys, but he had seen no water bill. He advised us everything would be okay and that there would be no more trouble until Monday. He told us Toup wanted to have me arrested, and I volunteered to submit to his arrest, but he refused my invitation. At least in the jailhouse, there was running water. I could eventually get a shower!

Deputy Ingress said he thought Toup LaPrix was a strange, dangerous person. He advised me to try to get some rest and to contact an attorney on Monday morning. He suggested I get an injunction against harassment issued for my protection. He assured me that the lock Jerry had put on the valve in the open position was appropriate, and that it could remain until Monday when things could be settled. I was not to worry.

The next day (Sunday, June 1st) at about 11:00 a.m., Toup appeared at my water connection along with two sheriff's deputies in two different sheriff's vehicles. I looked out my window, and it looked as if there was going to be a raid on my house. Terrible fears went through my head. I did not know what was going to happen next. After all, my battle was with one of the County's favored sons. I was no one special, and Toup had accused me of stealing water. Maybe this time it would be me who was accused of committing a drug deal that went bad. I was really scared.

I called Kathy screaming. She came over immediately. My heart was pumping overtime. I knew the officers were not coming to my home to play poker.

Through the window, Kathy and I could see Toup and the officers standing around in the street. They talked for a while and then a big, buxom, blonde, female officer, named Susie Que, came into my garage and knocked on my back door. The male officer accompanying Susie Que preferred to remain anonymous.

I answered the door and she said, "Give me the key."

"What for?" I asked.

"Toup LaPrix is going to shut off your water."

I was so scared that all I could say was, "I don't have the key."

Susie Que's words came out of her mouth in a rude and threatening tone. She gave me an awful, threatening look, spun around on her heels, and went back towards the back of the house and started visiting with the other men.

I did not have a key. Jerry had put it in his pocket, and he never returned to give it to me.

In Susie Que's report, she said I refused to give up the key to the lock. My side of the story was that I did not have a key to the lock to give to her. She was in such a hurry, she did not take the time to find out the truth.

These two law enforcement officials had never seen a bill, never bothered to check any records of the water company, and never cared to justify their actions. They had not reviewed the deputy's records of the events that went on the previous day. They simply did what Toup LaPrix told them to do. No questions asked.

I think if that big, blonde storm trooper had been told to shoot me, she would not have had the guts or moral values to question the order. I had the impression that she was trained to shoot first and ask questions later. She and her partner couldn't care less whether I lived or died.

I closed the door, grabbed my camera, and went into my office where I could take pictures of the officers and the activities going on. Both officers stayed right there in the road and watched as Toup not only trespassed on my land and shut off my water, but also cut the main PVC house lines (my private property) several times and shoved them full of mud. They laughed with him and then they drove off. Susie Que and her partner were both so stupid that they wrote a police report stating their direct involvement in the criminal acts of that day. The report said, "We observed as Toup LaPrix cut the main water lines several times."

Imagine these so-called representatives of the law in their office laughing and typing a report that could eventually hang them. There was no water utility easement anywhere near the area. Toup never recorded any easements for the water company. My pictures were worth more than a thousand words.

Kathy Mazur and I went next door and explained to Mike what had happened. I wrote a check to Toup for all the embezzlement money (homeowner's dues) he requested. I asked Mike Mazur to take it to him. I called my son to come to the house and help Mike reconnect my water. That afternoon, Mike called the sheriff's office and explained that he had the extortion money Toup wanted so badly and that he would appreciate someone coming and giving Toup the check. At that point, we were all scared to death of Toup and the sheriff. Sergeant Sniper explained they could not do that, but he told Mike it would probably be all right to re-connect my water. The sheriff's office would not interfere if I paid Toup LaPrix the extortion money.

Sergeant Sniper said he was aware of the activities of his deputies and that the sheriff himself sent the officers for a Civil Standby. He explained that their job was to keep the peace between Mr. LaPrix and Mrs. Lewis.

I took the phone and asked if Sergeant Sniper would keep the peace by sending an officer for Civil Standby while Mike Mazur and my son reconnected the water supply. He said he could not arrange that unless the sheriff's office had time to prepare for the standby.

I suggested he hang up and prepare for the stand by. I explained it would take the men about 45 minutes to repair Toup's damage to my personal pipes, and we only needed the stand by for about five minutes to actually secure the connection.

Sergeant Sniper refused to consider sending an officer, as he had done for Toup LaPrix. His report of Toup's "Civil Standby' did not say, "Upon recommendation of the sheriff..." I went to the sheriff's office and bought a copy. I read in the report that Sergeant Sniper was the male officer at my home protecting Toup LaPrix on that Sunday. It seemed strange he didn't mention that in our phone conversation!

On that Sunday evening, Toup had left his home, and there was no one to take possession of my check. Mike Mazur kept possession of the check. He and my son repaired the pipes and reconnected the water lines to the valves. Because of the weekend and the evening hour, parts needed to restore the water were not available, but at least by early morning I would have my water turned back on.

Toup did not return home that evening. He spent a lot of time in the lounges, and it was virtually impossible to reach him any evening. In the small community, it didn't take long for me to learn that Toup LaPrix was in the local bar that night, bragging about cutting off my water. He even blabbed to my friend Jay Lint about how the sheriff had sent deputies to protect him while he destroyed my lines and what sort of fools worked for the Sheriff's Department.

I went without water that night. It is awful when you need to use the facilities and there is no water to flush. It was June and the weather was hot. My nerves were shot. I kept showing up at Kathy's door. She just gave me a key to her house.

The next morning (Monday, June 2nd) at 6:45 a.m., Kathy took my little check and her big check, for five months of dues that were in arrears plus five months of penalties, to Toup's house. Mike Mazur did not want any more trouble over dues. Cowboy Joe, the new secretary of the homeowner's association, met Kathy in the driveway. He took the checks from her, explained Toup was still sleeping, and that he would give him the checks as soon as he woke up. He told her not to worry; he was sure everything would be okay. He said he only worked for Toup. He had no control over his actions.

I knew I needed an attorney right away, so I called Attorney Law, the local attorney we had visited earlier that month.

Kathy said, "Don't you hire that fat fucker."

"Kathy, he is the only attorney in the area I have ever used and I need protection." I said, "I'm too damn sick to fight these bastards. I need help and I need water."

"Well, you won't get either from that fat fucker," she replied.

Attorney Law made an appointment with me for 11:30 a.m. that day. I went into town at 11:15 a.m. and paid Attorney Law the $1,000 retainer he demanded. I expected him to keep me out of jail and secure my water connection rights. He advised me he would bill me by the hour. He knew of the problems we were having at the Lake Juniper Subdivision, and he felt sure he could help. He asked me to have my neighbors call or write a letter to him stating they were unaware that their homeowner's dues were paying for water service.

I called both neighbors and they faxed the information to Attorney Law. He suggested the only way we could break into this problem and get it solved fast was to contact the media. I was to seek as much publicity as I could. I really thought he was just trying to keep me busy and my mind off the dangers that were at hand. Then again, perhaps he was trying to show me that the political ring I was a victim of had complete control over the media as well as the state and governmental officials. The news media were not interested in my vendetta with Toup LaPrix. After all, they heard I had not paid my water bill.

When I got home from the lawyer's office at 1:30 p.m., Toup had already come to my house, cut my pipes again, cut up more of the main water lines to my house, and thrown them all over my yard. He had also destroyed the female connectors to his company's pipes so that the water could not be reconnected without closing a water main from the well. The site looked like a maniac had been there. Mud from the dripping lines had been thrown all over my yard. All my plumbing had been raped, but those pipes put up a good fight. What a mess he had made! I was scared. Only a madman would cause such destruction.

At the request of and with instructions from Attorney Law, on Tuesday June 3rd, my son took me to the justice court. I filed a form asking for the court's protection from Toup LaPrix.

Jerry went with me into the courtroom. Together we explained the manic offenses Toup had committed as well as the harassing letters he was sending. We asked the court to issue a harassment order for not only myself but also for Jerry.

The judge explained that the order could be signed for me and my property, and it would be in force for six months. He told Jerry that if Toup LaPrix came after him, he should return to his court and get his own order administered.

We then had to see that the constable served the order on Toup LaPrix. Her name was Pam Bibich. She was the only democrat elected and serving in the Republican-dominated county at that time. She was a very sweet lady. She was on my list of favorite people. I think the reason Pam got that distinction was that she thought a lot like me. She was a hard worker and rather opinionated but honest. The county clique was always giving her a hard time because of her political affiliation. She had no intention of changing political parties.

The court clerk also gave me a set of orders, signed as originals by the judge, to take home in case Pam was unable to reach Toup and in case I should have another visit from the sheriff's officers. I had explained to the judge that the officers were really making me feel like a criminal. He instructed me to give the full set of papers to the officer and ask him to serve Toup LaPrix if the constable had been unable to do so. I kept my copies in a file and I put the sheriff's originals on my dining room table in case an officer should come to my house again. Pam had her set of originals, and I thought I was well covered.

I felt sure the sheriff's office had been informed by the court that the order had been issued. Two officers (one a sergeant named Webb) came to my house the next day (Wednesday, June 4th). I had not heard from Pam, so I knew she had not yet served the notices. Only Officer Webb spoke. The second officer stood inside my doorway, but he never said a word. His eyes seemed focused on the polish of his shoes. Sergeant Webb told me the county attorney had sent them to our homes on a peacekeeping mission. He had been ordered by the county attorney to instruct me to stay off Toup LaPrix's property and not destroy anything else that belonged to him.

After hearing his little speech, I was madder than hell. I, not so politely, explained to Sergeant Webb that the only thing I had destroyed was a $.79 lock, and if that bastard cared to repair my pipes and hook up my water properly, I would pay him for the lock. I told Sergeant Webb, "He tore up my property and he is running like a scared rat from Pam Bibich. Since you haven't been over to his house yet, take these papers the judge gave me and serve that rat. The judge's clerk gave me this extra set of papers, just in case you came by before Pam could get him served." I did not say please.

He looked at the papers I handed him, threw them back on my dining room table like they were burning his hands, and said, "I can't serve those. They are not signed. No way am I going to take photocopies of an order to serve on Mr. LaPrix. I'm just going over to tell him the same thing I told you and not to serve papers on him."

"Thank you for delivering the county attorney's message," I said rudely, as I opened the front door. "The next time he starts to send you here with a message, tell him to contact my attorney."

The officers took the clue and left. I called the judge's office. I told the clerk exactly what had happened and what Sergeant Webb had said. I asked her why she would give me papers to give to the sheriff for service that were not valid or properly signed by the judge.

She asked me to get the papers and look on the second page. She asked if there was a black stamp on the paper, which included the judge's signature written on the stamp in black ink.

I said yes, the signature and stamp were there. She said, "Lick it."

"What?"

"Take your finger, lick it, and carefully try to smudge the judge's signed signature."

"Okay, it smeared and it is real ink. You convinced me. Now what?"

"Hang up and I'll call you right back. I promise," she said.

Pam Bibich called me instead. She said she could not understand why Sergeant Webb believed he could not serve the papers. She said she could not believe that the sheriff's force was that afraid of Toup and that I was not to worry. She promised to get him served right away. She explained she had tried three times, she had left notices on his door each time, but he had failed to answer her.

When Pam called me that afternoon to ask when Toup picked up his mail, I explained to her where the mail was delivered and that he usually picked it up about 4:00 p.m. At about 5:00 p.m. that very day, Pam called to relate her experience. She sat out on the highway until Toup picked up his mail, then she followed him. When she pulled into his driveway behind him, he spotted her. He jumped out of his car and ran into his house through the front door. She waited a minute and noticed him running out the back door. She jumped out of her car and ran around the house to the back. The heels of her shoes kept getting stuck in the grass, and when she stopped, she looked up and saw Toup loping down the grassy slopes in his yard. She started laughing and almost lost it. Toup's toupee was bouncing up and down as he ran. She yelled to him and threatened him with arrest. He stopped and came back to where she was standing. She handed him the judge's order.

Toup asked her which judge would have the nerve to serve him those papers. She told him Judge Imus, then she left. She was still laughing when she called me. Every time Pam dared to buck the clique and stand up for what was right, they would get hostile.

I knew after the call, Pam could be in for more trouble with the clique. The County Board of Supervisors later voted to cut her pay by about $6,000 per year. They blamed the pay cut on "lack of budgetary funds." To my knowledge, no one else received salary cuts, but there will always be some honest Americans who care about public safety. They are so dedicated that they will face all kinds of trouble to protect the American citizen's rights. Pam fits the bill.

I called Attorney Law and explained what had just happened. "You tell your buddy, Billy Willy Jr., that if he wants to talk to me, he's to call you," I said. I explained to him that the sheriff's Sergeant Webb would not serve Toup the judge's papers.

I told Attorney Law the papers were still on my table where Sergeant Webb had thrown them down like a hot potato. He could come and see them if he did not believe me. I also explained that I needed my water reconnected and that it was not fun living in a house without running water. I suggested he should try it sometime.

"Go out and turn the water back on."

"I can't. Toup destroyed not only my pipes but also his own service connections. In order to re-connect the service, I have to shut down the entire system first. I can't do that. Toup would kill me first."

"Now come on Patti. Surely you know how to do those repairs. You are a licensed landscape contractor. Those water connections are easy."

Thinking in my heart that this man was a male chauvinist pig and we would never communicate without a man's assistance, I had to get my son to explain to him exactly what I had said and what the situation looked like, before he would believe me. I knew then that this lawyer was not going to take my "female" word for anything. This was the third time I had to prove my words to him in two days. I knew I was in a bad situation.

When the sergeant's report came out in print, the sergeant accused me of trying to force him to serve my copies of an order on Toup LaPrix. The force charge did not say "brute force," but it was a rather ridiculous statement.

Later that same day—June 4th, Jerry and I went to my backyard to examine the damages Toup had done to my main water lines, hoping to figure out some way to get my water restored. I picked up a piece of one-inch PVC pipe. It was about eight inches long, and it was full of blue-green crud. In all my years as a landscaper, cutting pipes and making water connections, I had never seen anything like that before.

The piece of pipe in my hand was from the same area where we installed the back-flow preventer to protect the house and the main water supply from contamination from fertilizers, animal urine, and other nasty things that might seep into the lines through sprinkler heads and yard lines. Originally there was one back flow preventer and six one-way check valves installed on the system. In Arizona, everyone drinks lot of water, and I sure did not want to be drinking dog urine. How was I to foresee that Toup's water company would furnish the crud coming into my house? The backflow preventers had been useless, but more important, they were nowhere in sight.

After seeing the contaminated PVC pipe, I began to realize why Toup LaPrix had shoved mud into my pipes when he cut my lines. At first glance, it had appeared to be manic destruction. At second glance, it looked like he was trying to hide that blue-green crud. Taking the pipe piece into the house, I called the County Health Department. I asked Sandy Mander, the health inspector, what the sediment might be.

"I have no idea," she said. "You should call the ADEQ (Arizona Department of Environmental Quality). The County Health Department is too small, and it is not equipped to test the pipe's contents."

Toup immediately learned of my complaint. He began telling everyone I had crushed up copper vitamin tablets and put them in my pipes. It had never occurred to me that something could be added to the water supply. It was obvious, even before I had any verification of the pipe's contents, that Toup knew what had been found. He also knew no one had taken any videos lately and he, therefore, could not be prosecuted for anything.

The supervisor of the ADEQ, in charge of the Lake Juniper area, said he had no idea what the crud might be and asked me if my house water was coming from a private well. I explained my house was connected to the Lake Juniper Water Company, and it was a public utility located in Mohave County.

"There's no water company called The Lake Juniper Water Company in that county. I know, because I have never heard of it, and I am in charge of all the water companies in that area," he said.

"And I suppose you don't know that my water was disconnected by Toup LaPrix and that he destroyed my plumbing, right?" I asked.

"What are you talking about?" he asked.

I explained everything that had happened, including the sheriff's civil standby. We talked some more about the dirty pipe, where it was found, and why the pipes were destroyed.

The ADEQ supervisor said he was sorry for the trouble I was having, but he could not test the pipe for me. He said the water company had to serve 15 homes and 25 people before his department could get involved. He insisted the water company had never been listed with the ADEQ as a public utility and suggested the foreign matter in the pipes might be algae of some kind that had settled into the pipe after it was exposed to the air.

I called the EPA (Environmental Protection Agency) in San Francisco. They too, seemed indifferent to my problem, but they would act if the State of Arizona requested their services. It was explained to me how expensive an investigation would be and how they would have to go way back into the mountain to start their investigation. They would have to try to locate the source of the problem.

That made a lot of sense. There was an old copper mine on the opposite side of the mountain from my house. The mining company had leached for copper with natural acid on a regular basis. There was no visible leach field lining required by the State of Arizona. The State got their big money from the mining operation. Nothing else seemed to matter.

All I wanted to know was what that blue crud was hanging in my white pipes, how it got there, and how to get rid of it.

CHAPTER 12

On June 7th, I took the pipe to my dad who lived in New Mexico. He was working for the University of New Mexico in the engineering department, and he would be able to get the pipe's contents tested by an honest, decent lab.

He took the pipe to the Assaigai Analytical Laboratories in Albuquerque on June 11th. They did an analysis on the pipe's contents. It took ten days for the results. Before faxing me the results of their tests, a lab technician called me. She told me if my drinking water was being supplied through those pipes, I could be in big trouble. She faxed me the results of her testing and suggested I take the results to my doctor right away. She told me to stay away from the water. (No problem there. Toup had that solved.)

When the laboratory faxed the results to me on June 21st, they were well worth the wait. The PVC pipe was full of heavy metals.

The report read like this:

METALS-ICP/SW	RESULT	UNITS	LIMIT
Barium, Ba	38.5	mg/Kg	.50
Chromium, Cr	43.1	mg/Kg	1.0
Copper, Cu	2030E	mg/Kg	.50
Nickel, Ni	46.7E	mg/Kg	2.0
Lead, Pb	135	mg/Kg	2.0

The "E," according to the report, meant the scales could not register any higher counts.

After having been so desperately ill since January with no one able to diagnose what was wrong with me, I went right to the old home remedy book that the *Parents Magazine* people had sent me as a present when my first son was born. The book was old and it was not in the best of condition, but it was still accurate. I looked up copper and lead poisoning.

Looking up copper, lead, and heavy metal exposure, every symptom I had been having was listed in that book. I took the book, a piece of the pipe, and the lab test to Dr. Cooper on June 22nd, and I asked him to run a blood test on me for copper and heavy metals. He knew we had been unsuccessful in determining what my medical problems were, and he said something to the effect that he hated it when patients diagnosed themselves. He was laughing when he said it, so it was evident that he was not really offended by my request.

We had the lab tests run, and sure enough, the copper levels in my blood were very toxic. My blood was coming in with a strong 211 mcg/dl, and the toxicity levels begin at 155 mcg/dl. Acceptable range for copper in the bloodstream is 70—155 mcg/dl. If there was a doctor who understood copper poisoning, he had not surfaced when all the testing was done on me.

I showed the pipe to my neighbor, Martin. We went to the spot where Toup had cut off my water. The water company's pipes that Toup destroyed had been dripping water for several days. They had corroded over with blue sediment. I explained to Martin Coole that the blue crud had been tested, and it was lead and copper. I suggested he have his water tested for copper. He explained he had sent his water samples to a water-testing laboratory on June 14th, but he had not received the results.

As we stood there in front of the pipe connection talking, we noticed that the dripping water had settled in a hole, and there were two sand frogs bathing in the small pool. The sand frogs (which are normally gray in color) had noticed us, and they jumped out of the pool and hopped under an electric transformer. They were the prettiest purple frogs I had ever seen. They were the only purple frogs I had ever seen! I asked Martin Coole if he thought the copper would turn the frogs purple. He said he had no idea how they got that way, but he had never seen frogs that color either. I just knew those poor frogs were doomed!

After receiving my lab reports, Dr. Cooper called the Arizona Department of Public Health and asked for the source of the copper. That was on June 24th. He asked for a conference with the state toxicologist. He received no immediate response. "Drink a lot of bottled water and stay away from the water being supplied to your house by that water company," he said.

"No problem. Toup shut it off three weeks ago. I have not found anyone brave enough to repair the connection, and Toup's brother, the one that owns large the water company nearby, refuses to check out the quality of the water or to get the water re-connected. He has refused to get involved. It seems he is afraid of his own brother."

"How are you surviving without water?" Dr. Cooper asked.

"Well, my son takes me to his house to bathe. Kathy Mazur lets me use her bathroom all the time, and Mike takes me to wash my clothes. After drinking all the bottled water you ordered, I am not very hungry, so there aren't many dishes to wash, but I have buckets of hauled water in the garage and I heat the water on the stove when I need to."

"You need to move to an apartment somewhere until this is over."

"I cannot afford to do that. All the medical and legal bills are cleaning out my bank accounts."

"Let the State pay for it. They are in charge of the Lake Juniper area," he said.

"Right," I replied. Dr. Cooper is from Canada. Maybe in Canada the State would pay for it. I live in a county where the government officials have shown me that they have no interest in my problems.

When neighbors in the surrounding area learned what was happening, they shared stories with me regarding Toup's past, and they warned me he was dangerous. They told me rumors about children Toup had beaten up. One boy spent two weeks in the hospital for operating his ATV on Toup's roads. Their stories sounded like nightmares. One man living near the subdivision stated that when Toup was building his dam in 1994, he placed underground spikes in the road to keep people off it. The man did not know the spikes were there, and he ran over them, ruining his tires and causing a lot of damage to his vehicle. He said the County had refused to do anything about Toup's activity, but he felt lucky to be alive.

I didn't feel lucky to be alive.

One solution to the water problem I had been considering was to set up a water tank. Attorney Law, however, had warned me against doing so. He said water tanks were not allowed in the subdivision, and if I set one up, it would cause more trouble. It appeared to me that he was not worried about me getting a water supply as much as he was worried that I would start a real war.

Mike Mazur told me, "Go find the tank. Kathy and I will find us a real attorney."

Norv Elkins had a friend who was a rancher. He loaned me an old beige-colored irrigation tank to set up behind my house on June 27th. Jerry did the plumbing for it, and he purchased a $200 pump to get the water into the house. The tank could hold only 150 gallons, but it was better than nothing. We had called several suppliers of tanks, but no one wanted their tanks delivered to Lake Juniper Subdivision. Martin Coole said I could use his garden hose to fill the tank when it got empty. (That 200 ft. of hose was heavy!) He did not want Toup LaPrix to see what we were doing, and he told me to fill the tank only after dark while Toup was at the bar.

Jerry took the tank into town in the back of my truck and filled it from the city water supply at the plant. When he arrived at my house, we hooked the tank up to the new main lines Jerry installed. The location we found to hook into was further down the hill and closer to the driveway than the original connection, so we plumbed a one-way check valve into the line to protect the tank and sealed what was left of the old line. The old tank leaked, and we patched it, hoping the patches would hold.

When we got everything fixed and we turned on the water, the clean water flushed the lines throughout the house and my toilets received blue water. My tub had chunks of blue sandy material that flushed out of the lines, and all the water coming from the faucets was turquoise blue. My icemaker was producing vivid blue ice cubes. Lab tests showed that the copper count in those ice cubes was 319 mg. All the water entering my house was blue. My two Oscar fish were immediately distressed. The automatic water leveler activated and before I could shut it down, copper entered the aquarium. Even the small amount of copper they were exposed to in the aquarium through the leveling supply, had started to affect them. I tried to get them into good water, but it was too late. They lost their battle for life. They were big fish and they tried hard, but they could not fight the copper intrusion. Even my poor fish had become victims condemned.

I knew Toup's house was being serviced by the same well, and I wondered why, as owner of a water company, he didn't realize there was a problem. Did his house have a problem?

June 27th also happened to be the day that the restitution hearing for Jack Tattoo had been scheduled. Not only was I mourning the death of two fish that I believed loved me, but I had to go to a hearing for a man I had learned to hate. When I went to the hearing, there was no one in the courtroom. The hearing had been rescheduled to another date three months down the line.

Three days later on June 30th, I woke up deathly ill. My son Jerry came to help. I was throwing up and had diarrhea so bad that I did not know which end to put in the pot. A deadly heat was in my neck, and my knees felt like jelly. I needed to go to Dr. Cooper.

When Jerry arrived, I was in the bathroom, and he called Dr. Cooper's office for an appointment. Even after learning Jerry thought it was an emergency, the doctor's receptionist insisted Dr. Cooper could not see me until 5:15 p.m. I told Jerry I did not think I could wait that long, but I would try. The bathroom floor seemed to be the safest place to stay, considering my condition at the time. Jerry went to get me a pillow. When he returned, there was white foam coming from my mouth, my eyes were open but unfocused, and I was struggling for breath. I was not able to respond to him at all. He called 9-1-1.

When I later listened to those emergency tapes, I cried. Jerry was so scared. He had assured the dispatcher he could do CPR if necessary. She talked and talked to him and sent him doing busy things for me like getting my medicine out so the ambulance attendants would know what I had been taking. She had him cover me up to keep me warm and to generally keep checking on me.

I came around enough to hear Jerry talking on the phone. His voice seemed distant, as if he was in another world somewhere. At least he was close enough for me to hear his voice, and that was comforting. He told the dispatcher I lived in "that damn Lake Juniper Subdivision." I could hear him saying the gates were locked and the ambulance would have to come in the back way. Jerry had not lived in Mohave County long enough to remember the street name that the ambulance driver would have to turn on, but it did not matter; there was no visible street sign anyway.

The dispatcher asked him if that was Toup LaPrix's subdivision. She knew about the locked gates. Everyone knew of the problems, but no one would get involved, including the emergency departments. She asked him how to get into the area. He explained the directions the best he could. When the dispatcher said the ambulance had turned on the rural street that ran southeast of the subdivision, he hung up the phone and ran two blocks on foot to show them the "alley passage." The rural road was empty of traffic. He ran back and called 911 again. He explained that the ambulance was not in the area. He screamed as he explained to the dispatcher that the ambulance was obviously lost.

The dispatcher suggested that Jerry not hang up the phone again until the ambulance was in his sight. He was determined to find that ambulance. He laid the telephone receiver on my chest and took off again.

As it turned out, the ambulance had gone past the turn-off point at the alley and had proceeded up into the mountains behind our subdivision. Jerry got into his car, went and found them, and brought them to the house. He had left the phone receiver in a position where the dispatcher could hear my breathing. I kept mumbling into it when the dispatcher hollered at me. There was someone trying to talk to me, but I did not know where she was. I kept trying to respond to the voice, but it seemed my brain shut down. All I could muster was a good grunt now and then. At least she knew I was still alive. The total response time for the emergency vehicle was over an hour.

As the paramedic and Jerry entered the house, I heard Jerry say, "She's got copper poisoning. She's been real sick for a few months."

The ambulance had a visiting doctor on board. He lifted my head and the room turned over a couple of times. My head began to clear and the attendant explained the doctor's presence. He took my blood pressure. The numbers were abnormally low. I told the doctor what my normal pressure should be and how high it had been running lately. I asked him for his opinion of my situation. He was hesitant to say anything, so I asked him if I was bottoming out. He nodded.

That was enough for me. Kathy Mazur had told me if that happened, it would be a sign that I was getting into big trouble. She had warned me of all the bad signs to look for, and this was the sign she had described as the worst. I did not want to die in the house. I agreed to let the ambulance driver take me to the hospital. I told Jerry to call Kathy right away. She had no faith in the city's hospital. She would see that I was protected from any medical malpractice.

The ambulance took me to the emergency room. I kept telling the emergency room personnel that I was copper poisoned. They responded as if I was still delirious. They started an IV, and the emergency room physician treated me with antibiotics. Jerry could not find Kathy Mazur. By 5:00 p.m., the emergency room doctor came in and gave me prescriptions for an inner ear infection. The IV probably saved my life, but I knew my problem was not solved.

I had Jerry take me over to Dr. Cooper before we returned home. We still had the 5:15 p.m. appointment made for me, so I just kept it. I showed Dr. Cooper the prescriptions I had received from the emergency room doctor, and he just wadded them up and threw them away. He said, "You do not need those. Did you tell them you had copper poisoning? That medicine will not help you, and I do not want you taking anything unless I prescribe it for you. Keep drinking bottled water. I am still waiting for instructions from Arizona's toxicologist. Evidently, they do not think your condition is serious. Here is something to prevent your vomiting problem. Go home. You need to rest. It has been two weeks since I sent my inquiry to the state's toxicologist. I do not know if they will ever answer, but we will get through this, I promise you."

After hearing that a client of the Lake Juniper Water Company had been copper poisoned by the local water sources, everyone politically connected was suddenly curious. Dr. Cooper said his file was already "a foot thick" with telephone messages from state and county officials. I was sure glad *he* wasn't charging me by the hour.

CHAPTER 13

Remembering what Attorney Law had instructed me to do, "Write to everyone, contact the media, and get outside help," I sent faxes and e-mails to every state and federal official representing Arizona at that time, pleading that someone help. This list included the governor of Arizona (Governor Jane Hull), both of Arizona's United States Senators (Senators John McCain and John Kyl), United States Representative Bob Stump, State Representative Joe Hart, and State Senator John Wettaw.

Senator McCain sent a response letter stating he had referred my complaint to our mayor. The letter concerned me. We do not have a mayor. We live in the county, and no counties in Arizona have mayors. The signature on his letter was an original. I licked my finger and checked it out.

My friend Heidi Lueck is an 84-year-young woman who moved to the United States from Germany when she was a much younger woman. She was concerned about what was happening with my health, water supply, and how the bureaucrats were treating me. When I read Senator McCain's response to Heidi, she and 200 friends signed and sent petitions to Senator McCain asking him to please come to Mohave County and see if he could help. His reply to that petition stated that he appreciated the invitation, but he no longer involved himself in local affairs.

"I know I am not born and educated in this country," Heidi said. "I thought this man represented the people of the State of Arizona. I know he is a busy man because I see him on television, but he should take time to service the people at home who need him. I am so sorry we failed."

"It's not your fault, Heidi. The Bible says we should not love money more than we love God, but more and more I see that happening. Indifference to a person's needs if the person has no money shows up every day in our political circles. If there is not big money involved, few care. Mr. McCain is not interested. He doesn't even want to know what is wrong with the water," I said.

Tipper Gore replied to my letter. She wrote that she was sorry about our water and the harassing attacks we had been receiving from Toup. She said she was forwarding my letter to the Equal Rights Commission. She felt perhaps if they could not lend assistance, they would know where to forward the letter. No other federal officials replied.

I was naïve enough to believe that the elected officials would respond to the fear I expressed in the letter, and at least attempt to find out what was happening to the taxpayers that they represent. Even though I am only an American citizen, if I had received such a letter, I would have done everything I could possibly do to protect and help the citizen who wrote it. The author of such a letter was either a victim in desperate need of assistance, or a mentally deranged person capable of doing harm to the community. It would be my responsibility, as an American, to find the truth.

Representative Bob Stump's administrative assistant contacted Attorney Law, who told the assistant that he (Law) could handle the problem himself. After the assistant's one visit in July, it did not matter how many times we wrote letters to the representative, we never heard from his office again.

The American Civil Rights Commission called in response to Tipper Gore's inquiry. They said they were referring my letter to Housing and Urban Development (HUD). The Civil Rights Commission explained that if I could prove discrimination because of my age, sex, health, or race, they could get involved. I knew that would go nowhere. HUD sent my letter and lab test results to the EPA, but their letter explained that until I got the water reconnected, there wasn't much they could do. It also explained that the ADEQ could not find anything wrong with my water, but they had promised the EPA they would continue checking for the problem. Arizona had not invited the EPA to get involved, but they assured me that my lab tests were of a concern to them.

On July 10th, a meeting was held at the home of my neighbor, Martin Coole. One of the county supervisors, Supervisor Golf, had arranged the meeting. He was a short, fat person who came into office in 1996. My friend Jim called him "an obese rhetoric spouter reminiscent of the 1920s Chicago era."

When he was first elected to the Mohave County Board of Supervisors, he seemed ready to help all the people. In the beginning, he was always well dressed and exhibited a happy, positive attitude. To his credit, he was the only supervisor who seemed to care about the residents of the Lake Juniper Subdivision even though it was not located in his district.

He was the only elected official in the room. His position as supervisor placed him at the top of the executive branch of county government, but because he was not from our district, he did not have to worry about getting our votes.

Supervisor Negate should have held the meeting because we live in her district. She could never make any fast decisions, and she voted against most everything complicated that came before her. The Lake Juniper problem was getting complicated. She had been in politics in the area for a long time. At one time, she was a mayor of the nearby city. She knew double talk.

Nine years earlier, in 1988, I had gone before the local city council seeking a conditional use permit for the night watchman's quarters on the six and one-half acre parcel I owned and used for my landscaping business in an area zoned light industrial. At her insistence, I paid for and presented the council with laboratory reports showing that none of the fines (leftover, unusable crushed rock) left on the property by a previous operation were dangerous to human health. Those reports cost me over $2,000. After a four-month review, she was the only council member out of seven who voted against the project. Evidently, this lady could not read those laboratory reports, did not believe them, was just plain stubborn, or afraid to be involved in my new venture.

The physical damage I received from the Lake Juniper Water Company was much greater than any damage that old rock product would cause my employees or me. Supervisor Negate was the supervisor assigned to the Lake Juniper Subdivision's district, and she did absolutely nothing we could detect to help or support the needs of the residents of the Lake Juniper Subdivision for the entire four years she sat on the Board of Supervisors.

Right after her election in November 1996, she told Kathy Mazur and me, "I am going to do everything I can for you people."

At this July 10th meeting, Kathy said, "I met Mrs. Negate in the office last Friday. I asked her why I hadn't seen her in the subdivision. She told me that she was instructed by the county attorney not to get involved in our problems. Chock up another liar lost to the clique and write her name on our list. Far be it from Mrs. Negate, who was the county attorney's boss, to defy the county attorney's instructions and help a group of taxpayers in desperate need."

"To be truthful Kathy, I'm glad she's not here. Maybe we will see some positive action today," I said. Through all our problems, Kathy had kept a list of people who had lied to us or in some way, just generally, "pissed her off." Kathy's list kept getting longer and longer.

Other people present at the meeting represented various departments of the county. Lieutenant Warfield, Captain Bulletin, and paid employees of the sheriff were there to represent the Sheriff's Department. They explained the sheriff was too busy to attend. In over three years, we never had the pleasure of seeing or talking with the sheriff himself, except at the Republican's yearly Lincoln Day Bar-B-Que. No one living in the subdivision had ever seen the sheriff within the boundaries of our subdivision. Since the sergeant had declared that the sheriff called for the civil standby so Toup could cut up my plumbing that Sunday morning, we all felt it was a cop-out for him not to attend the meeting and face us himself.

Two employees from the county attorney's office were there. They were Attorney Whiner and Deputy Attorney Nogut. Also present was Director Mallard, the director from Planning and Zoning and Acting County Manager Toup Faurget, both employees of the County.

Thankfully, there were still only four homeowners. All four were present. We were not about to miss that meeting!

As I sat in that meeting, I wondered why Supervisor Golf was getting involved in our problems, while our own elected representative had chosen to stay away. Because there were only three supervisors in the county, two could not be together at any time unless a public meeting had been noticed. The open meeting laws are strict, but when followed, they keep down some of the corruption. I giggled, leaned over to Mike, and said, "I wonder why they didn't notice a public meeting today."

Mike laughed, "You don't suppose they are hiding something, do you?"

At the meeting, the homeowners were told by Deputy Attorney Nogut that he had advised my lawyer, Attorney Law, to obtain a permanent injunction from the court forbidding the discontinuation of my water and the locking of the gates. He said he could not understand why Attorney Law had not done that already. (When later confronted, Attorney Law adamantly denied that Deputy Attorney Nogut had advised him to do anything. He said no one ever suggested he take such action.)

It seemed strange to me that if I was paying Attorney Law for his legal knowledge, why did he not know to ask for the permanent injunction? And why would he be following the advice of Deputy Attorney Nogut in the first place?

Attorney Whiner explained that the County could not get involved in civil issues of this type unless there was a permanent injunction in force. If the water supply were discontinued after the court order, the issue would become a criminal matter. As the criminal prosecutor, Deputy Attorney Nogut could then have Toup LaPrix arrested and the water restored.

Deputy Attorney Nogut agreed. "It is the only way I can get your water restored. Of course, I would honor any permanent injunction immediately. At this time, it is only a civil matter and I have no authority to intervene."

In the State of Arizona, there is a law that declares it a felony if a person blocks a waterhole intended for the use of cattle. I was not impressed by the thought that a cow's life carried more weight in the state than a human life.

We explained to the sheriff's representatives that the problems we were having with their department were quite unusual. All their staff seemed to be able to find their way into the subdivision to warn and threaten us against hurting Toup's feelings, but when we needed assistance, none of them could find their way into the subdivision because the gates were locked.

Three times we had called when we found Toup trespassing on our property and stalking our homes. Three times we had been told that the officer could not help because he couldn't get into the subdivision because the gates were locked. On Monday, June 2nd, when Toup completely destroyed my water pipes, they couldn't find their way into the subdivision to investigate what he had done because the gates were locked.

Captain Bulletin advised us he would notify all his personnel, including the entire emergency services, how to get into the back door of the subdivision in case of emergency. "You will never again receive the excuse that anyone from my department could not help you because the gates are locked."

Toup Faurget said, "I will have a sign built showing the new way into the development, so you people won't have any more problems receiving emergency services. I'll place it on the corner at Jordan Ranch Road."

Director Mallard said, "I will look into the possibility of obtaining a permit so you can drill your own wells."

Mike Mazur reminded the group that they held assurances for the subdivision's completion. He said, "I suggest you pay each one of us $200,000 today and we will leave the area. If you don't want to do that today or anytime soon, you can then pay us that same amount for every year you put us through this hell."

"Mr. Mazur. We are not putting you through hell. Our hands are tied," replied Deputy Attorney Nogut.

"Well, if you are not going to admit liability right now, you can do that later. Just remember what I said about the money," Mike answered.

The County did not keep even one of the promises they made that day. There was no sign placed on the main road showing directions to our alley. The gates weren't unlocked and they did not have the guts to force the opening of those gates. The gates remained chained and locked until April 2001.

It seemed the County maintained the attitude that "If you don't like it, leave. If you don't leave, we will break you." I was not about to be broken but I was quickly becoming a financial prisoner of the County. I was too sick to go to work and replenish all the money that was being spent, just to keep me alive.

The ADWR (Arizona Department of Water Resources) had told me earlier in July that if Mohave County approved a well location, I could have a well of my own. The man said that my property boundaries were large enough to meet state law. He explained that the application had to be approved by the County Health Department. With a well of my own, the water could be treated properly and any copper removed with the use of filters.

At the request of the ADWR, I filed an application for a well. In accordance with the rules, I filed the application with the Mohave County Health Department for review. The ADWR had been kind enough to help me compile the application. The County held my application (and check) for over a month then returned both items to me. There were no marks of any kind on the application and no explanation. The application never got to the Arizona Department of Water Resources. It seemed no one wanted to go against the wishes of Toup LaPrix and the county clique. Everyone showed indifference to our health, safety, and welfare.

I was beginning to learn that when civil, legal, or human rights are in question, the County does not put their decisions in writing.

The County continued to deny any wells. The Sheriff's Department continued to find it impossible to locate a way into our subdivision. Over a period exceeding three years, the locked gates were always used as an excuse for denying police protection for any of the homeowners. Considering the County's bias in favor of the local Good 'ol Boys, it was probably just as well. When the sheriff's office had appeared, the homeowners were treated as criminals.

The single thing I felt the county representatives had accomplished at that meeting was to satisfy their curiosity. Perhaps they wanted to be sure the Lake Juniper residents were suffering. My skin had taken on a gray pallor. I had bags under my eyes, was losing my hair, and appeared to be dying. That should have been good enough assurance for them. It didn't appear to them that I would be a problem much longer. They certainly did not want any taxpayers outside the subdivision to know what was going on at Lake Juniper.

Everyone has pet peeves. Mine deals with people who lie. If a person wants to make me angry, all they need to do is lie to me. In my teenage years, I learned the truth is better. Lies just make matters worse. In my adulthood, it had become evident I was attempting to be truthful in the midst of a den of thieves.

I had trusted the officials—taken them at their word. Mike Mazur explained to me that believing in government officials was not a possibility when getting involved with the Mohave County government. When we asked questions, they refused to respond. If we dared express our opinion, we were considered crazy. When we wrote to them, they put our mail in a cabinet under the rest of the junk, then they ignored us, hoping we might give up and move away.

Straightforward answers were an impossible feat for the people representing the county. It appeared many officials could not give us a direct answer because they first had to check out everything with Billy Willy, Jr., the elected county attorney. When Billy Willy, Jr. failed to respond, it seemed all the other political flunkies got lockjaw.

I had hired Attorney Law on June 2nd. On June 27th, his office sent me another bill for over $500. By July 2nd, he had been unable to secure a water supply for me and he went on vacation for a week. The man had been trusted and had been paid $2200 to restore my water service and he left town while I still had no water supply! Perhaps my attorney needed more money to finance his playtime! I was beginning to realize that Kathy Mazur might be right about him. He certainly had not shown me he could get off his fat butt and get my facilities reconnected.

I waited very impatiently for the legal process to take hold and restore my water, even though I knew I could not drink it nor bathe in it. It was hard to believe that the call Attorney Law said he had made to the Arizona State Corporation Commission had not produced water for me. I needed enough to flush my toilets, do dishes, and wash clothes. I did not think that was asking for too much, considering the legal fees charged.

By July 20th, after being without a decent water supply for nearly two months, I was sure Attorney Law was not going to get the water turned on anytime soon. I knew I could not afford $2100 per month in hourly fees for him to continue talking to the bureaucrats. I went into his office and asked to see my file. The file consisted of a pile of pink memos written by his secretary and the one letter he had written to Toup. I discontinued his services. My only request to his secretary was that she ask Attorney Law to get the tapes of the 9-1-1 calls for the ambulance Jerry summoned for me on June 30th. The tapes would substantiate my complaint about the locked gates and our lack of emergency services. I agreed to pay for the tapes and the time it took him to retrieve them.

The sheriff's clerk had advised me that Attorney Law had to retrieve the tapes and that they would save them for him to pick up. "Those tapes are not public record. Furthermore, most of those tapes are destroyed shortly after they are recorded," she explained.

Attorney Law said the sheriff's clerk was wrong and Law refused to go get the tapes. He said he did not have time for that sort of thing. He warned me against using the neighbor's water. That activity would be considered an illegal act. He said, "Even though the water company has broken every rule and law on the books, Toup will not be arrested, but you could be."

That was the second time I had been warned that I could be arrested. They couldn't arrest me. They knew I was too damn sick from the copper. Had the sheriff arrested me, the County would have been responsible for the $138,000 worth of medical bills I faced.

Mike Mazur asked me, "Did you fire that fat fucker?"

"Yes Mike, I did. He was quickly bankrupting me. He would not believe anything I told him. I can't tell what he's accomplished in two months, but it doesn't look like much."

"Good. I am going to put a line from my house to your garden. You spent too many hours working in that garden to let those plants die. I am tired of watching you carry buckets of water to them. If you want to extend the line to your toilets, be my guest. Jerry said he would do that for you. All these bastards have gone too far. Let 'em arrest us. It may bring on that publicity the famous lawyer of yours wanted you to get," he said.

I had to take a five-gallon jug and refill the back of that toilet because there was not enough water pressure to fill it properly. In my new $200,000 home, I kept large pans of hauled water on the stove and I would heat them for washing dishes and cleaning up. That hurt. I had invested a lot of money in a new washer and dryer and nothing worked! I cried a lot. I bought a lot of paper plates and TV dinners. I was seldom hungry and my weight dropped drastically. I knew I had to do something different before I lost my strength to fight the criminal system ruining my life.

I went alone, back to the sheriff's office, and the clerk refused to supply me with the tapes again. She refused to call Attorney Law. When I asked her to call Supervisor Golf, she complied. Supervisor Golf talked to the sheriff and I was given the tapes. I didn't even have to pay for them! Supervisor Golf was able to get the tapes for me because he was the supervisor who understood the sheriff was exceeding his budget every year by millions of dollars. He had the power to stop the sheriff's rape of the County General Fund. The sheriff had the time and personnel to respond to every request made by Supervisor Golf.

After Supervisor Golf presented my file containing Toup's activities to the county attorney, appeared at our meeting, and used his clout to get me the emergency tapes, the clique shut him down. We seldom heard from him again and when we did, it wasn't good news.

It appears in the financial records of the County that after almost two years on the Board of Supervisors, this public representative received a County-paid trip to Hawaii. Following that trip, he appeared at all the board meetings in brightly colored Hawaiian lounging shirts, and his attitude changed to match his attire. It was all a game for him. He merged into the political game with ease.

He managed to avoid or ignore voter input and answered all complaints with snide remarks. He spent public meeting time doing his best to disgrace anyone who appeared before the board with an opposing opinion. He insulted and interrupted as many people as he could. In my view, his demeanor became disgraceful and his appearance became slovenly.

In the last week of July, the Mazurs, Martin, and I set out to find a virgin attorney. We wanted one who did not live in the area and had not been corrupted by the clique. Our neighbor, Martin Coole, first called a local prominent attorney. Martin was sure the attorney was not corrupt. The attorney said he did not want to "mess" with our case. He said he was planning to retire. What an excuse! After five more years, he was still practicing law.

I called another prominent attorney in the area. His office was in Lake Havasu City, Arizona. He said he would look into the situation and call me back. He never called. The Arizona Bar Association faxed me a list of referrals, and in three days, we had exhausted the list. I sent emails and letters to 144 lawyers throughout the state. I only received 12 responses. They all had different reasons for not wanting to take our case. For the most part, their answers were, "The only part of this case where you might retrieve your funds is by suing Mohave County and the State of Arizona, and that would take years and a lot of money."

One of the lawyers sounded honest and reasonable. He said, "I'm sorry. I don't want to work in Mohave County. State officials and departments would be of little or no help to us because their offices are located too far from your rural area." People in Phoenix refer to Mohave County as "that foreign section of Arizona."

I even wrote to Jerry Spence. I had read that he does pro bono cases for people who have big problems such as the ones I was facing. The copper in the system and the lack of governmental response would be his cup of tea. He also is an author of several fine books.

His office gave me an answer, but it was not what I wanted. My case interested his reader. The group would review it. They could only take one new case. If mine was chosen, they would contact me, and I would have to travel to their office in Wyoming. Mine wasn't chosen at his roundtable.

We continued to search for an attorney, and after we made 156 inquiries of Arizona law firms, on August 2nd Mike found a law firm in Mesa, Arizona. It was a large, expensive firm, and he and Kathy went to talk with them. Many representatives of the firm sat down at a conference table with Mike and Kathy and listened as they explained how Toup LaPrix was harassing the residents of the subdivision. They explained my water supply problems, my health problems, and the non-completion of the subdivision that was ruining everyone financially.

Even though the firm's lawyers were finding the story they were hearing rather hard to swallow, they assured Mike they could do the job. They explained that a superior court judge, Judge Schneider, had previously ruled that three years was a reasonable time in which to complete a subdivision. They did not want to sue the County until they had exhausted a suit against Toup. If Mike still insisted the County be sued, they would consider the case later, but they would make no commitments or agree to sue the County.

Mike and Kathy paid the firm a retainer of $2500, with the understanding they would look for the resources of Toup LaPrix that could be used to pay for the damages he had caused everyone. If they found Toup had resources available, they would proceed with the lawsuit against him. If they found he had none, they would not go any further.

The one lesson we learned while searching for a lawyer is that if the firm asks for a $10,000 deposit, they do not really want the case, but they will take your money. Many lawyers licensed to practice in Arizona but residing in another state fit that bill.

Mike and Kathy headed for home believing they had found an honest law firm in Mesa. The homeowners would finally have good legal assistance. Mike Mazur was convinced the firm would be able to help. Kathy was not so sure. However, they had received a more positive response than we had been getting from other firms throughout the state.

When they returned from Mesa on August 3rd, Mike said, "I still think the lawsuit should include Mohave County and the State of Arizona."

"I think the reason no one else would take our case is because they didn't want to sue the governments," I replied. "At least we can get the ball rolling now."

"You just work on getting well. If the law firm files a suit against Toup, you and Martin Coole can join as plaintiffs. The first thing the firm wants to learn is how to get their hands on Toup's money," he said.

The firm must have felt there was enough money available because they wrote a demand letter to Toup, Cowboy Joe, and The Brats Consulting Group on behalf of Mike and Kathy Mazur. Later, after they received no response to the letter, they decided to file a lawsuit. The time had come for me to join in the action. I paid the requested fees for myself. The Mazurs and I split the fees Martin Coole had to pay. Martin did not have the money at the time, but we knew he would pay us when things got better. Later, he paid his share back to us in full. That is what honest people do!

By early August, we homeowners felt like prisoners in our own development. We were all pretty confused as to how long we would be locked up. It was an awful feeling knowing a developer had the power to lock the gates and leave them locked at his pleasure, but we were informed by the county attorney that we could not unlock the gates. If we destroyed Toup's titanium locks, we would be arrested.

The ADEQ (Arizona Department of Environmental Quality) had their neck on the line over my copper poisoning. With Dr. Cooper at their heels, they stayed in touch, ran tests (fake or not) on my neighbor's homes, and spent a lot of time trying to keep us from suing them. The ADEQ's position remained firm: they did not know where all that copper came from; they would help me run tests on my house when the water was restored, but the State could not get involved with Toup or Toup's system; it was too small.

"Are you telling me that 24 people could get copper poisoning, but they could not get involved until that 25th person surfaced? Is that really the law?" Mike asked.

"That [ADEQ] inspector told Patti that if there were deaths, they could do more," Kathy added.

"Well Patti, when are you going to die? We all need Toup's garage and the system inspected," Mike joked.

"Just don't drink the water, Mike," I replied.

I knew Kathy wasn't drinking the water, but Mike was.

After Dr. Cooper questioned the County, the Health Department claimed they did not have the facilities to test for corrosive materials in water. According to the County, everything that was happening to us was the fault and responsibility of either Toup LaPrix or the Arizona Corporation Commission (ACC).

In the time periods between June 1997 and January 1998, all the state, county, and federal health departments we called had been unable to help with the water situation, with the exception of the ADEQ and the ACC. After several pleadings by my physician, the laboratory technician, the Mazurs, Martin Coole and me, the individual departments within the State and the County began to simply ignore our calls. The state toxicologist, after Dr. Cooper waited over a month, telephoned him and suggested

I continue drinking only bottled water. Dr. Cooper demanded state testing of my water supply. That was rather a difficult request. The bulk of the water my house was receiving was not coming from the water company, and the State had not been invited onto Toup LaPrix's property.

Under doctor's orders, I was drinking about a gallon and a half of bottled water a day. Even though there was no drinking, bathing, making ice, or cooking with the contaminated water, my blood tests continued to show elevated copper.

Dr. Cooper said, "I told you not to drink or bathe in that water. If you continue doing that, you will die."

"I'm not drinking the water. I haul water in and I buy bottled water," I replied.

"The tests show these levels are not getting any better," he said.

"Well, fix it. You're the Doctor," I said.

In August, Mr. Ruleworm, the health director, explained the monthly denial of a well was based on two rules. I had asked for his reasoning to be put in writing, but he refused my request. In a public meeting, he insisted our subdivision was a "wet" subdivision. (That was reason number one.) He then stated that I did not own a full acre of land. (That was reason two.) The County's regulations stated you must own a full acre or you get no well. That rule had been waived many times for the Good 'ol Boys. I made a list of wells located on less than one acre with a septic system and located in a wet subdivision. I gave it to Mr. Ruleworm. He said he would look into it.

The State regulations did not require the one-acre rule. The only thing the State required was one-half acre of land and the well must be a minimum of 100 feet from any septic system. My land met that require-ment with a hundred feet to spare.

Mr. Ruleworm quit his position and moved away, so in September, I contacted Director Mallard. She agreed that exceptions to the rule had been made before in the County. She said she would look into it and see if an exception could be made in my case. Since there appeared to be a valid health problem, perhaps the Health Department would reconsider their denial for a well. I waited for her return call. After about three weeks, I called her again. With a lot of aggravation in her voice, she told me the County would not allow me to drill a well. The clique had won again.

"Nobody cares, Patti. You will just have to sue the County and bring all this crap on the table. No employee will get involved; they have families to feed," Mike Mazur explained.

"Mike, Arizona has a criminal statute that carries a very heavy felony sentence for a man if he is caught blocking cattle from reaching a watering hole. What about people? I cannot find any criminal statutes that cover human beings being cut off from their water supply. There were some regulations, but the Arizona Corporation Commission is in charge of the regulation enforcements. Their attorney explained to me that they could not get the county attorney to assist them in taking any action. After writing several scathing letters to the county attorney, the lawyer for the Arizona Corporation Commission told me the most they were authorized to do was condemn the water company. They could withdraw the certificate of need and necessity permit acquired from them, but they would have to close the wells. That would mean everyone in our development would be without water. There must be other alternatives. If I shut up, at least the State won't shut off your water supply."

"Keep trying. They won't do that," Mike said

Every time we attended any county meetings, no matter where our problem showed up on the printed agenda, our issue was postponed, making it the very last issue to be heard, if it was heard at all. This became so obvious to the chairman of the Planning and Zoning Commission that he made a public statement. He explained we had faithfully sat all the way through each of the meetings for several months, waiting our turn. At the next meeting we would be heard first.

It was very obvious that the county Good 'ol Boys did not want the public to hear of our problems. If the truth came out and it was made public, many big names would be destroyed. If they waited late enough, most of the people would be gone and the taxpayers wouldn't learn what was going on within our subdivision.

Several times Director Mallard had explained our item was always last on the list because, "people who live in other areas in the county need to be heard first so they can get home before dark." It was not unusual for the commission meetings to last until 10:00 or 11:00 p.m. On one occasion, we got home at 2:00 a.m. We appeared at several meetings only to find a statement under our portion of the written agenda that read, "Continued by Staff," so we would go home and wait another month. They never told us, prior to the meetings, that we would not be heard. We would give up our days of work (or nights) to go to the meetings only to find we were Continued by Staff or referred to executive session.

Previously, on July 14th, two of the planning and zoning commissioners had finally visited the subdivision. They had talked with Toup and got an on-sight view of the situation. Not many people have ventured into the locked subdivision, so that alone was a big plus for their efforts. They next appeared at the September 2 commission meeting and explained what they had seen. (The August commission met on August 5th, but they put "Continued to Staff" next to our issues.) The chairman had a prepared speech that he handed out to each of the interested parties present. It was very surprising for us to find that the chairman of this committee felt the homeowners in our subdivision were interested parties and had the right to know what was going on. (The following proposal includes a reference to Toup having had over thirty days to sign a proposed agreement. The agreement referred to was written when the "new" Board of Supervisors hired Attorney Whiner in June to write a contract specifying Toup's obligations to complete his subdivision. The contract was presented at the June meeting. Toup walked out of that meeting and refused to sign the proposal.) The new proposal was as follows:

LAKE JUNIPER ESTATES PROPOSAL

We see no reasonable excuse for your prior non-performance for complying with the subdivision improvements. Our agreement or non-agreement to continue the assurances has not prevented you from fully performing, during the over six and one-half years (6 1/2) since your subdivision was given Board of Supervisor approval.

You have had over thirty (30) days to sign the proposed agreement and related documents proposed by the County related to a proposed extension of assurances. You have chosen not to sign or to propose a compromise. For that reason, and your prior non-performance, the assurances for Lake Juniper should not be extended, and should be called.

Nonetheless, as Chairman of this Board, with the help and concurrence of the [vice-chairman] we are making certain observations and are bringing forth a proposal for your consideration and the consideration of the other members of the Planning and Zoning Commission.

Our observations include the following:

The [vice-chairman] and I were informed by you at our meeting of July 14, 1997 that you have been mining and storing AB [aggregate base], which you state will be used on the roadway. We also saw that apparently, in the last few weeks, a pressure tank has been moved in for the water system. These are positive signs. However, in calling the paving company and talking to the owner, I have been informed that he will be unable to pave your roads, as he is not in a position to take lots in lieu of cash, as you are proposing.

In talking with [*the engineering firm he's used*] regarding the projected costs for completion of the subdivision improvements, there appears to be a question in regards to him doing any more work as the engineer of record without being paid in a timely manner.

On Monday, July 14th, when [*vice-chairman*] and I met with you, your statement to us was that all the lots left that have not been sold to individuals were put into a trust for liability reasons and to protect your investment. You also continued on and said that the assurances that were put up were absolutely valueless. In checking with the State Real Estate Department and with your own attorney, I am told that:

#1. Any encumbrances or conditions for the benefit of the County are not changed nor negated in any way by the property transferring into a trust or by a change of trustee.

#2. Any person, trust, corporation or entity that is selling or owns more than 6 lots is considered a sub divider and falls under State Law and must provide a public report.

You then offered three (3) lots as assurances that the road paving would be done (because you firmly believe that the county assurances are not valid). My response was that if the lots are in a trust and you cannot touch them, then how could you give three (3) lots as assurance for the paving? Your reply was that you could cause it to happen.

We believe the lots are not acceptable assurances. We understand that your lots are not legally saleable or transferable.

The agreement and other documents proposed by the County Attorney's office, which you have now refused to sign, are designed to confirm and clarify the assurances for the benefit of the County. They are not for the benefit of individual county personnel, as you have described at our last commission meeting of July 9, 1997. Any extension must require the confirmation and clarification of those assurances.

I feel you are not getting adequate legal advice in regards to those issues. I also have no choice but to vote no to any extension of time unless you are willing, on an immediate basis, to provide Mohave County some cash assurances and a time line to finish the work, with verifiable performance.

The proposal we have includes the following items:

1. The gates from Stockton Hill Road to Anchor Drive must be immediately opened and remain open.

2. The AB must be put on all roadways to comply with proper construction standards and as promised by you.

3. All the roadways must be fully paved within three (3) months, to existing homeowners, Lake Juniper and within six (6) months, the entire subdivision.

4. The electric work and the water system must be finished; it can be done in phases if need be, but the entire project must be finished within one (1) year, including the filing of the "as-built."

5. Your Arizona engineer must give the County a cost estimate, which is signed and sealed according to Mohave County Subdivision 5.2.

6. You must provide the County with a cash bond in amount to assure the monies for payment for the performance, which we currently understand is not less than $165,000.00. This fund will be administered and disbursed by an oversight committee.

7. An oversight committee consisting of Ms. Ballard, a Supervisor, an Engineer, the Environmental Health Division Director, and a commissioner will be formed and will meet every quarter to assess the work done and continuation of the assurances the next quarter would be contingent on progress. Otherwise, the assurances may be terminated and called.

8. As stated, the cash monies to be provided will be held in an account to be controlled by the committee, and payment for work performed and/or completed, will be from such an account.

9. All new work will be performed in conformance with all applicable statutes, codes, ordinances and regulations, as well as in conformance with all Uniform Codes. All existing improvements will be brought in to conformance with all applicable statutes, codes, ordinances and regulations, as well as in conformance with the Uniform Codes. Any defects and deficiencies identified must be immediately corrected, including those electrical prob-

lems identified in a May 27th, 1997 letter of Citizen's Utilities, directed to you.

10. These Agreements, together with confirmation of the current assurances, must be confirmed in writing, by signed Agreement and confirming documents prepared by the county attorney's Office, and the cash monies posted, not later than August 7, 1997.

The chairman who wrote this decision for Planning and Zoning had volunteered his services. The Planning and Zoning Commission is a volunteer and advisory group, even though their recommendations are required. He was tired of messing with Toup. He later telephoned my home and explained to me he was not paid for the work he was doing and that he was sorry for all the problems I had faced.

At that meeting, the Planning and Zoning Commission voted to deny the application for extension of time to complete the subdivision.

That was the first planning and zoning meeting that we got to leave early because the unpaid planning and zoning commissioner had demanded we be the first ones heard that night. He said he was tired of seeing our issue on the bottom of the agenda every time there was a meeting.

Toup never signed anything nor did he post any money, new bonding, or any other alternative to the original assurances received by the County. He did add more aggregate base (AB) to all the roads located near our homes on the south portion of the subdivision. He had added AB to this same portion of the roads every year he had to apply for an extension of time to complete. The roads kept getting higher and higher. The gates remained locked.

Following the Planning and Zoning Commission meeting, however, Toup knew he would have to face the new Board of Supervisors on September 15th for the final decision on his subdivision. (Even though the new board had been meeting since January 1997, they had been ignoring every issue involved with the Lake Juniper Subdivision until March, when they hired Attorney Whiner to write the first contract with Toup. That contract was the one presented to Toup in early June.)

Toup took a belly dump (a dumb truck that opens on the underside) and spread AB over the roads, then he took a grader and spread the product around. He paid no attention to the engineer's staking that was still on the roads; he just laid product. He came to my street (Coral Bay) and raised the road level to at least ten or 11 inches above my existing land. He covered one of my drainage pipes with dirt and removed the second one completely. This left a three-foot deep ditch in front of my house, and I could not drive across the ditch to get into my driveway. Anyone coming to see me had to park on the road, jump over the ditch, and walk to the house.

Perhaps he was seeking someone's support at that meeting, so that he could report work was in progress toward completing the Lake Juniper project. In reality, he never agreed to any "deals" Attorney Whiner offered him. He was not prepared to face the Board of Supervisors again, and he had never looked at nor followed the engineer's construction plans.

Three days later, it rained. The water and mud came down the roads onto the lot behind mine. Then it moved down my walls and driveway so fast there was no blocking it. The mess came right through my living room, destroying my carpet and leaving watermarks on my furniture. It smothered my lawn and tore out a major portion of my landscaping. The right side of the electric transformer connected to my home sunk and it sits lopsided. Because a non-licensed contractor was doing the roadwork, there was no insurance, bond, or state recovery fund to help me absorb my $20,200 in losses.

CHAPTER 14

All this time, I remained very ill. The recommendation to flush out my body with water wasn't working. The results were as inconvenient as they were ineffective. Every time I moved my body, I was either vomiting or sitting on the toilet. My water buckets got heavier and heavier. The doctor kept telling me to eat more. I was not comfortable going to a restaurant to eat because of my need to stay near a bathroom. When I forced myself to eat, the sickness would start all over. I blamed inaction of my mind on stress. Stress had a lot to do with my problems, but there was much to learn about the effects of copper poisoning.

When Toup moved in a different pressure tank for the well in mid-June, the tank was very old, rusted, and dirty. He sandblasted the interior of the tank. What he failed to do was clean out the silica sand he had used.

The total dissolved solid counts in the water tests increased to 1500 ppm, and the water was eating away at the copper pipes in the homes. No matter what tests were performed, the large copper count found in my water in June was not found in the other homes. The silica sand was causing a lot of damage to my neighbor's appliances. The Mazur's shower tiles continued to turn green, and they had to replace the guts of their toilets on a bi-weekly basis. Our neighbor, Martin Coole, did not want to admit that there was a water problem. His main objective was to sell his house, and the more talk about bad water, the less chance he had to make a sale. He ended up replacing his dishwasher. His fixtures in the bathrooms were all eaten up. He blamed that on cheap fixtures.

When Dr. Cooper suggested chelation therapy, he asked me to go to Dr. Song. I saw dollar signs. In September, I went to the fine doctor, and he ran tests on my liver. I did not know where the money was going to come from. Many insurance companies will not pay for this sort of treatment for an adult, but I believe they should. People believe that the politically powerful and well-established branch of the medical profession speak against chelation therapy because the process is cutting into their profits. Many medical doctors are scorned by their peers for prescribing the process for their patients.

I found very few articles on the side affects of the process. Many say it won't help a bad heart or circulation problem, but they have been using it since 1945 to remove lead and other heavy metals from the body. Good naturopaths know what replacements need to be made in that area and they design vitamins containing good minerals to replace the bad. Dr. Cooper cared about my successful recovery more than he did his reputation among his peers.

Kathy Mazur had suggested I might find Dr. Sweet, in Lake Havasu City, to be less expensive. She said he was a very good naturopath. Upon hearing of my problem with the copper poisoning, he took me in right away. I was instructed to get all the silver fillings removed from my teeth because of the mercury content in the fillings.

Dr. Sweet told me that in addition to the chelation therapy, I had to do something to control the stress my body was going through. He suggested I spend time writing about the things happening in my life. He promised things would work out and that my writing would make a difference in my recovery.

When stress began to get the best of me, my sister also suggested I write down everything that was happening. By seeing the words on paper, I would be able to decide if I had any control over the situation or if the control belonged in the hands of God. I was to put the lists of things I could not control in a *God Box*, and I was to take the rest of the list and fix the things I could. She said if I would do my part, God would do his.

With hope in my heart for better health and for a better world in which people would care for one another, I gathered my notes, started up my computer, and began writing.

When I spoke with Dr. Cooper about my choice for the new doctor, he questioned my decision to go to Dr. Sweet when he had recommended Dr. Song. I explained the difference was $1800 versus $8500 for the same EDTA administration. Ethylene diamine tetra-acetic acid (EDTA) is a man-made amino acid chelating agent with a particular affinity for toxic metals. In my case, the metals were copper, lead, and nickel. When EDTA meets up with the toxic substances in the body, the materials are sequestered and then secreted in bodily wastes. The product each doctor purchased came from the exact same supplier. Dr. Cooper understood and approved of my choice of physicians.

The removal and replacement of the fillings in my teeth cost another

$1,000. Considering the alternative, the price tag was still very acceptable. I was wondering when it would all end. Kathy kept encouraging me on. I had suffered so much, I was game for anything. The dentist had taken the silver fillings out and replaced them with composite fillings. They work just as well as the silver.

By September 22nd, two major class action suits had been filed against Toup LaPrix, and they had him so confused, he did not know where to turn. The suits were in two different courts with two different judges. The first had been filed in November 1996 (ten months earlier) by six of the people who had bought lots in the subdivision (the lot owners). Their judge was based in La Paz County. The four people who had built homes in the subdivision filed the second class-action suit against Toup in September 1997. Their case was to be heard in Mohave County. I was one of the plaintiffs in the homeowner's case.

The suit that Kathy and Mike Mazur, Martin Coole, and I filed on September 22nd in superior court listed Toup LaPrix, the title company, the water company, the homeowners association, and any and all partnerships, heirs, and wives or ex-wives Toup might have or had, as Defendants. The suit claimed, among other things, fraud, civil racketeering, and damages both medical and financial. This list was quite long. The claim requested that all defendants be ordered to pay the cost we expended for our homes plus damages, and left room for additions to the defendant list. I thought our attorneys knew all the deeds to Toup LaPrix's lands had been changed to include Cowboy Joe and The Brats Consulting Group. The demand letter had included these defendants by name, but the lawsuit did not. Failure to include Cowboy Joe and The Brats Consulting Group on the original lawsuit proved to be a costly oversight.

Our attorneys found that in the beginning, no judge in the county was willing to hear a case involving Toup LaPrix. The lot owners who were suing him had found a judge in La Paz County who was willing to hear their case, so our attorneys applied for a hearing in that court. Toup made a smart move and took his "one time shot" and excused the La Paz judge for cause (requested a different judge for a reason). Toup felt the judge would be prejudiced because Toup had appeared in front of him before with a similar case. The La Paz judge had already reviewed Toup's frivolous filings in the property owner's case. If Toup allowed us to have the same judge, that judge would have been able to finish the case in no time flat. Our case was then moved back to the Mohave County Superior Court.

Many of Toup's filings had been stored in his computer, and exact replicas were presented to the court over and over. They made no sense, but the court was required by law to read them and act on them.

Toup LaPrix never answered the charges in the lawsuit. He instead submitted papers requesting a Motion to Define, and he submitted many questions to our attorneys that, according to our attorneys and the judges, had nothing to do with our lawsuit. For example, he wanted to see our bank statements!

When he cited legal interpretations made by previous courts (stare decisis), the cases were always very old federal cases. Many of the cases involved plaintiffs who had filed lawsuits against states and counties (sovereign entities), and had failed to file the notice of claim before filing the lawsuit with the superior court.

Toup LaPrix claimed he was a sovereign entity and that we had not filed a proper claim before filing the formal complaint and he was immune from civil action.

When I read Toup's pro se responses to our lawsuit, I told Mike Mazur, "We sent a demand letter. That is the same as filing a claim. He ignored our demand. I think the lawyers did everything they should have done."

"Yep. They know what they are doing. Toup is just an ass. Since we have learned how royal he is, we should call him "King Toup." I understand his brother said he would help him pay for an attorney and he refused the offer. After we prove in court that this bastard is a felon, I am going to prove that the County is at fault. We are fighting bigger crooks than King Toup, and there are more of them."

"Do you think we can prove that?" I asked.

"You bet," he said. "You just get well. Kathy and I will work with these lawyers. When you get better, we will file a lawsuit against the County. They are responsible for this mess and they can pay."

"If we end up suing the County, the taxpayers will be the ones who pay. I don't think I like that idea," I said.

"Okay. Look at it this way. You are a widow. You have been without water for several months now. It has been published on the front page of the newspaper that one house out here has no water. Have you seen any taxpayers come to see which house it is and what the hell is going on? Has anyone brought you as much as a bottle of water?" Kathy said.

"Well, you and Mike are helping when you can and Jerry has been busting his butt to help," I replied.

"The County has a lot of money and they can pay to keep their promises," Mike said. "When we get through suing the County, the taxpayers can make some political changes."

As of September, Toup LaPrix had refused to sign or negotiate either the contract that Attorney Whiner had presented in June or accept the proposal written by the chairman of the Planning and Zoning Commission. It was explained to the public at the board meeting that the papers were only a draft and that Toup would be given the opportunity to respond to Attorney Whiner and negotiate a final contract.

Toup reviewed the draft of the new contract and got angry. The contract was a farce. It was very wordy and very restraining. He was expected to sign a contract that prevented him from declaring bankruptcy. It looked to me like the County was trying to violate every civil right the man had. I read the contract and I knew that Attorney Whiner had no idea what he was facing. Toup had some extensive negotiating to do. No way would I have signed that piece of dictatorial trash.

When we went to the Board of Supervisors meeting on September 15th, the board chairperson at that time was Supervisor Negate. She asked us if we had anything new to add to our comments previously given to the board. She explained we had told them enough already. There were several people in the room, and it appeared she did not want the public to hear our complaints. The local newspaper had made the situation look bad enough already. None of the supervisors had been able to change anything, and Toup was not going to sign their new contract. They had been told by the Good 'ol Boys to stay out of our problems. The board was not to get involved.

I raised my hand and explained I had more evidence of damage I would like to discuss with the board so they would understand why we needed Toup out of the picture. It seemed the only way the County could warrant having the subdivision completed by professionals. I told the board that I never dreamed Toup would get away with doing anything else to hurt my property or my person. He had already lost his credibility with me. He did manage, in the past month, to build the roads too high with

AB causing the drainage patterns to change. I told them about the flood damage he had caused and that I still had no water supply to clean up the mess. I stated that I felt it was time to call in professionals to complete the subdivision.

Prior to voting, Supervisor Negate asked that everyone in favor of the County calling in the assurances, please stand. Everyone did.

The board voted and made a resolution for the second time, to call the assurances, and auction the land put up as assurance for the completion of the off site improvements.

Toup stood up and read the Board their Miranda Rights. "You have the right to remain silent…"

Unfortunately, the deed the County took as assurance for completion of the subdivision was not the deed to the land within the boundaries of the subdivision track where we lived. The County spent many hours in litigation before they earned the right to foreclose on the assurance land and clear the clouded title in March of 1999. That trial caused the County much more trouble.

They still had to gain the rights to enter and improve the land within the subdivision boundaries around my home. There were no court records showing they sought that privilege.

After the County decided to pull Toup's assurances, he placed several huge boulders across the main road in the subdivision. He placed them just past Martin Coole's property. This activity prevented anyone from entering through the back of the subdivision and driving through. The people who owned homes in the subdivision could still get in and out by the back road and reach their homes, but only 12 out of 73 lots had access. The county attorney showed indifference to the problem. Deputy Attorney Nogut said, "As long as you can get to and from your home, he has broken no laws."

Toup was still ruling. He was riding on the county attorney's immunized power to do nothing.

In October, Toup LaPrix went on a talk show on K-AAA, the radio station in Kingman Arizona. The host was one of those men who have their own ideas of what is best for everyone, and if a person had other thoughts, they just weren't very bright. He allowed Toup to spout off about the bureaucracy and the time restraints they had imposed on him. He was not about to negotiate.

He said it had taken him ten years to get his permits together so he could begin construction. He claimed that just at the time he was ready to complete his work, the County had stepped in and refused him another extension of time to complete the subdivision. He accused the County of trying to steal his land. Toup told how the County would take his land and sell it. He believed they would keep the money, and the subdivision would never be completed. He said the County would take the money, put it in the general fund, and forget the landowners just as they had with the "Valley Vista" subdivision.

Cowboy Joe was on the show supporting Toup. He explained these activities were commonplace in the county. He has witnessed how property purchasers in other areas of the county had gotten what he called "the shaft" and that most assurance money ended up in the budget of the county attorney.

When Toup began blasting the county attorney, Attorney Whiner, called in to defend himself, his boss (Chief County Attorney, Willy Billy, Jr.), and the contract he had written. Attorney Whiner explained how the County had gone overboard to try to help Toup, but he would not cooperate and finish the subdivision. He called Toup a liar and the war was on. Fortunately for the host, the show time had run out. He invited the attorney to be on his show and tell his side of the story the next morning.

On the show the next day, we were to be more educated about what had happened and where the County had failed the homeowners in the subdivision. Deputy County Attorney Whiner explained the County had shown favoritism to Toup in allowing the subdivision land to be sold prior to completion of the infrastructure. Supposedly, because Toup's families were long time, respected residents of the county, the County extended special considerations to Toup when they accepted land assurances as a bond for the completion of the subdivision. (He did not mention that land assurances were an intricate part of the *Subdivision and Road Maintenance Regulations*). I did not think they wrote those regulations just for Toup LaPrix.

Attorney Whiner expressed his concerns for the people who had paid high prices for their land in the subdivision and still had no improvements. He insisted that when the assurances were called, the County would complete the subdivision with the funds received from the sale of Toup's land. He said that if Toup would just try to sit down and explain to the County that he was short of funds, the County would work with Toup to get the subdivision completed in a timely manner.

Many of the things Attorney Whiner said sounded sensible, but considering the exalted position Toup LaPrix held in the community, nothing this attorney said would really come true. He was dreaming, and any listener involved in the subdivision dilemma knew the man was dreaming.

Each day I prayed for the strength to go on and for the patience to deal properly with Toup, Mohave County, and the bureaucrats.

Even though I found many untruths in what Toup was broadcasting around town and on the radio, I was beginning to believe many of his statements were correct regarding the county's political corruption. It was scary. What I had originally perceived as a small, safe, law-abiding community was, in reality, run by money-grabbing, arrogant, selfish dictators. It appeared I was about to lose the $200,000 investment I had made in my house. I was already out $38,000 in medical bills, $60,000 in income, and I knew there would be more medical bills to come.

I was gradually losing my independence. I could not drive myself anywhere because I never knew when that ball of fire would creep up my neck and I would pass out. I couldn't fly my plane, and my $500,000 investment in my business was in jeopardy. It was frightening to be at home alone and unable to take care of my investments. I feared the stress I was under would end my life, just as it had ended the lives of Jerry and Phil.

Everyone reacts differently to stress. Jerry ate, Phil drank, and I was not eating.

One big misinterpretation of the federal laws by the County was found within the "Freedom of Information Act." The legislature of the State of Arizona picked up on that act, and when they voted in the state law, it was even stricter than the federal act. In general, the law states that public record in Arizona is to be made available for review immediately on request. Tagged to that law are all the fees that are to be charged for reproduction of documents.

We found that if the county clique did not want the truth about an issue known, the written documents got lost, misplaced, or destroyed. An alternative would be for them to say they would get a copy made and call when it was ready. They might say they would contact the county attorney and see if a copy or review of the information could be released. They would promise that when the attorney approved the review of the public documents, they would call. If we asked to review an entire file, they would hand us boxes of material that had obviously been inspected and altered to protect their interests.

After listening to the radio and hearing both sides of the story about the fate of our subdivision, I decided to look into Toup's claim that our subdivision improvement money would be used for the County just as it had been in the past at Valley Vista. The county financial department could not produce those documents for me. Low and behold, the financial director knew nothing about the funds that were to be used for the completion of the utilities in the Valley Vista subdivision.

I have a client who owns a lot in the Valley Vista subdivision. She showed me papers that stated that in 1994 the Federal Trades Commission entered into a settlement with the sub-dividers at Valley Vista. The money the land buyers received in the settlement would be turned over to Willy Billy, Jr., the county attorney, for disbursement to the offended landowners for use in completing the utilities in the Valley Vista subdivision.

Nearly six years later, according to the homeowners in that subdivision, that money had not been disbursed. It did not appear that it would ever be used for the benefit of the victims, as the federal government planned.

Main gates locked from 1997 to 2001

Actual installation of water system after project certified as complete by Arizona Licensed Engineer.

Electric placed under water distribution line

Water, boards and boulders

Sanitary Conditions

Rusted pressure tank

Water line ready for meter installation

Meter Box 5' underground

Pictures taken after project was certified as complete by Arizona Licensed Engineer.

Torn down street signs

Construction Garbage

Felled trees left on site

Trespass and destruction

Trespass and destruction

Lot stripped of trees

VICTIM CONDEMNED
Final installation of "Perfectly good roads."

Flood damage.

CHAPTER 15

On October 12th, the victims of Jack Tattoo learned that the restitution hearing was held a month earlier on September 19th. Evidently we weren't invited.

We received a copy of the court's order, which included both the judgment and the restitution.

In the court's judgment, the defendant was found guilty of aggravated assault (a Class 3 felony), possession of marijuana (a Class 6 felony), in violation of three stated laws of the State of Arizona, all of which are *non-dangerous* and *non-repetitive* offenses.

After obtaining the information from the Arizona Revised Statutes, we were able to decipher what crimes were involved in the plea agreement and what crimes Jack Tattoo committed that had been pled away. The laws covering a criminal who carries a previous conviction were set aside, as were the laws covering the production of marijuana. Three counts of theft, one count of possession of drug paraphernalia, and driving under the influence of intoxicating liquor, were all dismissed. No mention was made of the guns, and no mention was made of the fact that this was Jack's fourth felony offense involving firearms violations. The report made reference to *non-repetitive, non-dangerous* offences! What does that mean? The criminal had done the same thing before, and I believed, if given the chance, he would do it again.

It was actually pathetic to read that the five- and three-year probation periods would begin one day after Jack Tattoo's release from the California prison and that the California prison system "forgave" a sentence of one year of parole because Arizona had ordered the probation to run five years and three years respectively. The restitution ordered paid to the victims did not begin to cover the damage they incurred, but the fees ordered paid to the Probation Department, the County, and the court were quite substantial.

As I continued reading the court's order, I felt sure Jack would fail. He could not follow the rules imposed by this probation. He would not even try. He had demonstrated a lack of discipline all his life. He had three children but was not married. He had quit school after the eighth grade. He was only 27 years old.

The State of Arizona does not reveal prior felony convictions to victims. I had received Jack Tattoo's rap sheet by mistake. The paper said that he had already been in prison twice, in jail six times, had four other felony convictions under his belt and one misdemeanor conviction. Each of the previous felonies involved the misuse of firearms.

I wondered why a criminal would be so well protected by the system. Who might have reason to hide such reports other than criminals?

Some of the probation requirements would be hard for even me to follow, especially the one about supporting all his dependents—three children, a girlfriend, a sick mother, and an elderly father who claimed he needed help with his wife—and paying all his financial debts. He had no education to speak of, and, in his spare time, he was to complete 500 hours of community work service (a little more than one hour a week through the length of his probation), obtain a GED within 18 months, and complete an intensive drug treatment program. If that didn't keep him busy enough, the court had ordered satisfactory attendance and participation in Narcotics Anonymous and/or Alcoholics Anonymous.

Laws are written with two key words: shall or may. When "shall" is written, the law must be followed. When "may" is written, any victim might as well give up on any argument they have to present. The lawyers play around with laws containing the word "may" like a tennis ball on an open court. I made a promise to myself that I would go to school again and learn more about how laws are read and interpreted by the legal practitioners of today.

By January 3, 2001 Phil had received $560. I deposited all the checks in the savings account he had set up for his son. I received no more funds to deposit. The man was dead. Who was going to complain?

CHAPTER 16

The years 1997 and 1998 turned out to be hectic for Toup as well. During this period he had fought the County to save his land and he was losing. On top of that problem he had begun to irritate the city police and municipal courts.

Toup filed a lawsuit against Municipal Judge McCoy and Officer Poor. The officer had arrested him for a traffic violation. Toup contended in his filings that the judge had no right to suspend his license for not paying the fines she had imposed on him or to fine him at all. He stated Officer Poor was fraudulent in filing his police report. He accused the officer of not being trained in federal law. The filings he submitted to the court contained the same ramblings he used in all his other court cases. He asked for a jury trial. He was suing them for $1 million in gold. I have the arrest report. The rest of the information was given to me by County Attorney Billy Willy, Jr. He wrote they had no right to arrest him or to fine him for driving without a license, insurance, or tags because he had immunity as a sovereign entity. He also claimed the Corporate State of Arizona had no authority over him because the state was in bankruptcy.

After the fines were ordered, Toup offered to pay the fines with a promissory note. The clerk refused the note, and Toup got angry. He asked the clerk his name and the clerk responded, "Carl." Being unable to get the clerk to give his last name, Toup immediately went to Maricopa County and filed a lawsuit against Carl Doe.

In the end, as in everything Toup was involved in, his victims won their case but lost their money to the courts and lawyers.

If the police arrested and prosecuted Toup, they would end up with boxes and boxes of costly legal paperwork. Those lawsuits do not enhance an officer's personnel file.

It was not unusual for me to get a call from someone who had seen him driving drunk and speeding from bar to bar. Calls were made to the police reporting his activities, but nothing ever came of them. Mothers Against Drunk Drivers (MADD) did not have an organization in the area, so there was not much help if the police would not respond.

It must be extremely depressing for officers to go to all the trouble associated with arresting someone, knowing the county attorney will throw out the arrest. It certainly was depressing for me to watch the courts put felons back out on the street on probation. An officer could soon learn that arresting people was a wasted effort.

There are plenty of openings for officers in Mohave County. I noticed over several years that there were always ads seeking new officers in the local papers. The only real job requirement was a moral attitude that condones ignoring victims' rights—victims condemned by the policies enforced by the Good 'ol Boys of the county.

In his self-serving mind, Toup concluded his rights as an American were denied whenever he could not get what he wanted. Toup wanted to shove the laws back to the times when there were no taxes, no maintained roads, no street lights, and one room schools. In his fantasy world, Toup had forgotten his Porsche would be gone and he would be riding a horse with the cold desert wind blowing up his pant legs. I imagine had they found a way to make money putting a license plate on his horse, Toup would have been back in the pokey again.

On October 29, 1997, Toup LaPrix stuck a letter in the front door of Kathy and Mike Mazur's home. The letter stated he would shut off their water in 24 hours if they did not disconnect their water line from my house. The line was in the Mazur's back yard and there was no way Toup could have seen the line unless he was trespassing on our properties.

Because of his previous behavioral pattern, I was sure there was not much we could do to prevent the water disconnect. All he was doing was warning them that their water was definitely going to be shut off.

I used my saved e-mail addresses and sent a plea for help to every state and federal official representing Arizona at that time. My neighbors were going to suffer if we couldn't get protection for them and their property.

State Senator John Wettaw wrote to me. He said he had read my previous communication and that my current letter sounded even more distressing. The letter explained that I was not in his district, that he was not allowed to cross boundary lines, but he would like me to keep him informed on the problems and how they were handled by the county officials.

I started to believe that maybe, in addition to being a victim in desperate need of assistance, I might be a mentally deranged person capable of doing harm to at least one bastard in my community. I was frantic. My neighbors knew the truth and they were just trying to help me. It hurt even more knowing they were the only ones trying to help me.

Kathy asked me to watch her house, and if Toup shut off her water, I was to turn off the hot water system and call her friend John to come and secure her appliances.

Toup went to Kathy and Mike's house and cut off their water. When he arrived, I told him the water was not connected to my property. I knew he could see that.

"I gotta turn it off anyway," he said.

Kathy called the sheriff's office and the dispatcher said she would send an officer out.

"While you are doing that, would you put that damn sergeant on the phone? I am hot!"

"Yes ma'am," she replied.

When the sergeant came to the phone, Kathy explained, "Look, we have all had just about enough. Mrs. Lewis was sitting on my porch when Toup LaPrix cut off my water. The judge issued a protection order for her against Toup, and he totally ignored it. He scared her to death. Can't you do anything about that?"

The sheriff's sergeant explained to Kathy that the county attorney had informed his department that a Protection Order was not critical. If a person should break such an order, the charge was only a misdemeanor and if the sheriff's office was busy, they were not obliged to respond to such an order! He said he would send an officer to look over the situation.

The next day, Kathy Mazur and I discussed the fact that Toup had been harassing her, knowing her husband was not in town. Mike would get home from a trip, find out what had happened each time he was gone. He began to worry. Friday nights and Saturdays were perfect times to harass everyone. The public officials were out fishing, and we, Toup's victims, couldn't get the necessary help until Monday. According to the county attorney, everything that was happening at Lake Juniper was just a neighborhood spat and was to be considered a civil issue.

We waited hours, and no officer appeared. I got mad and went home. I checked my answering machine for messages and there was a message from a dispatcher. She stated that the officers could not come into the subdivision because the gates were locked and they had no way to get in.

My anger was beyond description. Captain Bulletin had promised us that we would never get that response from the sheriff's officers again. He promised that every officer would be trained to know the back road entrance.

I wrote a letter to the sheriff and filed a formal complaint against the captain. I asked the sheriff to understand that the situation was very unstable in our area and that we were all scared to death. Ultimately, the County would have to bear the responsibility.

On November 1st, I bought a bigger water tank, hoping it might make our lives easier. We ran Clorox through the new tank to make sure it was clean. I used the tank for two weeks or more, then on November 17th, someone put some kind of diesel smelling junk in the tank, and it messed up my entire plumbing system. When I found the gunk in my water tank, I called the sheriff. Deputy Ingress responded, and he took a sample of the water and gunk to the sheriff to see what the additive was. A week later, I received a call from Deputy Ingress. He informed me, "The crime labs in Arizona are not equipped to test water. I won't be able to investigate and find where that stuff came from. We don't know what it is."

We cleaned out the tank, sterilized it several times, and tried again. A month later, the plastic tank received a three-foot cut about midway across the tank. I had no proof regarding who was trying to destroy my water supply. We all had one prime suspect; however, I wasn't able to get videos of the events. The lieutenant told us that the sheriff could not begin an investigation without videos or witnesses, but the sheriff preferred videos.

I decided I needed a small gun, lessons, and a license to carry a concealed weapon.

Is it any wonder that the Timothy McVeigh's of this world would choose to reside in Mohave County? Almost every legal infraction committed in the county will be considered either a civil issue or a misdemeanor that is not worth the time and money it takes to investigate and prosecute. Mohave County proves to be a safe haven for criminals to set up shop.

McVeigh lived here in 1993 and 1994. He lived in a trailer park on the south side. He purchased the ammonium sulfate that produced his bomb from a local hardware store. When the investigation led the FBI to Kingman and to the store, the owners received a lot of bad publicity. Since I had one of the largest landscaping firms and I purchased the fertilizer regularly, the owner called and told me he had about 100 bags of the stuff and if I would take it, they would deliver it to my plant for $1 a bag. To this day, I still have some of it stored in my shed. When we prepared a yard for new sod, we would spread a very small amount of the product on the new soil. It helps the sod take root faster. It is so powerful that if you use too much, it will burn the roots.

Our lawyers asked me to prepare an affidavit, explaining the events that took place at the Mazur house. I did that, faxed it to them, and they sent my affidavit to the State Corporation Commission on November 1st.

I still hoped there was a reporter out there somewhere who would help. I went to the Internet and found a weekly news writer who was writing stories about northern Arizona. I explained to her, through e-mail, some of the problems we were facing in the Lake Juniper Subdivision. On November 3rd, I went to Williams, Arizona and picked up a man who wrote articles for the website. We traveled back to my home, and he arranged for interviews on November 6th with Deputy County Attorney Whiner and Toup LaPrix.

When I went to meet the journalist after his appointment with Toup, there was tape across the edges of the hood of my son's car. The writer had borrowed the car to go to his interview with Toup. After only three days in the area, he had learned so much that he was scared for his own life. He explained that if the tapes were broken, he knew not to start the car. Investigative reporters had lost their lives when they got too close to uncovering mob-connected political situations. He told me a chilling story about one of the reporters who lost his life in the Phoenix area. He seemed so scared, I was beginning to get worried for him.

After the interviews with Toup and Attorney Whiner, the journalist wrote two great stories. They were damaging to the County. He told me he had more to write, and I waited for months for the next issue. His writing stopped, and I never heard from him again. He just flat disappeared!

Before his disappearance, he explained to me that Toup LaPrix had stated on his tape that he would not have received approval for the Lake Juniper Subdivision had he not bribed the planning and zoning director with drugs. Toup explained that the director had lost his job and entered a drug rehabilitation clinic.

The writer told me he was going to research the truth and print the entire interview he had with Toup. That never happened. I was told by Billy Willy, Jr. that the man did not have a problem; he just took a job in another state. I wondered why Toup would tell such a lie about the planning and zoning director.

Kathy, Mike, and I sent money to the writer in hopes that it would encourage him to finish his story. The first $200 check was received and cashed. The rest of them were returned undeliverable.

"Gosh Kathy, I hope we did not get that man hurt," I said.

"Nah, he just got shut down like everybody else," she replied.

"I do not believe that. He wanted to help. He said there was much more to write and that we should keep watching his website for new stories. He has written articles about his views on the corruption in his own town, why would he stop writing now? Where did he go?"

"I do not know, but I still say he got shut down. Maybe they paid him more than we could. He said he needed money when he was here. He did not even have his own car," she said.

"Kathy, maybe he was right when he said the situation was dangerous for any outsider who gets involved. He watched his back every moment he was here. He told me that no one from outside the area would help us because it was too dangerous. I'm sure my frantic pleas for help from all the news people and politicians didn't help his efforts," I said.

Our struggles to maintain health, safety, and welfare against all odds were not looking favorable. Kathy and Mike had no water for their toilets. Kathy was faithfully bringing in buckets of water to flush her toilets. She was not happy. She had to shower at a friend's home before work each morning. It was a terrible situation. I had been without adequate water for almost six months. Kathy had dedicated her guest bathroom to me, and now, she too, had to use someone else's facilities.

I felt so guilty. I was not in a position to return the favor the Mazur's had given me and supply them with water. I tried to send what water I could over to their house, but the little tank and pump I had couldn't get the water all the way over there. Supplying them with an outhouse was all I could do. Kathy Mazur had just had surgery, and her doctor had not removed the stitches, but she had to haul water in five-gallon buckets from our neighbor Robert Gillam's house. At night, when Toup was out drinking, Robert would take a hose to Kathy's and fill up everything he could.

On November 4th, I wrote a letter to Judge Imus, explaining that Toup was still stalking our property and still trespassing on my land, and that the sheriff's office wasn't inclined to do anything about it. Judge Imus wrote that even though he was not indifferent to my problems, he had no authority to make the sheriff follow his order. Only the county attorney had such authority. His letter stated that he had neither power nor control over his orders once they left his courtroom. I learned that in a rural county, the only thing a Protective Order is good for is to piss off the person who was served with the order. Attorney Law had failed to explain to me that the sheriff would not enforce it.

When I showed the judge's letter to a friend in the area FBI office November 1997, he shook his head and said, "My God." He had also tried everything he could to get us some help, and he was just as frustrated as we were. By then, I looked like someone headed for the undertaker, and I think my appearance frightened him.

Kathy had taken me to see him. She had begun taking me on most of my errands. She asked the agent, "Can't you do something?"

"If I could, I would. This is not a federal problem yet. If you ladies will just hold on a little while, our office is working on making some changes. If Ms. Lewis was my mother and I was not wearing this badge, I would have eliminated the problem already. I do promise you, we are working on the problems the County has. Where is her son? Can I talk to him?" he asked.

"He's here in town. You can talk to him if you want to, but I remind you, he is not a fighter and his life is worth more than mine or Toup's," I said. "I've thought about taking care of my own problem, but I couldn't live with myself if I succeeded. They have threatened me with jail several times and I would rather not give them the chance to lock me up."

A young woman living in the county had received an Order of Protection shortly before I applied for the injunction against harassment. Her boyfriend was not willing to accept the fact that she did not care for his company any longer. He had beat her, and she obtained the order to afford the police the legal means to protect her if the boyfriend came anywhere near her. She was living in a safe house, and she was working at a truck stop.

The boyfriend showed up at her workplace and killed her. Who was protecting her? What good was that order? She had alerted the officers that the man was stalking her. Had there been ten orders against the kook, such paperwork would not have saved her life. Police will not assign full time protection to an individual. Had the girl been armed, she might have saved herself. Hundreds of victims of abuse are murdered every year because they refuse to face the fact that they are in a situation that requires self-defense. Most people believe that if they can defend themselves and take action against their aggressor, they will most likely be prosecuted for it. In any case, they are condemned if they do and condemned if they don't.

On November 5th, the sheriff sent Captain Bulletin to my home to say, "I'm sorry. I posted a notice on our bulletin board explaining to our officers how to enter your subdivision. I guess no one bothered to read it."

Lies, lies, and more lies. I believed that every man in that department knew how to get into the subdivision. Most of the officers had been in the subdivision before. I had taken pictures of some of them. They had no problems getting in when "King Toup" called them.

It is unlikely Captain Bulletin would ever come to my house again. Being tired of the lies, I chewed him out just as if he was one of my children who had lied to me. There was no question by now that Mohave County politics were enough to give a brainless sloth a nervous breakdown.

That same day, after Captain Bulletin left, I called the Headquarters—a company that rents portable toilets. I asked the secretary if they had an old toilet that was clean on the inside but ugly on the outside. I suggested one with a lot of graffiti might be nice.

"We had one come in yesterday that looks pretty bad. What do you need it for?" she asked.

"We live in a subdivision and the man who owns the water company has shut off everyone's water. He is not going to be happy when he sees an outhouse in my front yard, but we need something. If you send an old one, I won't feel so bad if it gets damaged," I replied.

"How long will you need the unit?" she asked.

"Well, I don't know. I have been without water to my home for over five months. The Corporation Commission said they could not help me get water until I released the injunction against harassment I have on the owner of the water company. There is no dedicated easement on my property for a water company connection, so I guess that until the failure of requiring such an easement is corrected, Mr. LaPrix cannot trespass on my private lot. I know the order will expire in another month or so, and if it will help us all get water, I won't renew it."

"Won't that be dangerous for you?"

"Nah. The sheriff hasn't paid any attention to the order yet. It just pissed everybody off," I replied.

"Well okay," she laughed. "We will be out there today with the unit, and if it gets damaged, call us and we will bring you another one."

By the time I had carried the buckets of water to my plants to save them from the new drought, the toilet was delivered to my front driveway. It was rather old and nasty looking on the outside. It was light blue and had black marks where it had received scrapes and bumps over its years of service. The inside was spotless, so I approved the unit and the delivery-man left.

At the previous, September 18th Planning and Zoning meeting, in addition to the issue of putting wells on the subdivision, I had questioned Director Mallard, the planning and zoning director, about the flooding of my home. Two months later, on November 10th, she finally sent me a letter, explaining "...the height of Coral Bay has been built according to the approved plans." She even sent me pages and pages of the engineer's original calculations. What she failed to send me was the "as-built" heights of the roads (what the heights really were). As director of the Mohave County Planning and Zoning Department, she had to know the papers she sent were useless without the as-built plans. Even with these discrepancies evident, she still defended Toup's actions. If she had admitted that the County had failed to inspect the work for seven years and had no idea what the road heights were, the County might have to help me pay for the damages caused by his actions and the County's negligence. It had become evident that almost anyone associated with the corrupt system would, in time, also be corrupted.

Toup had managed to raise the road next to my home five feet higher than the approved plan. One more foot and he could easily flood Martin Coole's house as well. He sure wanted us out of his sandbox.

The Mazurs had a hearing date with the Arizona State Corporation Commission on November 11th. Our attorney said she would try to get them water before that time. Now that the water situation involved more than just me, our attorneys finally decided it was time to apply to the superior court for a permanent injunction prohibiting the discontinuation of our water.

Since the harassment order wasn't worth the paper it was written on, I did not get it extended for another six months, and my hearing was scheduled with the Corporation Commission for the first meeting in December.

The State Corporation Commission meetings (SCC) began on November 11, 1997. We were scheduled to have two hearings each. One was to be in front of an officer and a court reporter, and the second before the commissioners as a whole body a month later. The Mazur's went to the SCC first. The hearing officer's order stated that the Mazur's water was to be turned on in 24 hours and it was not to be disconnected again. If the water was not restored in a timely manner, the Mazurs could take any steps reasonable to connect their own water. The water was to stay connected until the commission hearing scheduled for the Mazurs on December 4th.

The Mazur's had to pay to have the State's papers served. In five days, the Commission was not able to get a letter delivered and acknowledged by Toup. Kathy hired a man to serve the papers, and they finally got served on November 20th. The 24-hour stipulation couldn't start until Toup was served.

Either Toup ignored the authority of the Commission or he couldn't read the papers. Whatever the case was, he failed to comply with the order. On Thanksgiving morning, after giving Toup 26 hours to turn the water back on, Mike Mazur went outside, cut the lock and opened his water connections. He tossed the lock in Toup's front yard so he couldn't say Mike Mazur stole it.

On December 1st, Toup approached the Mazur's water connection again. My son and Mike just happened to be in the front yard visiting when they saw that Toup was headed right to the water box! Toup didn't see the two men when he drove up. They went to the back of the house and there he was, squatting down over the water connection. Mike Mazur was 6 ft. 7 in. tall and wore size 14 shoes. He did not have an ounce of fat on him, but no one would dare dispute the fact that he was a big man. He walked over, stood above King Toup, and asked, "Just what do you think you are doing?"

Since it was a day Mike usually would have been on the road somewhere, Toup was not expecting any interference. He jumped up and backed out of Mike's reach: "I'm shutting off the water. I, I have to shut off your water," he stammered.

Mike Mazur explained to him, "You cannot shut off the water until the commission hearing, and you might, right about now, want to call the sheriff for protection."

Toup wasted no time grabbing a cell phone from his truck, and he made his call. While he was phoning, Kathy Mazur got out the orders from the SCC, and she too, called the sheriff. She explained, "I am in possession of a state order requiring Toup LaPrix to keep my water turned on. I know you have a copy of that state order because my lawyer sent the damn thing to you. You are to see that my water supply continues until our hearing on December 4th. Toup LaPrix is at our house trying to shut the water off. My husband is a big man, and I suggest you send the biggest officers you have because if you wimps don't help this time, Toup is going to get hurt. Now don't you tarry. You get here now 'cause my husband is hot."

Two large-bodied officers and one not quite so large arrived within minutes. None of the men came near to being as big as Mike. We didn't know if the officers came at Toup's request or at the request of Kathy Mazur, but considering the size of the officers, we think someone listened to Kathy. In the past, the sheriff's office had proven to be very responsive to Toup and much less responsive to his victims. Mike Mazur wondered if the two big officers were there to protect him, "King Toup," or the smaller deputy who did all the talking.

Toup explained to the officers that he had a right to shut off their water because the Mazurs had a lawsuit against him. He explained how they had been listening to the lunatic next door (that's me!) and that he was going to see that we were all evicted from our residences.

The officer explained to Toup that in the meantime, the water had to stay on, per the state's command. He showed him the paperwork, and after looking over the papers for quite some time, Toup handed them back to the officer. He told the officer that nowhere in those papers did it say he could not disconnect the Mazur's water.

Mike had to read the instructions to Toup aloud. Even after reading the papers, Toup still contended that nowhere in the papers did it say the water was to remain connected. He refused to believe Mike Mazur had been given the right to reconnect his water. His view was, the water company was his property, and the State had no authority to make such an order.

The officer took Toup aside and spoke with him privately and then sent him away.

Toup got in his old truck and drove up the road. He turned the truck around and headed back toward his own house. The officer blocked his way and asked him to step out of his truck. He advised Toup that he was, once again, under arrest this time for driving his truck without a driver's license or tags. Toup claimed that the officer could not arrest him on his own private road. The officer explained to Toup that as long as the gates to the subdivision were locked, the road Toup was on was the only entrance to the subdivision, and the public had to use it, and therefore, it became a public road.

I guessed that would be one of those civil issues Toup would have to straighten out in court. They took him to jail again. The county attorney ruled against the officer, and Toup was out of jail in no time flat. When he got out, he immediately telephoned the ACC and chewed them out for allowing the Mazurs to restore their water supply. The officer was not impressed by his call. She called me after talking with Toup. She asked if I was okay, and then she told me about Toup's call to her office. I assured her that I was nowhere around when the incident occurred but that Mike, Kathy, and my son were entertained by the event.

My turn for a hearing with the ACC was on December 11th. Toup failed to appear at the hearing. Scott Savler, the hearing officer, listened to my testimony. He said he would take my case before the commissioners next month in January 1998. That meant I had to go through the Christmas holidays without water. I asked my attorney if I had heard Scott Savler correctly. I couldn't believe that after all I had been through, they would allow me to go through Christmas without water! I wanted to know if anything could be done about the water situation before the holidays.

My attorney said that was impossible because the commissioners had not put my name or case on their agenda for the meeting in December. I would have to wait until the January meeting.

Scott Savler sat there and listened to us talk. He shook his head up and down in agreement with my attorney's words. I began to cry. He lowered his eyes toward the carpet, then jumped up from the table, and ran out of the room.

With all the stress I had been under, the thought of having to use an outdoor toilet for another cold month made me feel as though someone had just signed my death warrant. By this time, I was so desperate that I was prepared to go to Washington and sit on the capitol steps with a sign pleading for water and protection. I decided that if I had a sign stating I was from Arizona, perhaps I could ruin Senators Kyl and McCain's Christmas.

I told my attorney of my plan and explained my motive. I had been through almost six months of hauling, going without, or sharing water, and I couldn't believe I had more of the same to face. My grandchildren could not visit me in the summer because my house had no water, and my life was in danger from Toup's actions on a daily basis. Because of the lack of funds, there was no carpet on my concrete floors, and carpet tacks lined the walls. My home was not safe. Tears welled up in my eyes again.

Somehow, our attorney managed to get a written order allowing my water to be restored. Scott Savler signed the order. I had to wait about five more days until December 16th while the paperwork was prepared, and Toup could be served. The paperwork gave Toup 48 hours to reconnect my water, and if he failed to do that, I was allowed to connect it myself.

Toup ignored the order, just as he had ignored the Mazur's order, and I was faced with the problem of finding a way to repair the water company's equipment so a connection could be made. My employees and I searched for the water company's state-required shut off valves. There were none. The well had to be shut down before repairs could be accomplished. The plumbers tried, in vain, to reach Toup.

On December 20th, the neighbors were notified that the water shut down was necessary to accomplish the repairs. The well was shut down, and the men installed the state-required equipment to my lines and to the lines belonging to the water company. They went back to the well to start it up again, and Toup approached them. He was very angry and told them to leave the well alone; he would turn it back on.

The men argued and explained that they needed the water turned on so they could check for leaks before they left. Toup told them he would turn the well back on when he got "damn good and ready."

The next morning, December 21st, at 4:00 a.m., I received a call from Kathy Mazur. The water had not been turned back on, and the neighbors were all in a panic. I apologized for the inconvenience, and I explained that there had been plenty of time for Toup to turn on the pumps the previous day.

I asked one of the men who shut down the well to call Toup and ask if he could help him turn the well back on. Toup refused the man's assistance and explained that he would turn the well on later in the day. It was too early, and he was surely not going to the well at 6:00 a.m. He said, "I have no intentions of ever supplying Mrs. Lewis with water."

The man was very kind when he talked to Toup on the telephone. I knew he really wanted to kill Toup for what he had done to my neighbors and me. He told me that he believed Toup would sabotage all the work the men had done. If Toup even looked towards my house, I was to call. By 2:00 p.m. in the afternoon, everyone had their water restored, including myself. Thankfully, there were no leaks.

I decided I didn't trust the situation, so I decided to keep the outhouse, just in case. I was glad I did!

When I left the house that day to go to my doctor, someone had gone onto my property and dug up the underground water shut-off placed on the line as required by law. My men had not returned and I thought it was pretty gutsy for someone to mess with my property like that again. I set up my system so that if the pressures from Toup's water company exceeded 65 psi, my regulators would prevent the damage my home and appliances had experienced in the past.

Since I had questionable water coming into my home again, the doctors wanted it monitored regularly. I had learned how to test my tap water with pool testing kits, and the water quality was awful by the time it reached my kitchen sink. The little testing strips showed the pH levels to be too high. According to the instructions on the bottle, the ideal range for pH would be 7.2—7.6. A high pH count in water can be very destructive. Following the instructions of my physician, when the levels appeared out of range on my testing kits, I was not to bathe in the water. I was to wear rubber gloves when handling the water, and I was never to cook with or drink the tap water again.

Toup then began cutting off the entire system. For days on end, he claimed he was unable to restore the system. We complained, but we knew our health, safety, and welfare were just a joke to the county, and they did not intend to cross Toup. The new deputies had tried to help the day Mike met Toup at the water connection, but the sheriff had put them in their place.

My house was a wreck. The pipes under the concrete leading to my kitchen began to leak. The leaking problem was blamed on the high TDS (total dissolved solids) in the water. The floors had been jack hammered up and the pipes repaired. Everything was extremely depressing. The plumber said that eventually I would have to re-plumb the whole house. Christmas was right around the corner. In an effort to make the best of a bad situation, I went out and decorated the house with Christmas lights. I lit up the outhouse and placed a star on top of it.

By January 1998, I had been doing chelation therapy for 16 months. Even though the treatments were uncomfortable, they seemed to have done wonders. After several weeks of intravenous treatments, many more tests, and a lot of vomiting and visits to the outhouse, my body began shedding the toxic copper levels. I replaced the bad copper with good copper through vitamins and zinc supplements. It was explained to me that there are 36 forms of copper. The good comes from nature and vegetables, and the bad comes from copper pipes. The zinc supplements, when taken in tablet form, had a tendency to hit the bottom of my stomach like a ton of rocks. There were many times I would take them, then just go to bed.

If one wanted the process to work as it should, the chelation treatments had some side effects that could not be completely controlled. It is designed to rid the body of the heavy metal. The only outlets through which the copper can be eliminated are through the bowels or through vomiting. If the copper got into my kidneys or liver, it was so heavy that it would just sit there and destroy them. Our main objective was to protect my kidneys and liver the best we could.

My body must have been babysitting those organs on overtime. The chelation therapy caused an experience that was like a drunk going through the DTs. I had seen a movie that showed what drunks go through while ridding their body of alcohol. I can honestly say the experience I had looked just the same.

Later, when all the men who worked for my company got sick with the flu, I was the only one who remained well. During the chelation therapy, zinc was added to the EDTA along with other vitamins. It was explained to me that the zinc works like a magnet to copper and helps pull it from the system. When my body received the necessary zinc through the intravenous feedings, the stomachaches stopped. Zinc also protects the system as it moves around collecting the heavy metals, so my liver was getting extra good protection.

Chelation therapy has been used since 1945—shortly after the war—to rid a child's body of lead poisoning. Many paints produced in the United States had a lead base. Children would peal the paint off the walls and put the paint in their mouths. They would get very sick with lead poisoning. Testing a child for heavy metals is a requirement of the State of Arizona's low-income medical program; however, it is not a test required of adults. Because I owned my own home, I did not qualify for any program the State had to offer. Even though I could not go to work or even begin to make a living for myself, I still wasn't broke enough to qualify for state assistance.

The chelation therapy caused drastic changes in my body. I found myself allergic to many of the foods I used to eat on a regular basis. Hives had become a common occurrence in my life. Many times, I had to take medicine to gain control of the problem and stop the itching. It was assuring to learn that as soon as I got rid of the nickel in my system, things would get better in the hives department. After a year, things did improve. I lost a lot of hair, but I could not tell if it had fallen out because of the copper, the chelation treatments, or the stress. The muscles in my body became more sensitive during the treatments, but the condition was tolerable. My mind reacted slower at times. I did not know if the copper poisoning or the stress of all I had been through caused that problem either. Whatever it was, I knew I did not like it.

Two inspectors from the ADEQ (Arizona Department of Environmental Quality) came to the house in January 1998. They were worried about the results of the field tests they had previously taken on my water. They left my home with a list of tests they wanted to run on the wells and my home. The two men explained the tests might not be approved because they could be very costly, and the Lake Juniper Water Company well was not an ADEQ approved system. Instead of receiving the ADEQ's permission to do the testing, one inspector retired and the other was transferred. The subdivision was assigned a new representative. He was a very nice man, but, of course, he could find nothing wrong with the water tested at the well. His reports showed that there could be a problem in our homes. He stated in his report that the distribution system of the water company might be causing the problems; then again, it could be our water softeners causing the problems. He just could not tell for sure. He could not understand why the Mazur's white bathroom tile was stained green. He couldn't understand why there was turquoise blue water and sand in all the toilets. The Mazur's house did not have a water softener. He suggested that the people being serviced by that water company should do their own investigations to find the truth regarding the water quality and why it was destroying the homes. The ADEQ refused his recommendation that pH tests be performed. No commitment for that testing would be forthcoming. Funding for such a project was not to be made available.

The County Health Department's representative had one test run on my water in 1997. The only place she found copper was in my ice cubes. They measured 319 mg. The cubes I gave her were a beautiful blue. Because of their distinct shape, it was rather obvious they came from my icemaker, but because I had handed her the cubes in a baggie, she refused to admit in her report to Dr. Cooper where they had come from. This same blue water had shown up in my home and the homes of my neighbors many times. When Kathy Mazur offered the blue tainted water she took from her tap to the County Health Department in February 1998, they refused it. They told her the container she had put the water in was not the right kind of collection container.

There are many different types of filters and reverse osmosis systems that can be used at the well site or at the meter site to keep the corrosive materials (TDS) from entering a house. There seemed to be no way Toup or his brother would spend the money necessary to supply our homes with potable water much less a water meter. The County Health Department refused to intervene, and they continued to deny private well applications. They remained mute.

Martin Coole's reaction to the State and County's indifference to our health problems was to keep his mouth shut and get out of the development as soon as possible. Kathy opened her mouth. When the County Health Department refused her water sample she said, "Those bastards aren't going to do anything about the water supply. They don't want to know the truth because they would be forced to do something about it. That costs money. Our lives aren't worth anything to them, and if we die, oh well. I told that bitch she could come and take blue water from the back of my toilet anytime she was in our area. How much do you want to bet she never comes? She'll never come out here because if she found bad water she would lose her job."

"Kathy," I said, "Do you really think the State will allow our homes to be destroyed by this water?"

"How sick did you get? Did you see anyone lined up on your doorstep with solutions to the problem? Did you sign any medical releases so the bastards could read your medical reports first hand? No. They don't give a shit. It is all a civil issue, remember?"

Back in September 1997, Kathy and Mike Mazur, Martin and I (as homeowners) had filed that class-action lawsuit against Toup LaPrix, the water company and the homeowner's association. A portion of the case—the part that involved the water company and the homeowner's association—came to court in January 1998.

Our attorneys had managed to get all our water restored through the ACC, but they amended our lawsuit against the water company to include in the hearing scheduled, a request for a court injunction to prevent Toup from continuing to turn the water off. Because the original lawsuit included complaints of negligence and fraud against the Lake Juniper Water Company and the Lake Juniper Homeowners Association, Inc. as defendants, that portion of the case was to be heard and decided by Judge Wise, a judge pro tempore.

Roger Arms was chosen by the law firm to represent Mike and Kathy Mazur, Martin Coole, and me in that hearing. Before the trial began, Toup refused to approach the bench. He sat in the jury box and spoke to the judge. He said he was not prepared to address the court at that time. He would not give the judge his name. (I learned that Toup's refusal to go through the courtroom gates and sit at the defendant's table is the legal equivalent of failing to appear for the hearing.)

Mike Mazur was called to the stand. He testified as to what he was promised when he purchased his home. Roger, our attorney, showed Mike a copy of the advertising we had all received regarding the subdivision. Mike confirmed it was the same literature given to him prior to his purchasing his lot. He explained the water disconnection and Toup's unusual behavior.

Judge Wise asked the "unnamed man" in the jury box if he had any questions for Mr. Mazur. He said he did not. Martin Coole was called to the stand, and he went through the same routine. The unnamed man didn't have any questions for him either.

Just as Roger called me to the stand, Toup reached into his briefcase. I couldn't see what he was doing, and I got so scared I started shaking. There wasn't even a bailiff in that courtroom. The closest thing to protection was a deputy somewhere in the courthouse. Someone must have believed that this was just a civil matter, and there was no need for a deputy to be in the courtroom. I was not so sure. Not surprisingly, the courthouse security issue was deeply connected to county politics. The presiding judge wanted the courthouse security equipment taken out of the basement, installed, and staffed. As of my day in court, that hadn't happened. My safety, then, had become dependent on the outcome of personal territory battles amongst the county politicos.

My heart was racing a mile a minute and my hands were shaking. I knew Toup was capable of hurting me; I felt like a sitting duck. I thought, "If he hates me so much that he would keep my water shut off for over six months, he must want to see me dead. He knew there was copper in those pipes he cut, and he knew how it got there." Then my mind began to repeat, "While I walk through the valley of the shadow of death, I shall fear no evil."

I answered Roger Arms' questions as best I could under the stressed circumstances. I was not a good witness. I sensed the judge knew I was scared. He leaned over his desk and asked, "Mrs. Lewis, could you explain to me what chelation therapy is? I mean, what are you going through right now?"

"Chelation therapy is intravenous feedings of EDTA. In my case, many vitamins and other things are mixed in that bag so I won't get too sick. I go twice a week and each session takes four hours," I replied.

"What is EDTA?" he asked.

"I really don't know how to pronounce its real name, but it works like a magnet and collects all the heavy metals in my blood and tissues. It has something to do with formaldehyde, but I am not sure what that is," I explained, wanting to keep it short.

Judge Wise then asked Toup if he had any questions for me. Roger Arms allowed him to ask me one question, but when he started to argue with my answers, an objection was made, and he was not allowed to ask anything else.

After the hearing ended, Roger Arms explained that he did not object when the court asked Toup to speak because we needed to show the court we could still be polite. The last thing on my mind was trying to be polite to Toup. I didn't want to be connected to a water system being run by Toup. The system he built was ruining my appliances, my pipes, and my house. I still questioned how the large abundance of copper (powdered) got into my lines. All I wanted was my own well and independence from the whims of Toup.

Roger asked the judge to issue a permanent injunction prohibiting the disconnection of our water supply. That is the order Deputy Attorney Nogut had required, and we were about to have the ability to put that prosecutor's feet to the fire. Roger felt a superior court order might carry more weight with the "good old boy" clique structure than a hard-to-enforce state order. He also asked that our case against the Lake Juniper Water Company and our case against the Lake Juniper Property Owners Association be decided by default.

Judge Wise agreed to issue the permanent injunction immediately, and he took the rest of the case under advisement. He instructed our attorney to submit the necessary papers for him to sign.

The permanent injunction was issued right there on the spot, and it was just a matter of days until Roger had a copy of that injunction delivered to each of us with a note that read, "Just in case you need it." We all felt we would be able to sleep knowing Toup would not be out shutting off our water supply.

I could see my water connections from my office, and from that day on, I kept one eye on the connection and a gun loaded on my desk.

While we waited for the judge to review the rest of our complaints, we learned Toup had other problems. The bank holding his mortgage filed a suit to foreclose on his house because he had not made his scheduled payments. None of us knew what was going on, but he was often away from the subdivision, so it got much quieter. Martin Coole had rented out his house and moved into town.

The condition of the Lake Juniper Subdivision had become an embarrassment for the county clique. The police had begun to arrest Toup for driving his vehicles on a suspended driver's license in addition to no vehicle tags or insurance. He had been breaking the same laws for several years without any noticeable arrests, but now his brother was continually bailing him out of jail.

In January 1998, the mortgage company began foreclosure on his residential note, and the public sale of his house was to be held on the courthouse steps. When Toup appeared at the sale in his Porsche, he was arrested again for driving without a license. He was paraded through the crowd in handcuffs, then put in jail. He had just gotten out of jail about three days earlier, and every time the police picked him up, they put his car in storage. He had to get himself and his car out of jail.

On two previous occasions, I had watched as a car-hauling truck delivered the Porsche back to Toup's driveway. The authorities would not let him drive it home because it had no license plates. On one occasion, the driver of the big car hauler became lost and tried to deliver the Porsche to my house. I refused to sign for it. He took it across the street to Toup.

My friend, Terry Augustine (the same man who had taken pictures of all of Toup's antics within the subdivision), was present on the steps of the courthouse when they auctioned Toup's house. All my friends wanted to see Toup dead, but in the meantime, they were prepared to watch him suffer. Terry said he had learned from the officials present that Toup was not taking his lithium. Blood tests taken by the jailers had showed no lithium. The officers told Terry that Toup could be very dangerous when he failed to take his medications, and the officers seemed concerned.

A medical book I have says lithium is a drug prescribed for the control of mania in manic-depressive patients. The officials of the county had known all along that Toup had mental problems, and they still allowed him special favors that were causing his victims a lot of grief. His parents must have been aware of his mental condition when they set him up with his sandbox. The bulk of his father's estate was left in the care of his brother when his father died.

During the auction, there were security people all around. It was obvious the County and the auctioneer were not going to take any chances on getting hurt. Mickey Bowles, one of my employees, went to the auction as well. He said there were even police officers hiding in the bushes.

The forced, public sale of Toup LaPrix's home was completed, and the bank owned his house. The judge had ordered Toup to move from the home immediately, but he ignored the court. In November 1998 the bank notified us that Toup would be removed from his home if he failed to comply.

We were not sure what would go on in the neighborhood because of the previous troubles, so we requested the time and date of the eviction—I wanted to be out of the area at the time of that event.

The bank understood our concern and gave us a date and time the eviction would take place. I went to New Mexico for a visit. When I got back, nothing had happened. Toup was still coming and going as he pleased. Kathy said he had not been spending many nights in the house. She explained that all his belongings were still in the house and he was still picking up his mail.

Toup swamped the court with filings. The courts read them and moved forward on the foreclosure. About a month and a half later, the bank notified us again that they would be taking possession of the house in January 1999.

I left again. I'd had enough of Toup's wrath, and I was just starting to get well. I didn't need to get into the middle of a war zone. By that time, the sheriff's deputies had been staking out Toup's house for several days. I swear I saw them hiding in the bushes on more than one occasion. Attorney Law, who was representing the bank, said they were acting like a bunch of Kamikazes! (You have to wonder what he was thinking here.)

Terry Augustine couldn't stand the suspense. He went to Kathy Mazur's house on the day planned, making a promise to me that he would detail the events. The minute I got home, he called with the details.

"There were at least 11 officers, including the county attorney himself, in bulletproof vests. They approached the house moving in like a bomb squad and secured the premises. What appeared to be a heavy, blonde, female deputy was standing guard on Toup's balcony. She looked like a Viking queen. The only thing missing was her battle-axe. I think the Sheriff's Department prepped Toup. Nobody had seen him in over 48 hours. My guess is that the only reason they had not taken the house sooner was because they couldn't find a way into the subdivision—the gates were locked."

Terry continued, "The moving company they hired to move Toup's personal belongings from the house found mercury and coffee cans full of a blue powder stored in his garage. They had to string plastic yellow crime scene tape all around the house and land. That moving company is not licensed to move hazardous material. Someone with a special license was called in for that chore. I don't know how long that yellow crime scene ribbon will stay wrapped around the area, but you stay away from there. That mercury is very dangerous."

At this point in my story, my editor asked, "Did anyone identify the copper as being the same as in your pipes? Did you take samples of the blue powder? Why wasn't a criminal investigation started? It sounds like you didn't make the connection between the copper poisoning and this blue powder. I think readers are going to want an explanation of why this bit of incriminating information didn't trigger anything."

My answer to her was, "No one tried to put the two together. Remember, the county said they could not test the pipe; their labs are not equipped. The state said they do not have facilities to test the pipes. I had to send the pipe to New Mexico for testing, and no way would the sheriff order a comparison of the two copper substances because the coffee cans belonged to a Good ol' Boy. After covering for this man for years, they didn't want to know. Case closed..."

CHAPTER 17

In February 1998 I had some extra time on my hands, so I decided to find out what was going on between the court and the County regarding the security in the courthouse.

As the community grew, the needs of the court grew as well. It appeared the supervisors and the county attorney were controlling the presiding judge and his court's operational activities, which the judge did not appreciate. The supervisors refused to comply with the presiding judge's order for increased funding and a legal battle ensued.

The presiding judge of Mohave County had gotten his budget slashed by the Board of Supervisors using the excuse that the courts had not used all the funds allotted in the past three years. The presiding judge had moved some six year-old metal detectors out of the basement and put them inside the front entrance of the courthouse. He had the protective devices on hand, but the courts needed proper funding to put that equipment to use. The presiding judge of the Superior Court filed a court order against the County, ordering the County to fund him another $800,000 so he could operate his court properly. In addition to other inconsistencies I had witnessed, the taxpayers had to pay for a federal court fight between the judicial and executive branches of Mohave County.

The Mohave County supervisors are elected officials and their terms are for four years, and there is no limit as to how many times they can run for re-election. As of this writing, one member of the board—Supervisor Snide—has been elected three times. This supervisor is a bald ex-cop from Los Angeles. He often appears at the board meetings in a polo shirt and blue jeans. He looks like he has a hot date waiting at the racetrack. Supervisor Snide makes it obvious that the public should get their concerns stated quickly, so he can then cast his vote and get the hell out. I believe his demeanor is vindictive and uncaring.

Terry Augustine had heard rumors about Mr. Snide and suggested I start my search at the courthouse. I went to the office of the clerk of the district court and asked for all files that included each of the supervisors. Two court cases were present in the files concerning Supervisor Snide that had a lot more in them than normal business problems. As I read the file, I found that Snide had a son, whose mother died and left a large sum of money for the boy's upbringing, education, and future. Snide was given custody of his natural son, along with guardianship of the trust money. At the age of 18, the child was to receive the balance of the estate left to him. The social security system was paying Snide about $350 per month to help support his child. There was another child from a previous relationship of his wife. Snide took his child and the other went with his natural father.

According to the court records, Snide's son was very intelligent. They were not able to live together successfully, so the son moved to another state to live with another family while he was completing his final years of high school.

After graduating from high school and preparing for college, the child requested his father release his inheritance so he could continue his education. According to the court records, the child had to sue Snide for the balance of his money. The presiding judge of Mohave County had to help settle the son's complaint. He ordered Snide to present an accounting of his trust expenditures and to turn over the slim remains of the child's portion of the estate that amounted to $49,000.

The second file showed that in 1997, after Supervisor Snide was elected, he was evicted from his home because he hadn't paid his mortgage payments. The same presiding judge signed the orders. Perhaps having two judgments against him, both handed down by the same presiding judge, Snide began to show a bit of animosity toward the county's court system. I asked the clerk to make me copies of both files, and I went home and read them again. The judge in both cases was the same judge who had filed an order for his court's funding.

I was taught that America is a democracy with three distinct divisions of powers: the executive branch (in this case, the county Board of Supervisors), the legislative branch (state senators and district representatives), and the judicial branch (the courts). The executive branch controls all the operational funding for the judicial branch. Salaries for the judges are determined by the legislative branch. The fact that the court's primary control—money—was in the hands of this particular Board of Supervisors did not set well with me. The circle of corruption was becoming more understandable.

Libraries, schools, fire departments, etc. have itemized tax distributions listed on all the property tax bills. Each entity prepares its own budget. Citizens who are unpaid board members approve the budget. If a tax increase is requested for a certain district, the final approval for the increase comes from the county Board of Supervisors. State law controls all excessive spending, unless a loophole can be found by the whining district. Each district has its own checking account, the money from which cannot be used by the Board of Supervisors to cover other needs of the county, as this board was planning to do with the judge's budget. Why the court system is not classified as a separate entity on my property tax bill so it can receive the same financial freedom afforded the schools, libraries, community college, etc. is unclear.

Snide may have had an axe to grind, and it appeared the courts were to foot the bill. The local papers as well as surrounding county newspapers said that Mohave County was generating problems that had never before surfaced in any other county in the state.

The Board of Supervisors did not consider that the security for the courthouse needed to be funded, and the judicial department was trying to save enough to install and maintain the security system and provide for security staff. The taxpayers would foot the bill for the entire litigation cost because the judge and the supervisors could not agree on how much money should be budgeted for the courts.

My friend Terry Augustine laughed and commented on the article written in the newspaper about the lack of security at the courthouse. He said, "Get this. Because the presiding judge has failed to waste the taxpayer's money as the sheriff does, his courts will take a huge cut in their budget. The board will probably turn around and give the money to the sheriff.

"If the courts knew how to manipulate the board like the sheriff does, that security system would have been up and running the day it was received. Instead, they stuck it in storage in the basement. The sheriff's office always goes over budget. The courthouse needs the extra money to protect us poor citizens. That is what that security system is designed to do, isn't it?" he said.

In March 1998 we received a written, partial judgment, against the water company and the homeowners association from the judge. I learned then that it was not all over. Judges can choose to rule on parts of a lawsuit as appropriate. Things were beginning to look a little better, but I was ready for the entire lawsuit to be over! The court ordered the water company to pay each of us the value we had invested in our homes and I was awarded $200,000 for medical damages. The homeowners association was ordered to pay us $5,000 each for fraudulently taking our dues and giving them to the water company.

It was exciting to learn that the court understood our problems and that we had won the first phase of this trial, but what did we really win? The water company was owned by Toup and his straw entities and, to our knowledge, owned nothing but improvements that owed nine years of back taxes, had previous liens, and were not capable of servicing the areas they had promised the Arizona Corporation they would service. If we took over the system, it would cost us over $400,000 to bring the system up to state law requirements before it would be functional and productive.

"When do we get the money?" Mike asked.

"I doubt that we ever will, but this partial judgment is a start. The attorneys will now have to fight Toup. At least we now have the injunction," I replied.

"How long will they drag this out?" Kathy asked.

"It could take another year or so, I guess," I answered.

"We'll all be broke by then," Mike said.

On March 12th, less than two months after we received our injunction papers from the lawyers to prevent him from disconnecting our water again, trouble started once again. I received a call from Kathy Mazur at about 8:00 p.m. just two days after we received the judge's order.

"Ya got any water?" she asked.

"Gosh, I don't know. Let me go see," I replied. The kitchen faucet produced only a small stream of blue/green water, and then the water spit a few times and shut off. "Nope, no water. Do the other neighbors have water?" I asked.

"They are the ones who called me. They were trying to bathe the kids and they don't have any water. I'm coming over," she answered.

Martin Coole's renters called Martin and he immediately tried to call Toup. Kathy called the sheriff's office at 7:55 p.m.

"I don't know why we bother," Kathy said. "The sheriff will call Billy Willy, Jr. and he will tell them to misplace the dispatcher's notes. Then they will erase the tapes of the call, and if we persist, they will call back and say that they can't get into the subdivision because the damn gates are locked."

"Now that the judge has started paying attention, you don't think they would pull that on us again, do you? We managed to get the injunction Deputy Attorney Nogut asked for. He said he would arrest Toup if we got the injunction and the water got shut down again," I reminded her.

"Talk, talk, talk. That wimpy blow-hard doesn't have the guts to stand up against Toup. What's the matter with you girl? Are you getting daft? Did that copper rattle your brain? Toup is mad because we obtained a judgment against the water company. He doesn't want to supply us with water, and no one will enforce the injunction. I don't care what Nogut told us at the meeting, he will not allow Toup to be arrested," she said.

The dispatcher said she would have the sergeant on duty call us back. After waiting for the sergeant's call for two hours, I called the dispatcher and asked about the delay in response. The dispatcher explained there had been a bad accident on the highway and a man had been killed. The sergeant was very busy and no one else was allowed to handle Lake Juniper matters.

I asked the sergeant's name. After a long pause, she said, "His name is Webb."

It seemed strange there was only one officer in the whole Sheriff's Department who could handle a call from Lake Juniper. What was the big deal here? All we wanted was to have an officer contact Toup at the local bar and steakhouse where he hung out and tell him to turn the water back on. Sergeant Webb never called. What I had failed to realize at that time was that Sergeant Webb was the same officer who had lied to me about the judge's signature being absent from my protection order. At the insistence of the dispatcher, at 10:00 p.m., I called Toup's brother and explained that the subdivision was without water. The response I received was no surprise to me. He didn't care, but he would tell Toup.

How much more fighting for water would be necessary to convince the bureaucrats we needed our own wells. That night, sleep did not come easy.

At 4:30 a.m. the next morning, Kathy Mazur called me. She was getting ready for work, and she just wanted me to know that she still didn't have any water. Martin Coole was to come to the well and see what could be done to get the water back on.

At 7:00 a.m. Martin Coole brought a big fiberglass tank to set up as an alternative water system for his renters and their three small children.

He worked most of the day setting up the tank and pump system. He brought his water truck, filled the tank, and got the system working. Funny I didn't know that Martin Coole owned a water truck.

Martin called and explained to me that he had called Arthur's Repair Service but that Toup's brother had already called them and threatened to discontinue using their services on his own water company wells if they even touched our well. Martin had then called A-I Well service. They agreed to come to the well site that afternoon.

Martin's secretary called the sheriff's office and asked for a Civil Standby, as ordered by Judge Wise. Hopefully, there would be no problems with Toup while the well was being repaired. The sheriff's office never came to the site. Evidently, they called Toup and informed him of the intended repairs. Being aware of the permanent injunction that had been issued by Judge Wise, the sheriff's officers obviously did not want to be anywhere near Toup. That action would have required an officer to arrest Toup for being in contempt of the court order. At that time there was no way the Mohave County Good 'ol Boy clique would allow such an action.

Toup came sailing into the subdivision. He went directly to the well site, slammed on his breaks, skidding his tires, and jumped out of his vehicle. He threatened the serviceman with bodily harm if he touched the system. He told him he would keep him tied up in the courts with litigation until it bankrupted him. The man explained to me that the rumors he had heard about Toup and Toup's threat of litigation was enough to convince him that repairing the well was not worth the risk.

Martin Coole and the man left the site and called the sheriff. The officer was loose-lipped enough to tell Martin to write his own report, but that nothing would come of it. Martin Coole explained the court's permanent injunction. The officer replied that they knew about the permanent injunction, but that the county attorney said the judge failed to tell the sheriff's office what to do if Toup broke the injunction!

Martin Coole's secretary called and talked to the lieutenant who let her know clearly that the County was not going to arrest Toup. Why they wouldn't arrest him remained a mystery to all the residents of the Lake Juniper Subdivision, but was becoming more difficult for the Good 'ol Boys to cover up. Once again, I wrote a letter to the county attorney and, as always, I believed it made no difference. This time I was wrong.

Since our water was still off and the county attorney had refused to keep his promise, Kathy and I called our attorneys, and they started the legal process all over. They attempted to file an Exparte Order on March 12th to have the water restored. It asked the court to find Toup in contempt. My attorney told me the term Exparte means "of a side" and refers to an application made to the court by one party without notice to the other party.

Our attorneys needed to act fast, and there was no way they could follow normal court procedures and get things done in a short timeframe. The motion was faxed to me. I made copies for everyone, and I took the papers to the court clerk for filing. I told the court clerk that our attorney was sending her signature by FedEx and that she would have it the next morning. The clerk refused to accept the filing. I went home, called the attorney, and told her of the situation. She suggested I just wait and they would get me an original signature.

I was grateful that I had finished the chelation therapy treatments and that I was able to drive my own vehicle again. I was running around the county like a chicken with its head cut off. The trip back and forth to the courthouse had become a very familiar route. I was discouraged because I had not passed the physicals that would allow me to fly again. It would have been easier to get in the plane and go get that required signature from our attorney.

On March 12th, the attorney's secretary jumped in her car and took the signature to the Phoenix airport where it was sent off to me in minutes. By 9:00 a.m. March 13th, I was back in the court clerk's office to file the papers. That afternoon, Judge Wise arranged a telephone hearing. At that time, it was decided we would have to have a formal hearing. Judge Wise set our time in court for 9:30 a.m. next Monday, March 16th. With the knowledge that our attorney was doing everything possible to get our water restored, and a court date for the hearing, the few more days we had to wait for water seemed tolerable.

When we arrived at the courthouse on Monday morning for the formal hearing, I was surprised by the visit of two of my friends—Patsy Cline and Lynna Palmer—from New Mexico. I had been keeping them apprised of the chain of events since I built my home in Lake Juniper. They had heard the story and seen my pictures. They had suggested I close the house and come back to New Mexico. They knew about every confrontation I had faced and had received copies of every nasty letter Toup had written to me. Finding the facts unbelievable, they had come to the courthouse to see first hand.

Our attorney of record that day was Attorney Dramaine. Since the firm first took over our case, she had been the most active attorney. Her name appeared on most of the filings with the Arizona Corporation Commission. Every time Toup had pulled another stunt, she immediately made the proper legal moves to stop him. Her ability to move fast on every problem Toup and the clique placed before us made us true believers that she was prepared to buck the establishment.

Deputy Attorney Nogut had made a big issue of the fact that Attorney Law had not prepared the proper legal way for a criminal prosecutor to step in and help. Attorney Dramaine had paved that way. There was no security present in the courtroom. I was worried that someone might get hurt. I believed our attorney's fear of the long hand of the clique was as great as mine. When Toup and the clique began their denials of our rights, Attorney Dramaine became livid. "Not in America," she commented. She assured me she had brought along her fiancée to protect her as she entered the courtroom.

After being in the courtroom a very short time, she came out and advised us that there would be a wait of about 30 minutes. She had to go obtain a warrant. I was grateful for her efforts. She seemed to have all her ducks in a row.

I was more comfortable knowing my friends were with me because by that time, the mere sight of Toup raised my blood pressure. My visitors got to meet my neighbors and talk about the Lake Juniper nightmare.

Deputy Attorney Nogut went into the courtroom. No one knew what he was doing in there, but he seemed to be moving pretty fast. Martin Coole's secretary had explained that the lieutenant from the sheriff's office had said that Deputy Attorney Nogut was the attorney who refused to allow Toup's arrest so we could reconnect our water in peace. Granted her words were a bit of hearsay, but his actions (or inactions) had given me plenty of reason to believe her.

We were all summoned to the courtroom. Attorney Dramaine opened, explaining the injunction and the threats by Toup. She revealed the facts that we again had no water and no attempt had been made by Toup to restore it. She did not hesitate to explain to the judge that we had received no support from the sheriff's office when the time came to enforce his injunction.

Toup, representing himself again, explained to the court his property had been taken from him, and he asked the court to accept the filing for the property's return. It appeared Judge Wise was getting pretty confused as to how to handle the situation.

Toup explained he had no tools to repair the well and that unless Judge Wise got him his belongings back, he would not be able to make the repairs. He demanded the court file papers ordering the return of his belongings.

Toup told the judge that he was being expected to pay the moving van and storage costs. He said that requirement was against the law. There was not any need for the judge to try to explain to Toup more than once that the stored belongings had nothing to do with the case at hand. We were to proceed with the hearing.

Our attorney called each of us to the stand. Each of us verified that we did not have any water and that the sheriff had refused to respond on the injunction, and that we were told by the deputy that the court had failed to tell the sheriff's office what they were to do if Toup did not comply with the injunction. Because of the confusion, they chose to do nothing.

Martin Coole explained how Toup had threatened him and the serviceman. He did a good job of putting Toup in his place. When Toup suggested that Martin Coole was not qualified to work on the well, Martin Coole reminded him that there was a certified well mechanic at the well and Toup had threatened him and scared him off. Toup objected to Martin's response.

During the hearing, Deputy Attorney Nogut remained in the courtroom. He looked at each of us, but his eyes would always turn towards the carpet and his shoes when we looked back. I just knew something was not right—I didn't trust him.

My mom always told me you could tell the success of a man by his shoes. Well, that was not true in Mohave County. Most of the honest people who had lived in the area for any length of time, could no longer afford good shoes. A man wearing sneakers or old boots and a suit might prove trustworthy. All the people with the expensive clothes and shiny shoes looked at the carpet rather than face me.

In the end, Judge Wise ordered Toup to reconnect our water. He gave him 48 hours to see that the repairs were accomplished. He got past the personal property issue by telling Toup there were other screwdrivers in the world besides his "golden" screwdriver that was in storage. He then told Toup he had until Thursday at 4:00 p.m. to restore the water to our homes, which meant Toup actually had 72 hours to correct the problem. Oh well, one extra day without water couldn't hurt too much. By this time, I had been without a steady supply of water for over eight months. What was one more day?

Judge Wise wrote a new, permanent injunction that stated if Toup allowed our water to remain shut down for 12 hours, we could file in the court to have him arrested for contempt, and he would be confined to jail until our water was repaired.

Now that sounded like a fair decision at first glance. Toup restored the water within 71 hours of the court's order on March 19th, but two weeks later on April 2nd, when the water went down again, Judge Wise had been assigned a permanent position in the criminal court system and our case had been moved to a Maricopa County Civil Court in Phoenix.

By the time the new judge reviewed our case, we had been without water to our homes for over two more weeks. Again we had to pay an attorney to protect us. That time we had the well repaired, paid the bill, and the judge could not put Toup in jail because we had fixed the well and our water was running!

Toup was never ordered to reimburse us for the money we spent repairing his system or paying our attorney fees. The attorneys felt it a waste of time to ask for the money.

During our March 16th hearing with Judge Wise over the first contempt case, he went over some of the documents he needed from our attorney that she had not filed for the balance of our case. Our attorney knew she had filed those papers at least 30 days prior. Her face turned red, and she asked the judge to be excused for ten minutes. He agreed, and she stormed out of the courtroom. She went directly to the clerk of the court's office, only to find the papers buried under the outgoing mailbox on the clerk's desk. They had been there, file stamped and dated, for over a month. It was a wonder they had not been filed in a wastebasket. She presented them to Judge Wise, pointing out the filing date stamp, and everyone left the courtroom. She had just been given a taste of the politics in Mohave County, and she didn't like it.

My son Jerry, Patsy Cline, and Lynna Palmer followed me outside. We were standing there talking about the case when Deputy Attorney Nogut approached us. He appeared very angry. He said he wanted to speak to me, and I acknowledged his presence. We distanced ourselves from the people around us.

From then on, all hell broke loose! Deputy Attorney Nogut raised his voice and pointed his finger to me, yelling, "How dare you send me a threatening letter. I am on your side. I have done everything for you I possibly can. What makes you think I am making decisions against you?"

I started to answer his question. I wanted to explain what Lieutenant Warfield had related to us when Toup ignored the court's injunction and cut off our water. Lieutenant Warfield had said the county attorney would never allow Toup's arrest. I said, "Lieutenant," and I was cut off. He knew exactly what I was about to say because Martin's secretary had already told him the same story. He sure did not want the witnesses present to hear that story again.

He shouted, "Don't you interrupt me. Don't you ever interrupt me. [The] Lieutenant did not say anything!"

His attitude made me wonder what other corruption he was shielding. When he stopped yelling long enough to catch a breath, I opened my mouth to speak again. "Shut up and let me finish," he growled.

I listened to him berate me and assault my intelligence for a few more minutes, and then I turned away from him. Deputy Attorney Nogut obviously felt I had threatened him. I had only written one letter to the county attorney's office prior to that date, and it was not addressed to him. It was addressed to the county attorney, whom I believed to be Billy Willy Jr. The only thing I asked in that letter was who was calling the shots in that office! I wondered how close I had gotten to uncovering something even more sinister within the Mohave County legal system.

Deputy Attorney Nogut had made us a promise that he would arrest Toup if we got an injunction and he broke that promise. Someone was pulling his strings, and I wanted to know who. Previous to our Lake Juniper Subdivision problems, Deputy Attorney Nogut had never been one known to lie, and I wanted to know who had forced him into becoming a liar at our expense.

My friends from New Mexico didn't understand why I just stood there and let Deputy Attorney Nogut ramble on.

Lynna Palmer said, "You should have slapped him."

"I've never heard anyone be so rude in my life. You must really be sick. If you were well, I know you would have kneed him where it hurts," Patsy said.

I had to weigh what Patsy said very carefully. Deputy Attorney Nogut had embarrassed me, accused me, and he shook his finger in my face. I am not one to stand back and take abuse from anyone. It was true that I was still physically weak, but my mind was okay.

We came back to the house, and I got out my copy of the letter I had written to the county attorney's office. Patsy Cline and Lynna Palmer both agreed there was nothing in the letter to spark such fury. I disagreed.

Perhaps the man had made a promise and he was forced to break his word. He knew he was now a liar in the eyes of several people. He knew those people relied on his honesty and he had let them down. He was unable to look any of the victims in the eye. Had I slapped him or busted his balls, as suggested, the bruises would have healed, and I could have been arrested for assaulting him. By remaining civil and reminding him of his shortcomings as a human being, his heart would take much longer to heal, and his conscience, if he has one, would never let him forget his actions.

Both Patsy and Lynna wrote affidavits stating what they had seen that day and their reactions to the event, just in case we decided to sue the County like Mike Mazur suggested. I do not believe either of those women will ever forgive that man for his outburst. I, on the other hand, believed that this man was pushed beyond his moral beliefs, by the Good ol' Boys. I believed he was suffering inside because he had lost the control afforded him by his position and he knew he was failing his public in order to keep his position. If my friends had the right to prosecute him for his activities, I believe they would love to see him hang.

After trying to settle down and failing to do so, Patsy, Lynna, and I compiled a letter to send to Deputy Attorney Nogut. That letter was lengthy and was intended to remind him of what he had promised, how his inaction, indifference, and lies were slowly destroying lives, and it asked him why he took the positions he did.

I had lost my husband, lost my foreman, had been cheated in a crooked land deal, and had been poisoned. I really hated being ignored.

Deputy Attorney Nogut, and indeed the county attorney's office, had made our lives hell through lack of protection and prosecutions from that office. It appeared his position required a dedication to certain people within the Good 'ol Boy clique. The injustices suffered by the victims he supposedly served seemed inconsequential. Perhaps I expected too much, but I felt he had condemned the very people he swore to protect.

The county flood control engineer had been studying the flooding situation for four months. My lawyer wrote him in February 1998 to remind him he had not addressed my flooding problem. He sent a reply April 1998 stating I should build an eight-inch high hump (speed bump type) in my driveway that entered my property from the side of the house to prevent future flooding. What he failed to address was how I was to prevent the water from pouring into my home from the lot behind my house and how to prevent the complete destruction of my electric transformer every time it rained.

To prevent the flooding, my neighbor, Martin Coole, sent his backhoe and operator out, and we dug a deep trench along my property lines, diverting the water around my house to a dedicated wash. We ignored the stupidity of the county's engineering suggestion for a speed bump, and we fixed the problem ourselves. The planning and zoning director informed me, if the trench we dug was over 100 feet, I had to purchase a permit.

When I asked if it was the same type permit Toup was required to have when he increased the designed elevation of my road five feet, I was ignored.

CHAPTER 18

All this time, Toup LaPrix had been representing himself in both civil courts, and the answers he had been submitting to the attorneys were not even readable. The words he wrote were rambling excerpts from items he had cut and pasted from the articles written by constitutionalists and placed on the Internet. A website called *The Militia Watchdog* has posted examples of the materials he used. They explain to the reader what the militia's political beliefs are and how this strange group is trying to destroy the United State's judicial process. Just like the web site reads, Toup LaPrix never answered the charges in any of the lawsuits against him nor did he admit to anything.

Back in 1979 Toup's father and mother had deeded a large portion of land in the area to their "beloved" son. It appeared his father believed that if Toup stayed busy digging and plowing the area, he would be more likely to stay out of trouble. After Toup started selling off lots, I believe he began to realize the game was no longer to his liking when the people he had sold property to refused to accept his status as "King of the Mountain." When the electric sign company was trying to collect on the judgment they won against Toup and he began to incur other financial and legal obligations, he took the deeds his parents had given him and rerecorded them. He marked on the front of the deeds, "Refused For Fraud" in large black letters. During our case, he submitted this altered document to every court. I wondered what sort of person would accuse his dead father and living mother of being fraudulent. The only thing his parents had made sure of when they transferred the property to him was that the property was free of debt at the time of the deed transfer. They had no power to keep his property free of property tax or legal obligations.

I never did understand what the website was trying to say about why the militia stamped gift deeds like that, but I was not alone; the judges didn't understand either.

Twice he counter-sued for $1,000,000 in gold (in federal court) everybody who had sued him for land fraud. He accused everybody of fraud, rape, mail fraud, and many other things. He accused the judges of being frauds, because the judges took their oath under a flag of war. The flag of peace, as he interprets the rules, bears no fringe. He claimed there was no judge in Arizona who had the right to be on the bench and judge him or anyone else. He always stated the state was bankrupt. I had the opportunity to compare his filings in the property owner's case with the filings in the homeowner's case. Except for the case headings, all the words appeared to be "cut and pasted." All filings were identical.

His observation of all the flags bearing gold fringe was correct, but I didn't know about his interpretation of the meaning of the presence of the gold fringe. Even in the county mediation offices, I found the American flag bearing gold fringe. As an American, I did not see that it mattered much. There are several different versions of why the United States flags should not have fringe on them. One man told me if your flag bore fringe it meant you were at war against your government. It was not much later that I found myself hanging a flag in my front window that was full of gold fringe, but we will get to that later.

One of the lot owners, Don Hamilton, laughed, "That bastard has filed so many papers, he probably doesn't have enough money left to finish the subdivision. The ink he is using on that computer is not cheap, you know."

The lot owners' attorney had to get all Toup LaPrix's legal gibberish dismissed in federal court before he could proceed with their lawsuit in state court. That action caused a delay in their legal process to April 1998. By the time the higher court made a decision and threw out Toup LaPrix's charges in that case, the homeowners' had a previous case to cite, and the homeowner's case progressed nicely for a little while.

I had become the watchdog. With my attorney's permission, the attorney representing the lot owners contacted me several times for progress reports on the development. All his questions were easy to answer. No improvements had occurred.

The pleadings Toup submitted to every court were very hard to read. Every other word was followed by the definitive article "the." When I tried to read what he was pleading, I couldn't understand very much of it. I would often find myself back on the computer looking for answers from the new website I found.

Toup LaPrix had previously been able to successfully negotiate with the State and the County. He could twist a few arms here and there. He had received all his clearances from the bureaucrats he hated. He was permitted to build not only a lake and a dam, but also a bonded subdivision. He even convinced the County to hold a deed to 69 acres of his land and a promissory note for $350,000 bearing interest at ten percent annually in lieu of posting a performance bond for the completion of his subdivision. He wasn't nearly as stupid as his court filings represented, regardless of his mental state.

Toup was financially ruining many people. It was blatant land fraud. All the people who had invested money in the subdivision were victims of the fraud. He had successfully lied to the county attorney about his financial ability to complete the subdivision. Any publicity surrounding an arrest of Toup would lead to a deeper investigation by the news media. The county attorney was too heavily involved in the approval process for the subdivision to allow that to happen. No charges were filed, no criminal hearings were held, and no restitution to the victims would be forthcoming.

In the courtroom, Toup always appeared to be following the advice of a group of people who disagreed with our judicial system and wanted to destroy that system. I believed he was much more capable of communicating than his computer-generated filings implied. After experiencing the county attorney's inaction in obtaining justice for many victims, my heart, eyes, and ears were turned to studying what Toup was trying to say and accomplish.

Paying attorneys, going to courts, and having my life turned upside down was very stressful. My financial plans for retirement were being wiped out, and I felt that criminal acts had been committed against us without proper legal protection. I was rapidly becoming hostile to the establishment.

Don Hamilton, one of the lot owners, was under the same stress. He had lost over $100,000 on the two lots he bought, and then suffered a heart attack in 1997. He joined the ranks of the County's victims condemned. He lucked out, though. They caught his condition in time, and he underwent successful quadruple by-pass, open-heart surgery.

The court sanctioned Toup several times for ignoring the court's rules and for frivolous filings. He never paid the amounts ordered by the judge, but the Mazurs, Martin and I continued to pay for the paperwork involved in preparing the lawyer's requests for sanctions as well as everything else they had to do.

Toup continued filing the papers, complaining how the county bureaucrats had caused him all his troubles. I found it ironic that Toup appeared to be blaming everything on the bureaucrats, even though they seemed to be the ones protecting him and de facto siding with him, whatever their motivations for doing so were.

What Toup had failed to explain in his filings was that the lake he was so proud of, and had spent years developing, had not been approved by the county bureaucrats for water storage. The state engineer approved it, but the county officials had different ideas. He had overstated his finances, spent too much time and money on the lake, ignored the commitments he had made to the people who had invested in his lots, and there was no way he could complete the most important parts of his project: the paved roads, the utilities, the fire protection, etc.

The completion of safety issues for that lake seemed more important to the bureaucrats than the completion of safety issues affecting the lives of residents in the subdivision.

Toup also "forgot" to mention in his filings that his water company had never received an approval to operate from the ADEQ (Arizona Department of Environmental Quality), because he never submitted his as-built plans for inspection. The approval he received to construct the system had been withdrawn by the ADEQ. After eight years, new laws had been written governing the construction of a water system, and his old plans did not meet new state laws. He also failed to report to the agency that people were actually hooked up to his unapproved water system.

Public record showed the right-of-way for the main road that passes in front of the subdivision and extends miles beyond the subdivision boundaries was obtained from Toup's family in the 1970s. The records substantiated that only a very small portion of land was traded to the county by Toup for the construction of Toup's dam. The records did not reveal how much the county paid to Toup's father in 1972, only that there was "a value received." It was possible that the county needed a wider space for the road than Toup's father sold them.

I had dealt with his father in mining operations. Both my husband and I knew his father. He was always nice to me and he respected us. I had been in his home, and I learned of all his adventures and his connections to the Hualapai Indian Tribe. His stories were extremely interesting. No one ever mentioned his black sheep son in our personal visits or our business ventures. I was well aware it was not customary for his father to give up something for nothing.

The main delay Toup faced was his inability to expediently dig the hole that was to become his lake. In his dealings with the County over the construction of what Toup called his "$2 million dam" for his lake, he not only agreed to give up some of his land for the road that was to be atop the dam (and form one side of the lake), but he also agreed to supply the County with screened aggregate base (AB) from the lake area for the road maintenance department. This also provided a good excuse as to why Toup's heavy equipment was never fined for being used for commercial purposes in a residential subdivision. When Toup started up that rock screening plant, the ground shook so much it cracked the paint on our walls in our houses. There was no need to complain, the county was getting free AB. According to the records, Toup supplied the county with 100,000 tons of AB.

For over four years, there were no bids let for road-base materials by Mohave County. When I, as a supplier of AB, asked for a bid sheet for the County, I was told by the road superintendent that the County did not intend to submit bids for AB because they were getting it free from Toup.

The construction of that dam and the problems with the under-the-table deals made by the County caused trouble for some honest employees. A former county supervisor who had experience with the secrets and the inside workings of the County revealed another scenario. Learning from a local attorney that I was interested in knowing everything about the lake and the subdivision, the former supervisor set up an appointment with me at the attorney's office April 2000.

At our meeting, he explained, "The County had a wonderful engineer in the road department. He had just a few years left before retirement when the County decided to help build Toup's dam across Stockton Hill Road to form a lake and enhance his real estate development. The engineer complained that using the money from the federally funded Highway User and Road Funds (HURF) for construction of the private dam would constitute an illegal act. There were no highway allocations in the fund designed to construct a $2.5 million private dam. When this honest county employee tried to stop the rape of the HURF money, he got his office moved to Lake Havasu City for the duration of his employment with the County."

He carefully explained at length that no employee was allowed to provide financial opinions or advice regarding the decisions of the use of federal funds made by the Good 'ol Boys. Honesty was a trait intolerable among thieves.

The former supervisor said, "Because he gave an honest opinion, that engineer's new office had nothing in it but a desk and chair. The County continued paying him his $98,000+ salary, and he showed up every day for the final year of his employment with nothing to do but keep his mouth shut and read the news. Had he done anything else he would lose his impending retirement. If you need help with that Toup thing, just serve him a subpoena. He'll talk."

I continued to ask more questions. Getting all the facts seemed important. It was just as my friend Jim said, "Corrupt systems must, of necessity, enforce corruption to survive."

"Does he know all about the dam, or did they move him before it was finished?" I asked.

"He knows it all. I'll give you his name and number, and you can send him a subpoena. He'll talk, I tell ya," he replied.

To this day, there is an argument between the state's dam engineer and the county's dam engineer as to whether Toup's dam was properly constructed in 1994. The county engineers trying to work with Toup refused to certify the dam because they accused Toup of moving their engineering stakes. The state's engineer stated he moved the stakes and he approved the dam, but Toup refused to pay the necessary permitting fees to the State. It was unlikely from the beginning that the lake would ever be more than the fantasy of a mental incompetent.

In 1990 the Planning and Zoning Department had allowed Toup to set aside the lake area, and it was never included in the boundaries of the subdivision. By doing that, the County would not be responsible for completing the lake as an off-site improvement, should the developer fail to perform.

It appeared on paper that the County's plan was to immediately start charging Toup big bucks for taxes on the lots within the subdivision. They allowed him to advertise the lake as an amenity of the subdivision so the individual lots would sell for a much higher price. That gave the county an inflated tax base, which they applied to every unimproved lot in the subdivision. It was false advertising because the lake was not part of the subdivision.

In April 1998 the lot owners' class-action lawsuit against Toup and his failure to complete the subdivision, finally got to trial after several delays.

Toup's feeble attempt to answer the lawsuit was nothing more than inept garbage. He suggested to the court that the superior court had no jurisdiction over him. He claimed he was a foreign alien! He claimed sovereign immunity. The judge asked Toup, under oath, where he resided. His answer was, "In my body."

If I had been on that bench, I would have let this man sit in the pokey for contempt, at least for as long as it took him to find his true residence.

I was called as a witness for the plaintiffs in that trial. My lawyer felt the homeowners had such a strong case that I could not hurt our case by testifying for the lot owners. I was a key witness. I was living in the subdivision, and I knew what was going on. Toup acted as if he did not understand why I was in that courtroom. It seemed his mind could not accept my presence. I do not think he expected me to be there. I owned a home, and in his mind, the rest of my case had not been set for a trial. (The homeowners' lawsuit had already attended their court hearing against the water company three months earlier in January and prevailed, and Toup got confused.)

When the lot owners' attorney called me to the stand, Toup objected every time I opened my mouth to answer the attorney's questions. When the attorney asked me my name, Toup objected. The session went something like this:

The Court: "What is your objection, Mr. LaPrix?"

LaPrix: "The witness doesn't belong in this courtroom."

The Court: "Well, let's listen and ask her the questions necessary for me to be able to decide if your objection is valid."

LaPrix: "I object."

The Court: "I have made my decision already and the witness may continue. Answer the attorney please ma'am."

After the attorney finished asking me about the conditions in the subdivision, Toup asked a few questions. Everything he asked me backfired on him, so he quit asking. Then he called for a mistrial. He told the judge that when the court allowed me to continue speaking on the stand, the judge had stated that he had already made his decision in the case, and the court had implied that Mrs. Lewis' testimony would not matter one way or the other. He claimed he had not been allowed to present a proper defense.

The judge said he did not believe that was what he had said, and he would review the transcript. If in fact he did say that, he would allow the mistrial. Toup lost the case. Judgment for the lot owners was issued in May 1998. Toup appealed.

For the record, Toup LaPrix was born in Arizona, went to school in Arizona, and has always done business in Arizona. When the mood struck him, he carried an Arizona driver's license and had Arizona tags on the vehicles he drove. The tags were often expired, and he drove on a suspended operator's license for many years. Police rookies arrested him five or six times for driving on a suspended license and driving a vehicle with no tags and no insurance. I do not know if the court ever collected a fine, but they never kept him in jail over a night or two. His affluent, politically connected clique (or his brother) always got him released right away.

In 1998 the County had begun their legal work, and they auctioned Toup's land to pay for assurance to cover his liability for completing the subdivision. There was a lady at the auction who was a true friend of Toup's. After she won the bid of $300,000, the auctioneer learned she needed to go to the bank and get her deposit. (The advertisement for the auction said that the bidders were required to present a deposit of at least 10 per cent of the auctioned price prior to bidding.) The woman had made no deposit but was allowed to bid! I couldn't understand why the County had allowed her to bid in the first place. The bid fell back to the original bidder, and the land was sold for the opening bid of $248,000. The county attorney complained and complained about having to respond to the paperwork Toup filed in the court. The County held the $248,000 for a year, and there were still no improvements to the subdivision. They did not have enough assurance money to do what they said they would do, so they sat on the money and did nothing.

As the homeowners' case moved toward the trial against Toup LaPrix himself in July, he asked the judge to dismiss my claim because I had sued him in another case, and that constituted double jeopardy. (Even though the case had been heard in January, the ruling had not been reached.) I am sure that claim kept our judge busy for a day or two because the homeowners had a different judge than the lot owners. Our judge could not figure out what Toup was talking about (I was only a witness, not one of the plaintiffs), and he could not find any other case I had filed against Toup. That one motion cost the homeowners added legal fees and extended the case another six months or so, while the homeowners' case was tossed around from one judge to another.

In Phoenix, the judges rotate from court to court. We got the privilege of meeting seven different judges. Each new judge had to read Toup's ramblings. I am sure they did not bother to read that mess any more than the federal judge did, when he threw Toup's ramblings in his trashcan. We were given six different reasons why six different judges could not proceed with our case. By the time our case needed an order on some motion filed, a new judge was assigned to our case, and extra time was needed for the court to get caught up on all the paperwork. The case took a long time, but the attorneys did not complain. They were making big bucks.

Because Toup never appeared in court or answered our lawsuit, our attorney submitted to the court an application for Notice of Default a submitted a Proposed Form of Judgment. Our attorney had told us the judge would submit a judgment against Toup or return it for corrections in a timeframe of 60 days. Our attorney submitted the paperwork to the court for signature on November 11, 1998.

Our judgment was in the hands of the Mohave County Superior Court (in truth, the substitute judge from Maricopa County), and Mike Mazur was impatiently waiting for the decision. All he wanted was to get the judgment against King Toup and to ultimately prove in another court that the Mohave County clique was the real cause of our problems. He truly believed there was a deep-seeded cover up. He was convinced King Toup was doing something for the Good 'ol Boys that allowed him complete immunity from the law and that we had gotten in their way and had thus become their victims.

We waited patiently for the judge to sign our final judgment against Toup. Well, most of us did. Mike got angrier and angrier because the judge had not signed the judgment for over 60 days. We began to receive more legal papers from the attorneys that were amending the lawsuit to include Toup's brother, The Brat Consulting Group, and Cowboy Joe. The attorney fees were choking each of us, and we did not believe the avenue the attorneys were taking on the case was in our best interest financially.

Every day Mike Mazur would ask if I had heard anything from the judge or the attorneys. My answer was always, "not yet." Mike was a bundle of nerves.

Kathy was working. All of my days were being handled one day at a time. Mike would come over to my house in the mornings for coffee. He exhibited no desire of going back to his truck-driving job while he felt Kathy and I were in danger. During his visits with me, we had prepared a claim for damages that we intended to file with the State of Arizona and Mohave County. Mike wanted to sue all the people who had ignored our situation and had so blatantly protected Toup.

Mike said, "While we are sitting around waiting for this judge's order, we should file a lawsuit against the County. I have already asked our attorneys if they would be willing to sue the County, and they said they wouldn't do that. Any other suggestions?"

"I doubt that we will be able to hire an attorney. I'm just not ready to start another lawsuit yet. My mind is not sharp enough, and my hands still shake when I get tired. Our lawsuits state that the claim is ongoing. As long as we have no secure water system, no paved roads, and inadequate utilities, I think our claim will remain current. As soon as I can, I will go to the university, learn more about reading and finding the laws, and filing lawsuits. If we can't find an attorney, I'll file the case myself."

"Okay, but the County should pay, don't you agree?" he asked.

"Yes I do. No one should be allowed to get away with what they have allowed in this subdivision. I know municipalities have some immunity against prosecutions and claims, but I think this County put themselves up as bondsmen and they should be held accountable."

"What do you think it will cost us to sue those bastards?" he asked.

"I have no idea. Once we get the judgment against Toup, our lawyers should be able to tell us where they found his money. They did promise you they would not sue if he had nothing to take, didn't they?"

"Yes. You are right, Patti. They did say that."

"Then maybe we are in for a good surprise. We'll get enough money to sue the County and we will do that. You have to be patient, Mike."

"If you promise you will go back to school, I'll be patient," he said.

"That's a deal." I replied.

In December, a news reporter from the *Mohave Standard* telephoned Mike Mazur. He requested an interview that was intended to give Mike a chance to tell our side of the story to the public. The reporter said he wanted printed information that came from an investor or homeowner who lived in the Lake Juniper Subdivision. Attorney Whiner had his day on the radio, and his side of the story had been printed in the *Mohave*

Daily Miner in September 1997. Toup had received the same privileges. The county attorney had his statements recently placed on the front page of the same newspaper. The people living and investing in the Lake Juniper Subdivision had never been asked to express their views concerning the problems with the subdivision.

Mike Mazur called: "Would you please come over to the house and help tell a reporter what is really going on in our subdivision? This guy is from the *Mohave Standard*, and he says it is time the public heard from the residents of the subdivision. I want the reporter to understand that Toup has threatened our lives. I need help in convincing a news reporter that our liberties are being ignored by the County. I'll call you when the guy gets here," he said.

"Okay. I'll do what I can to help, but he won't believe what we have to say."

Mike called me as soon as the reporter arrived, and I went right over to his home. The reporter gave us his business card and began asking us questions about the subdivision. When Mike pulled out all our files and showed him that we had saved written, tape-recorded, and video files of everything he needed to know, the reporter appeared very concerned. "What are you collecting and saving this stuff for?" he asked.

"The County thinks they can break us." Mike answered. "King Toup thinks he can break us. He has told that to the sheriff. He told the sheriff's deputy he would see me leave the subdivision with nothing more than a suitcase. With Patti's help, we'll prove them all wrong," Mike replied.

"I make him save everything," I told him. "We take pictures of events that occur and save every paper we get. I will eventually get it all together, and when it comes to a showdown, we will be ready," I said.

The reporter seemed very interested in what we had to say. I noticed he carefully examined our legal papers. He gave most of the files back to Mike as he read them, but one file he placed under his right arm. I kept my eye on that file. When Mike Mazur related some of the unbelievable events that had transpired, I continued to back up his words with the written files.

The reporter started steering the conversation towards our personal lives. "Now, Mike you are a truck driver, right?" he questioned.

"Right," Mike said.

"And your wife Kathy is a nurse?"

"Right," Mike replied.

"I understand you built this house as a spec house, and it has a significant mortgage on it. Is that correct?" he asked Mike.

"Yep," Mike replied. "I can't sell this house because of the lack of a constant potable water supply, and we have an idiot who runs around disconnecting everyone's water supply that the County keeps protecting with Civil Stand-bys provided by the sheriff."

"What's a Civil Stand-by?" He asked.

"Well, the sheriff sent two officers out to Patti's house to protect King Toup on a Sunday while he cut all the water lines to her house. They just stood there watching while he did his dastardly deeds, and they protected him so Patti couldn't shoot the bastard. When he was through busting up everything, they drove off. They called that a Civil Stand-by," Mike replied.

"And you Patti. I understand you are widowed and you own your home outright. You are not employed by anyone, but you own some businesses and have investments. Is that correct?" He asked.

"Why do you ask?" I said. "I don't think that sort of stuff should be written in your paper."

He shrugged his shoulders and began to talk about why we were still living in the subdivision. He said he would not be able to write about the bad water being supplied to our homes by the Lake Juniper Water Company. He knew the County had other wells that were just as bad as ours, but the paper was not allowed to write about such things.

I felt sure he would not be writing about any civil stand-bys either, but I kept my mouth shut. I was supposed to be an observer and a back-up for Mike, not a troublemaker.

The man commented on the Doberman that was standing in Mike's kitchen. Maggie was a beautiful dog. The reporter told Mike it was a very smart move to have a dog like that around to protect Kathy when Mike was on the road. He explained, "One never knows what might happen with all the drive-by shootings and everything going on in our world today."

Being from a large city like Chicago, Mike took that reporter's comments as a warning. Mike had started ruffling the feathers of the clique. Evidently, his indignation was not well concealed because the reporter suddenly decided to leave. I stuck my hand out for the file he was holding under his arm and he gave it back to me.

After he was gone, Mike explained his interpretation of the interview to me. I guess my life had been protected so much that I was naïve and unable to recognize such a threat.

Two weeks passed and the article the man had promised never appeared in the paper. Mike called the *Mohave Standard* only to find the man no longer worked for them. Mike asked if they would be running his story about the residents of Lake Juniper, and the man said he didn't know what Mike was talking about.

We began using Mike's idle time designing a landscaping plan for his yard. He said he really needed to do something besides standing around and waiting. Jerry brought him the supplies and helped Mike when he could. Mike worked every day. He spread the decorative rock, planted the sod and plants, and built the water barriers I insisted his yard needed. I warned them both to be careful and to watch out for drive-by shooters.

On January 14, 1999, while waiting since November 11th—over 60 days—for our judgment to be awarded by the judge, Mike seemed so jittery that he couldn't stand waiting around any longer. He wanted to get back to work. He had completed his landscaping project, and it looked great. He had also repaired all his vehicles. Toup seemed to be backing off for a while, so Mike decided to apply for a job at a plant in Clark County, Nevada. They needed drivers, and Mike was a good driver with a very good work history. Mike's best friend worked for the plant, and he told Mike he was sure he would be hired. For four days, Mike nursed a cold. Kathy called it pneumonia, but Mike insisted she was overreacting and that it was just a cold. When he began to feel better, I found him outside in the cold weather checking out his camper.

I was going into town for some groceries and bottled water, so I stopped to ask Mike if I could bring him anything. He accepted my offer and gave me a short list of things to pick up. When I came back to Mike's house with his list fulfilled, he asked me, "Isn't this your beauty shop day?"

"I just came from there," I said. Mike's face turned red.

Because of the loss of my hair, I still looked pretty bad. Mike apologized and we had a laugh. With what little hair I had left, I needed a magician more than a beautician.

For the next four days, Mike tried to stay in bed or at least inside the house. He felt weak, and Kathy had warned him against getting any sort of a chill. According to Mike, Kathy threatened his life if he went outside in the cold air until his lungs were better.

When Mike felt he had recovered, he told me he needed to go back to work. He explained he would be away for a few days and that he hoped King Toup would not find out he was gone and start harassing Kathy and me again.

I assured him we would look out for each other, and we had Jerry to help us.

We had still not heard from the court. Then on January 19th, 68 days from the day we believed the court had received our papers for review and signature, Mike died of a heart attack in Clark County, Nevada. He was 42 years old. This victim of Mohave County's politics never even had the chance to see the judgment he fought so hard for. The stress of having his financial life destroyed by Toup LaPrix probably hastened Mike's death. He had a bad heart to begin with, but the stress of all the problems we were having put too much strain on Mike's weak heart. Mike had also become one of those victims condemned by the county leaders' blatant disregard for their fiduciary duties to the community they have been chosen to serve.

My first reaction to his death came to me in the form of anger. I called the attorneys again. I was in the perfect mood to get nasty and demanding. I asked if the judgment we had submitted to the court on November 11th had been signed. Attorney Dramaine assured me that her office had been checking on the judgment every week and that they had communicated with the judge's office just the day before. I asked for the judge's phone number. She gave it to me. I called the judge's office and asked the clerk about the status of that judgment. She informed me that no judgment had been received from our attorneys to be signed. She said our attorneys had failed to send the required paperwork. I told the clerk someone was a liar and that I intended to find out who it was. I explained I would call her back if that would be all right with her. She agreed.

I called Attorney Dramaine. I explained the clerk's response. She seemed to sense my anger. Someone was hiding the truth, and I wanted to know who it was.

She quickly promised she would look into it herself. The next day she called and said that the paperwork she had submitted to the judge had been misplaced on the desk of Mohave County's presiding judge. I had to believe that story. It was not the first time the county's judicial group had misplaced our papers. Attorney Dramaine, along with the court clerks, made certain our judgment was immediately delivered to the proper Maricopa County judge for signature. I explained to her that I hoped she had learned a lesson. Mohave County was conveniently losing all her paperwork. I told her never to trust them again.

Misplaced for over 60 days? First, the clerk lost our papers. Next the presiding judge misplaced our judgment papers? I wondered why, not how, that could happen. No matter what obstacles were placed before us, I decided I was not about to give in. I learned a lesson. In the future, all filings made with Mohave County on my behalf would be copied and sent directly to the judge handling the case on the date it is file-stamped. I vowed then never to trust the county court system with any filings I made.

The circumstances surrounding Mike Mazur's death were extremely painful for everyone. He had gone to apply for a new job. He had given up his previous job to protect Kathy and myself from Toup, his family, and the Mohave County clique. More money was needed to support Kathy and pay his bills. Mike felt that with the judgment against Toup before the judge, the worst of our problems should be over.

Kathy described to me the events surrounding Mike's death.

Mike arrived an hour early for his appointment in Clark County, Nevada. He waited in his camper until the offices were opened. Kathy believed that because of Nevada daylight savings time, Mike had just forgotten about the time change. One of the men from the plant arrived at about 6:45 a.m. and went out to Mike's camper. He told Mike he could come in and fill out the necessary papers even though it was still a bit early. Mike answered the man and said he would be right there. The man went back inside the plant. Things got busy, and no one realized Mike had not appeared for his interview.

At 2:00 a.m. the next morning, a security guard noticed a light coming from Mike's camper. He went to tell Mike he should shut off the light, and he found Mike dead in the doorway of the camper. It looked as if Mike had died while descending the steps. The security guard immediately called the police and the coroner. Mike's body was then transported to the Clark County morgue.

At about 2:30 a.m., the coroner notified the Mohave County sheriff's office of Mike's death. The coroner instructed the sheriff to inform Kathy

Mazur of her husband's death, and he related all the information necessary to contact her. The coroner's audiotape of the conversation reveals that the officer agreed to complete the instructions of the coroner. The Mohave County Sheriff did nothing.

A friend of Kathy's came to her home about 8:00 a.m. after hearing the news of Mike's death from a worker at the plant where Mike died. Kathy had no idea why the woman was crying when she came to her front door. Without being prepared for this new tragedy, in addition to her previous suffering, Kathy suddenly learned of Mike's death. Still in a state of shock, Kathy called the coroner in Clark County. When she explained how she learned of her husband's death and revealed that the Mohave County sheriff had not notified her, the coroner was furious. The Clark County coroner then informed Kathy of the taping of his conversation with the sheriff's office. He told Kathy he would send her a copy of the tape.

After Mike's funeral, Kathy went to see the county attorney to set up a meeting between the county attorney, the sheriff, and herself. The county attorney's secretary assured her the county attorney would call her and set up an appointment for the three of them. Kathy said, "That never happened."

Kathy asked me to speak at Mike's memorial. All I could say was "I promise you. Mike Mazur that I will continue the project you started and are now unable to complete. I expect you to help me from wherever you are." I knew I would fight to protect our homes and see that in Mohave County, we all regained our rights as American citizens. I had finally started school in August, and I was learning how to find and read the laws. I was getting ready for a different legal battle.

Finally, the Maricopa County judge in charge of our homeowners' lawsuit signed the judgment order in a very reasonable length of time—February 10, 1999. That was not surprising. He was not related to anyone involved, and he lived in another county where political pressures from Toup's clique might not reach him. The court found Toup in default, and we were awarded well over $3 million between us on the second phase of our lawsuit for damages, breach of contract, intentional misrepresentation, civil racketeering, fraud, and other charges. The last phase of our battle against Toup and company was to get the judge to rule that Toup's business partners were either fakes or, if real, were also crooks. We needed to obtain the same judgment against them.

How to collect of the judgments would be a challenge. Except for the land he owned that was heavily encumbered by tax liens and judgment liens, Toup had no money. Our attorneys could not tell us how we were to collect on our judgment, nor if we would be successful. They had worked hard on the case, been paid well for their work, and now it was time to assess the damages to our pocketbooks.

I believed it was time for me to go after Toup's bonding agent. The County claimed that was a problem to be addressed by the State and Mike had claimed it was a problem for the County. So on February 24th, I filed claims with the State of Arizona Risk Management Department and Mohave County Risk Management for ongoing problems with and completion of the subdivision and damages to my property. Filing a claim means that persons believe they have been wronged, that they have financial damage, and that the State and County are at fault. A claim is a necessary filing with the body politic prior to a lawsuit being filed. I had promised Mike I would file the suits, and I felt ready for that battle.

The State's only response was to ask what I meant by "ongoing." I explained, and we never heard from that risk management agency again. An ombudsman wrote me a letter stating that the State had no control over our water situation, but his letter failed to mention the rest of our complaints. His letter stated that the State had done all they could do for us. Attorney Whiner wrote a long letter for the County denying any liability for the subdivision conditions and the damages we received.

In response to the claim I filed against Mohave County for $3 million, the county attorney, Billy Willy Jr., had an interview with the *Mohave Daily Miner.* That paper is like most of the newspapers in small towns; they print whatever the Good 'ol Boys in control tell them to print and not much more. In the interview, Billy Willy, Jr. stated that the people who purchased lots in the Lake Juniper Subdivision had taken a certain amount of risk. At least three years prior to the county attorney's statement, Governor Hull made a profound statement when she appointed the director for the Arizona Department of Real Estate. She said, "No one should ever be taking a risk when they purchase land in Arizona."

The rules of the courts have time limitations as to when a person must file a lawsuit. How could I timely file anything when the damages were occurring every day for years on end? Two and a half years after I filed the claims against the State and the County, my home sustained another $1700 worth of damages caused by the water system. I was replacing recirculation pumps every six months or so, and I had replaced the water heater three times in five years. No one from the county offices attempted to intervene in any of the problems that had been created by the developer with whom they had a contract. They had blindly entered into a contract with Toup that appeared to pave the way for Toup's land fraud.

After winning my case against Toup in February, I hired a private detective firm to bring me all the written documents they could find concerning Toup and his ownerships of property—real and personal.

They showed me papers that explained that after Toup's failed lawsuit against the judge of the municipal court and the police officer who arrested him for car registration and insurance violations, Toup applied for new plates and insurance on his vehicle in the name of The Brats. If the insurance company or the motor vehicle department had checked on the authenticity of The Brats, they would have discovered that The Brats was a company that could only be located in Toup's mind. He had used the names The Brats Consulting Company, The Brats Investments, Inc., The Brats Advertising, etc., none of which could be found on the roles of the Arizona State Revenue Department nor the Internal Revenue Service.

For many years, Toup had stated in court, under oath, that his contractual negotiations with an unnamed party forbade him from revealing the name of the person to whom he transferred his assets. His victims and the courts spent many hours and thousands of dollars to disprove his claims of the existence of a trust.

On a deed transfer filed in Mohave County in 1996, Toup had used the company name of an investment firm whose business address was in Las Vegas, Nevada. That firm was supposedly the receiver of his irrevocable trust. That deed transfer stated, "Due to an oversight, this deed is being recorded in 1996. It should have been recorded on March 17, 1993." At the end of 1992, Toup had filed for bankruptcy, which was immediately dismissed. I don't know why the case was dismissed. I thought that, just maybe, Toup had learned that falsifying financial documents in the federal court was too dangerous, so he stopped the bankruptcy filings. In a federal court, he would find no protection from fraud charges.

The New York-based investigators were hired to find out if Toup had deeded all his property into an irrevocable trust, and if he really had the foreign bank account he had bragged about. The investigators found two investment firms with the same name Toup had used in his recordings, but they had different addresses. Both firms had web pages on the Internet. Both firms professed the ability to set up an irrevocable trust. The company that bore the address that Toup had given for his receiver, turned out to be a company out of Las Vegas that was defunct. It was no longer a valid corporation in Nevada. A man with a name similar to that corporation's listed receiver was located on the rolls of the Nevada Department of Corrections as an inmate. The crime committed was fraud. The coincidence bothered me.

A second company the investigator found bearing the same name was a division of a large, well-known fidelity bank. Suspecting that Toup was committing felonies, the company agreed to sign affidavits stating no one in that corporation had ever had any contact with Toup. There was no foreign bank account found that could be connected to Toup or any of his associates. I learned a lot about Toup and the people and politicians he contacted regularly. It was worth every dime of the $10,000 I paid.

A full month had passed and Toup had not appealed the judgment. The lack of Toup's appeal meant I could move on to the moneymen. On May 20th—more than 3 months after the judgment in the homeowner's lawsuit against him—Toup finally asked for an appeal. Because I had decided back in February not to pay any more attorney fees to answer Toup's court ramblings, I decided I would somehow handle this appeal myself. At the hourly rate charged by our attorneys, we could be looking at another $14,000 for an appeal. I wasn't prepared to spend the money. If Toup was going to file all those weird statements in court to delay the ordered proceedings, I could continue school and learn enough to answer his trivial garbage without the need of a licensed attorney

I followed the Rules of the Court as well as I could and answered Toup's appeal. That part was easy. He missed his filing dates by months. I knew there was more to come because Toup had said he would keep me in court the rest of my life. I needed the knowledge to get him stopped. I needed to find time to go to school.

What could it hurt? Toup had already lost his case. He had no cash. His land was being sold in bits and pieces at land tax sales. It was not likely I would ever get my money back anyway, so I spent my time in school. I finished the business class, and enrolled in a paralegal class offered through the University of Arizona. If Toup's legal challenges were going to haunt me for the rest of my life, I should at least learn more about how to approach the judicial system. After my bout with copper poisoning, I decided to take the doctor's suggestion and reactivate my mental system by studying. I needed an attitude adjustment. Jerry had taken care of me when he was alive, then Mike Mazur stepped in and protected me when my body and mind were failing. I needed to take care of myself again. I hoped I could find someone who would represent us on a contingency basis and continue the collection process against Toup.

I had been thinking about taking paralegal classes, but I hadn't begun any classes yet. But just by reading the court rules I had ordered in preparation for the class, I responded May 30th pro se (for ones self) to the notice of appeal. The rules of the court stated that much more time had passed than afforded by court rules for Toup to request an appeal. I cited that rule. I stated that Toup's request was filed untimely and should be dismissed.

The ruling Good 'ol Boys next move was to decide that the landowners in the subdivision should form a Mohave County Improvement District. In August 1999 they notified the property owners that there would be a meeting to discuss the completion of the subdivision, and the formation of the improvement district. At the meeting, Attorney Whiner explained that by entering into such agreement with Mohave County, each landowner would pay an assessment, depending on the amount of land owned by each landowner. The money collected would then be used to complete the subdivision. It was the County's position that if we wanted our subdivision completed and our water system made legal, we would have to pay for it ourselves.

Toup still owned over 60 percent of the subdivision, and I wondered why the County would think that they could collect the improvement funds from him. An improvement district's liens come first, before tax liens and judgment liens. The County could file improvement liens on Toup's property and foreclose, and my judgment lien and the tax liens against Toup would be worthless. That financial move would ruin most of the lot owners and me.

When we explained that we had already paid a very high price for our lots in a County-assured subdivision, we were ignored. When the water system failed and shut down again in September, the Mohave County rulers suggested that if we would all come in and sign for an improvement district, we could then expect an adequate water supply.

This little act of blackmail, should it have been approved, would cost Kathy and Martin another $16,000 or more, and my assessments—because I was already purchasing Toup's land through tax deeds—would total over $70,000. Four other people who held CPs were looking at the same bill I was. Attorney Whiner said we could receive federal grants to help with the expenses, but he could not tell us where to investigate those grants. Of course the County would not be able to offer any advice or help in that area.

On August 21, 1999, I started school. I enrolled in a paralegal certification course given by the University of Arizona.

When I complained to Supervisor Negate that nothing was being done to correct the problems in the Lake Juniper Subdivision, she sent me a message through her secretary. The secretary said, "Mrs. Negate asked me to call and tell you that the County has done all they will do for the people of Lake Juniper, and they will do no more."

No improvements had been made or attempted. What about the assurances? What did the County intend to do with the money they received from the sale of Toup's land?

When I questioned Mrs. Negate about her statement that "they will do no more," she said I had misunderstood. How can one misunderstand when one is staring at all the unfinished problems and sees no one attempting to correct them? My supervisor did not help her constituents in the Lake Juniper Subdivision one iota. Neither Kathy nor I ever saw her in the subdivision. She never crossed the threshold of my home. During our time of distress, she certainly never came to my home to get any facts. Four years of indecision, uncaring, and failure did not present a good batting average in my book.

The landscaping company I started brought in sales tax receipts to the community based on a yearly gross of almost $333,000. This same woman gave no consideration of any kind to the revenue advantages a company like mine might bring to the community, if allowed to grow. My company was all but "out of business." The stress I was under would not allow me to actively participate in the company's operations. I spent over $25,000 of my inheritance money, trying to cover the company's debts, but the company could not survive with Phil gone and me spending all my time fighting the County and the crooks in court.

The appellate court denied Toup's appeal on August 30th—three months after he filed the appeal. When the appellate court mentioned my name on the determination, I was so proud! I knew then that some courts would truly pay attention to little people who had to appear before the court without an attorney.

Kathy and Martin were still getting bills from the attorneys. They decided there was no visible way to regain their expenses and they released the firm. When Toup filed with the Arizona Supreme Court, months after his rejection by the appeals court the court refused to hear his case. None of us were required to respond to that action. In fact, it was a year later before we were even informed that he had approached the Supreme Court. We were never noticed of such action even being taken.

The firm representing the homeowners had not won a judgment over Toup's straw entities. The case could continue for at least another year, and it would be necessary to fight harder if I was to clear the way for collection of the judgment. The clouded titles had to be corrected. All of the people and the governments who had liens filed against Toup's property, before my judgment was rendered, had to receive satisfaction on their liens before I could collect. All of Toup's indebtedness to other liens and then his act of changing and recording a change of ownership of his property clouded the titles to his property. I had a lot to clear up and pay before I could get a clear title to his property. Not only did he have liens against his properties that were incurred prior to our judgment, he also added, prior to our judgment, Cowboy Joe and The Brats Consulting Group as co-owners of his properties.

Before judgment was rendered against Toup, the attorneys had amended the lawsuit and added Cowboy Joe, The Brats Consulting, and Toup's brother to the list, claiming conspiracies by these defendants as well. That activity made our judgment against Toup another partial judgment. We still had no rights to foreclose or collect anything until the others were found guilty too.

I believed that all the defendants, straw companies, brothers, etc. should have been in one case and the lawsuit against all of them heard at the same time. Why waste years of the court's time, when it was one suit against many? The case was being stretched out and I could not accept the delays. Believing the attorneys should have handled it all at once, I was not about to go on spending $3500 a month in attorney fees to take on one case at a time. A judgment against the straw defendants could be obtained in a reasonable length of time if I put them all together. I could convince the court that they were created simply to protect Toup. For example, Cowboy Joe never paid a dime for the share of Toup's land that that he claimed he owned. The Brat's Consulting Group was a figment of Toup's imagination and there was no one to speak for that group that had ever paid a dime for their share in Toup's property. That group had no license to operate as a partnership or corporation in Arizona. That group had never paid taxes and had no tax numbers, no address, no licenses to do business in Arizona, no officers listed, and no statutory agent.

CHAPTER 19

On October 20th, I was notified by the Victim Witness Program that Jack Tattoo had jumped probation. He had been missing for several months, and I had never been told he was on the loose. Since I had made such a fuss, perhaps the victim's program leader (the county attorney) felt I should be aware that there had been a problem. Jack Tattoo was scheduled for a hearing on October 29th concerning his probation violation in the Mohave County Superior Court. The same judge who originally heard his case would be presiding. I had learned more about the laws of the state and how I wanted to interpret them, and I was hoping I would witness better enforcement of those laws than I had seen so far.

As I entered the courtroom for the hearing, I noticed my trusty professor from paralegal school was sitting in the prosecutor's chair. It seemed appropriate. He specialized in prosecuting drug offenders. He was the prosecutor for MAGNET, Mohave County's drug enforcement team. When I was attending his class, I had complained about the court's judgments and the indifference shown for the victims of Jack Tattoo.

"What are you doing here?" I asked.

"I'm just filling in for the prosecutor. He's out sick. This proceeding is only a formality. Nothing will be decided in here today," he replied.

"Do you remember my telling you in class about that felon with the long list of convictions?" I asked.

"Yeah," he replied.

"Well, this is that bastard," I said.

He began to thumb through the file.

Jack Tattoo entered the courtroom in shackles. There was a guard watching over him. There was another tall, rough looking, blond-haired man sitting in the second row of the visitor's chairs. I took a seat in the front row right behind the professor's chair. I still felt Jack Tattoo would have liked to get even with me for writing that victim's letter. I was afraid he might get the job done.

This day, as before, there was absolutely no courtroom protection. "I will fear no evil."

Jack Tattoo's attorney was involved in a case in another courtroom, so Jack's case was delayed for about 20 minutes. While we were waiting, Jack Tattoo asked the guard if he could speak to me. The guard said he could if I did not mind, and Jack Tattoo proceeded to ask me to forgive him. He explained he had married the girl he had been living with all these years and that he had three sons. He spoke as if each word was being carefully considered. His speech was slurred, and I was sure he was on drugs. His presentation suggested a con job. I could not find it in my heart to forgive him yet. No sentence he had received from any court had changed him one bit. He was still a drug addict and was still dangerous.

Jack Tattoo pled guilty to probation violation. As the hearing continued, another of those plea bargain situations seemed to be in the making. The judge assured Jack Tattoo that he could impose jail time in any bargain.

"Jail time? What about the eight years of prison time you promised him in the last hearing?" I thought. The judge had previously promised all of Jack Tattoo's victims, and Jack Tattoo, that if he failed while on probation, he could serve his full term in prison. Hearing the judge's speech, I got sick to my stomach. My head was pounding, and I wanted to scream out to that judge, "You are talking to a four-time felon who has proved that he has no respect for the court! You already gave him an easy ride, and he fell off the train. Why can't you do your job?" Even with my schooling, I wasn't beginning to understand what was going on.

The judge set bond at $5,000 then added a severance fee that brought the total to $8550. Jack Tattoo was a free man the next day. He was to go home to Yuma and report back to the court December 7th. The bonding companies were not so quick to cooperate this time, so Jack Tattoo's ailing mother covered his bond.

While there was five and a half weeks until the next hearing, the court needs time to review any papers I submit. So I had only three weeks to get my legal research done and try to convince the court that victim's rights were being ignored. It seemed the attorneys on both sides were hiding the real facts concerning Jack Tattoo's past from the judge.

This victim had many unanswered questions. "How can the citizens of this county expect the police officers to fulfill their duties with any enthusiasm when the officers of the courts are allowed to ignore the laws of the state? Have the honest citizens become victims condemned by monetary budgets? The Probation Department accurately said this man was not a candidate for probation prior to his last hearing. Was it all worth it?"

The judge had previously promised the victims and Jack Tattoo that the court would not go lightly on him if he broke the probation rules. Jack Tattoo had signed acknowledgements that if he violated any condition of his probation, the court *could* impose a maximum sentence. He did not care. He just lived a life of crime to feed his detestable habits.

What I wanted to hear was that the court *would* impose the maximum sentence!

I wondered what would happen to all the children involved in this particular matter. After Phil Fox died, his son seemed to lose all hope. Phil's brother told me the boy had stopped going to school at 14, right after his father died. The child showed no respect for authority of any kind. Perhaps he was unconsciously learning how to survive in a world of plea-bargaining that showed no respect for the laws written by legislators or for the victims of crimes. I wondered if Phil's son would someday leave victims in his path due to bad legal examples being set for him by the court at such an early age.

Jack Tattoo had sired three children out of wedlock. He told me he had since married their mother, but according to the records of the Probation Department, his "wife" did not know of Jack Tattoo's whereabouts for an extended period of five months. She had been unable to tell Jack Tattoo's probation officer where he was. Would his children become innocent victims condemned because the laws had been defiled by the judicial system?

Since arriving in Mohave County I had been the victim of five felonious crimes. Granted, they were mostly burglaries, but all but one of the suspects was still walking the streets. The one that was confined was in a New Mexico prison.

After the hearing, I went to the county clerk's office and looked at Jack Tattoo's file. Noticeably absent from the file was the paper the probation office sent showing Jack's criminal past. Near the front of the file, I found a report called a Release Questionnaire. An officer of the Yuma Police Department had completed it. It was a preprinted form with many questions concerning a defendant. The officer was required to fill in the blanks that applied. I found something that caught my eye. A question asked, "Was evidence of the offense found in the defendant's possession?"

The answer given was "yes. Small container with substance field-tested positive for methamphetamines." A question asked, "Is the defendant presently on probation, parole, or any other form of release involving other charges or convictions?" The answer was as follows: "Yes. Probation with 3—4 months left."

The judge had previously given Jack Tattoo eight years probation. He had not begun the probation until February 1997 and had been AWOL since April 1999. Where did the rest of the years go? Reading on, I found the report most interesting.

Question...Is the defendant employed? Answer...Yes.

Question...With whom? Answer...Self-employed/Tattoo's Engineering.

Question...How long? Answer...12 years

Question...Nature of employment? Answer...Engineer.

Question...Where does the defendant live? Address given.

Question...With whom? Answer...Wife and children.

Question...How long? Answer...1 year.

Question...What quantities and types of illegal drugs are directly involved in this offense? Answer...UNK (usable amount) of methamphetamines.

Summary...Probable cause for arrest.

The officer wrote, "Called to hotel for criminal damage. Contacted Jack Tattoo in room, and ran a warrant check. The check returned a felony warrant for probation violation. When we were explaining what was going to happen with the warrant, Jack Tattoo moved close to his girlfriend and handed her something. When she was asked what was in her hand, it turned out to be a small bottle with a substance that field tested positive for methamphetamines." End of report.

When I was in the courtroom (October 29th), the prosecutor had explained to the judge that the defendant had failed to report to his probation officer. He did not tell the judge that drugs were found in Jack Tattoo's possession. No mention was made of the lies he told the officer regarding the length of time remaining on his probation, his education nor his length of employment as an engineer. No mention was made about his being in a motel with a girlfriend and possibly doing drugs. Jack Tattoo had blamed the criminal damage on his dog! I was sure everything I had read in the report would be ignored at the hearing, but I had to try.

Hoping I could make a difference, I asked the clerk if I could have a copy of the report. She said, "Sure. Is that all you need?"

I took the report to my professor. I asked him if he had seen it. The professor explained that he had not seen it, but that the hearing Jack Tattoo had just had, did not include exposing the report or offense. That portion of the case would be heard during the December hearing and handled by Attorney Bargain. He asked me if he could make a copy of the report, and I agreed. He made two copies and promised me he would show the report to Attorney Bargain.

At the next hearing on December 7th, Judge Blinders discussed Jack Tattoo's case with the prosecutor. The arresting report I had read and delivered to my professor was not explained to the court. Before sentencing, the prosecutor, Attorney Bargain explained to the court a victim had something to offer for the court's review. I was surprised when he turned around and handed me the arrest report he was holding in his hand. I asked myself, "Why would Attorney Bargain ask me to give this report to the court? Why had he not presented this report to the judge himself? Who was preventing him from doing his job?"

I was again just a scared and angry victim. I asked the judge, "Have you had the opportunity to read this report in its entirety? Jack Tattoo was found in possession of methamphetamines. There are a lot of other items in the report this court might find interesting, and I am wondering if you have read this report." In my mind I kept repeating, "I will fear no evil."

The judge's eyebrows went up and curled in a bit. I sensed he had not seen the report.

Jack Tattoo's attorney objected. He said, "The agreement made does not allow that arresting evidence to be brought before this court. This victim has received full restitution and cannot be heard in this courtroom." Obviously, that was why they wanted me to be the one to present the evidence.

The judge explained to the defense attorney that my employee had lost his life and that the court would view my involvement as a victim as one of an employer who had the right to continue to try to protect the rights of her employee and his family. He then began to read the report.

The judge grunted as he read the entire report. He asked Attorney Bargain if Yuma had filed charges against Jack for possession. Attorney Bargain explained that the amount of drugs in Jack's possession was so small that Yuma did not mess with it. He explained to the judge that Yuma, being a border town, had so much drug traffic, the amount Jack had was something the police could not afford to pursue.

The judge thanked me for submitting the report to the court and went on to sentence Jack Tattoo to the bargained ten months in the county jail. If he did his time in the Mohave County jail, with no work release, the time would be counted two for one, for a total of five months. That saved the County money. All the time Jack Tattoo had avoided probation was to be added to the end of his probationary sentence. If he could convince the California authorities or the Yuma authorities to accept him on a work release program, he would be permitted to spend his time in either jail. If allowed a work release program anywhere, he would be required to complete the full ten months.

I had no idea what he had chosen to do, where he spent his time, or even if he had spent any jail time at all. I received no other notices. I felt sure the judge resented many of the plea agreements arranged by the county attorney, but I learned in school that he had the power to deny them. I had just become a thorn in the judicial system's side. As a victim, I was expected to "get over it."

CHAPTER 20

Five years earlier, in 1995, a group of people had gotten together and formed the Mohave County Economic Development Authority (MCEDA). The lineup of MCEDA's board of directors looked like a list of "who's who" in Mohave County.

These people explored every loophole available in the laws to promote their agenda. The infrastructure built for incoming corporate projects ran along, across, and very near lands owned by their board members. They proclaimed the area would be called the I-40 Corridor.

The public was told that The Mohave County Economic Development Authority (MCEDA) was a private corporation funded in large part by Mohave County out of the general fund. I couldn't find them listed as an Arizona Corporation, so I don't know how that business was formed. The policies maintained by MCEDA appeared so questionable, it was rumored that a state representative from the county's district called for an FBI investigation. The people heading MCEDA were either unable or unwilling to show to the representative any accountability for their actions and expenditures. It appeared taxpayer's money was being spent on corporate welfare as if there was no end to the supply. I wondered when they were going to start printing their own money. MCEDA was making any kind of deal they could make to bring industry to Mohave County. The major portions of those industries were very wealthy, well-established corporations. They had been denied residency in many American states because of environmental concerns.

Taxpayer's credit was expended to fund infrastructure for those wealthy corporations. Roads and wells were built with taxpayer's resources to accommodate the plants. In contrast, in residential areas, the property owners are always assessed for pavement improvements, and existing businesses always pay for their own paving.

The county was fiscally unable to support the new industrial growth. The taxpayers were assured through propaganda that some of those plants were capable of generating up to $1 million per day. That would produce a great return to the general fund in tax dollars. There was no promise given in writing by any firm that they ever would do that. The construction incentives provided for them were pushing the county towards bankruptcy.

One man who owned the major portion of land being developed by MCEDA on this I-40 Corridor had a large family. Each member of that family donated the maximum dollar amount allowed by law to the campaigns of Supervisors Snide and Golf when they ran for election to the Board of Supervisors.

On January 12, 2000, the radio station K-99 (owned by the same state representative who had called for a local FBI investigation of MCEDA) aired the facts about a man who was representing the entire community. The reporter explained that the man was hired by MCEDA to find new industries that could be placed on the I-40 corridor and then invite companies to the area. The reporter called this man, "One of Mohave County's most powerful and controversial public figures who heads up the Mohave County Economic Development Authority (MCEDA)." The reporter had a report before him that stated the MCEDA employee was a felon, convicted for counterfeiting federal currency in California in 1982.

The felon then tried to quiet K-99's charges through the allied station K-AAA. He attempted to refute the court-recorded facts regarding his felony conviction. He claimed he was an innocent victim of a counterfeiting scheme. He explained he had borrowed a car from a man in Las Vegas in order to drive it to Los Angeles. The owner of the car asked the felon if he would mind taking a box of copy paper with him to his (the car owner's) L.A. office. Having asked to borrow the man's car, the felon felt obligated to take the paper to the man's office. He stated, "After all, I thought it was just a case of office paper."

He explained that when he got to the office, FBI agents were there, and they arrested him for being in possession of paper used in counterfeiting. The felon pleaded with the people of Mohave County to believe him when he stated, "It was easier to plead no contest to the charges than to try to fight the arrest." He admitted to the people listening that he was caught red-handed with counterfeiting paper. He claimed he had no way of knowing beforehand what kind of "copy paper" he was carrying. More than once during the interview, he said he was never convicted of counterfeiting. He pled, "No contest." I am sure that if he had a good attorney, that attorney would have explained that his plea of "no contest" would be an admission of guilt to the felony he committed.

The United States Secret Service Agent's sworn affidavit regarding the agency's surveillance and arrest revealed a different story. The special agent (SA) working undercover said a man matching the felon's description and the felon's partner examined the counterfeit U.S. currency with a magnifying glass and discussed the quality of the printing. The felon's partner and the man matching the felon's description both said they wanted the printing to be of higher quality. The person matching the felon's description said he would bring a new camera to the shop [the next day]. The felon went by several names. Three of those aliases are listed on the agent's report, and they are comical.

The next day, they entered the shop carrying a new camera and lights and were caught. Inside the shop, the agents seized approximately $4 million in counterfeit currency as well as plates, negatives, and various printing equipment used in the manufacture of counterfeit currency.

After both men received their Miranda Rights, the felon's partner refused to make any statements to the secret service. The felon's partner had a long criminal record from his past, and he knew better than to utter a word. The felon waived his rights, gave the agent a signed sworn statement of his involvement in the manufacturing of counterfeit currency, and named the felon's partner as his partner in the counterfeit operation.

At trial, the felon pled "No contest." In a plea bargain, he received only a probated sentence. He had rolled over on his partner, allowing the man exposure to a prison sentence. Ultimately, the felon's partner only served six months in the pokey, with five years probation. The felon received only three years probation and 1,000 hours of "light" community service because the court believed he was in poor physical condition.

The reporter said he had questioned most of the economic development board members and they were not aware of the felon's criminal past. Some members later admitted they were aware of the felon's criminal past, but he was so successful in his job they saw no problem with his being on MCEDA's payroll. The two controversial supervisors stated in public meetings that the felon had done his time, and they felt he had paid his debt to society.

After the felon's criminal file was made public and began to circulate throughout the community, proving he had lied in the radio interview, he retired from his County-funded position. (For more about the MCEDA, please see the Appendix.)

After that counterfeiter was exposed, the two county supervisors who had repeatedly voted to drain the county treasury in favor of the Mohave County Good 'ol Boys and corporate interests acted quickly to give the felon a new image. In the year 1999, they voted to name one of the new roads they were building in the industrial corridor after him! The Board that was elected to office in 2000, however, in one of their first official duties, changed the name of the roadway with the felon's name on it. They changed the name to honor a water-guzzling power plant.

The convicted felon was still allowed to vote in Arizona. I contacted the court where he had been convicted of counterfeiting, the governor's office in the State of Arizona, and the Fair Elections Committee. Nowhere could I find evidence that the man had received Civil Rights Restoration, which is required if a felon wants to regain their voting rights.

The Arizona laws seemed to have two versions of this requirement. One law said the judge who convicted the felon must restore the felon's civil rights. A second law said if a first time felon had completed probation, the felon's civil rights were automatically restored. Since this man had been voting for many years, the secretary of state and the Mohave County attorney must have been aware he signed voter applications. On these applications, the felon had to attest, under penalty of perjury (a class 6 felony), that he had never been convicted of a felony, by signing the application. Not only on May 24, 1988 when he registered as a Democrat, but also on January 26, 1996, when he registered as a Republican. One could only believe he fell under the latter of the two Arizona laws.

The felon, using his partner as the qualifying party, made four applications to the Arizona Registrar of Contractors for a contractor's license. The first application was made in November 1998. (One was being classified as "C-41 Precast Waste Treatment Systems.") On each of those applications, under penalty of perjury, he signed attesting that he had never been convicted of a felony. He was issued a contractor's license. He was also issued four bonds to cover his new licenses. The bonding company's applications asked if the applicant had ever been convicted of a felony. He marked "no."

According to the laws and rules established in Arizona, if he had marked "yes" on everything, his background would have been checked. The secretary of state's office told me that background checks could take up to 30 days, but the usual turnaround time is ten days. Because his record shows only the one conviction and no other criminal activity, he would have been allowed to vote, allowed to carry a contractor's license if his offense was not too great, and most likely been able to obtain a bond. After reading all the facts about the felon, I wondered, "Why did he lie, swear, and commit more felonies when the state laws protect his criminal rights?"

This convicted criminal was highly honored by the same county and state that refused to prosecute the criminal acts committed against my neighbors, friends, loved ones, and me. A corrupt system can leave a trail of victims condemned. The taxpayers are left with the responsibility of coping with and often paying for the human suffering.

On January 13 I retained a different lawyer for the subdivision problems. He was willing to provide his services on a contingency basis and take a percentage of whatever he is able to collect. He was hesitant to take on the case only because he knew absolutely nothing about civil law. I believed that with his mouth and license, and my help, we could prevail. I gave him a retainer and he agreed to try. We wrote up all the necessary papers, asking the court to review the ownership of Toup's land and seeking fraudulent transfers of titles, and after much time and work, we obtained defaults against the other two parties, The Brat's Consulting Group and Cowboy Joe.

To accomplish that, I had to get past Toup's brother. I had had a conference with Toup's brother and his attorney, Mr. Duff, back on May 15, 1999. My new attorney sought and received a judge's order that forced Toup's attorney to communicate and answer the interrogatories he had been given. It was obvious that Toup's brother was nothing more than a man with a crazy sibling and that his attorney had been misled.

In researching old court files, I found a heated deposition given in 1996 during the electric sign company trial against Toup. In that deposition, Toup stated under oath that The Brats Consulting Group was his brother. When I later advised Attorney Duff of the contents of the deposition, Toup's brother declared the statement a lie, and he agreed to testify to that fact under oath.

The judgment against the straw companies was in my favor and obtained by default. The Court ordered that Cowboy Joe and the Brat's Consulting Group were responsible to pay the judgment to the extent of their holdings in Toup LaPrix's interests. The courts would not allow Toup to answer with any more of his trivia. One of the seven judges appointed to our case had silenced him. He was not permitted to file any more trash in the court without the judge's permission.

Toup and Cowboy Joe appealed to the Arizona Court of Appeals, and they lost. They next petitioned to the Arizona Supreme Court, and their hearing was denied. These courts had already dealt with Toup and to see filings from him and Cowboy Joe as a pair, fighting over the same case again, was probably not too well received. Receiving the final judgment I needed against the straw company and Cowboy Joe meant we could proceed with collection.

Just as things were looking up a little bit, both Kathy's dog Maggie and my dog Chogie got sick. Chogie seemed to have an awful stomach problem, so I called Nurse Kathy. She came over right away and suggested I give him milk. After he drank the milk, he was much better, but Maggie had begun to show signs of being sick. Kathy took Maggie to the veterinarian, and they ran a series of tests. Some of the lab work was sent to Phoenix, and when it was returned, Kathy learned Maggie had mercury poisoning. Maggie was allowed to go home for a while, but her body could never get over the bout with the mercury. She got so weak she could not get around at all, and Kathy had to finally give in and have her put to sleep. Kathy and I spent many days taking walks and looking out for meat thrown on the ground or anything else that could be injected with mercury and that would look appealing to our dogs.

Kathy finally found the mercury in her water fountain that was sitting in her own front yard.

With the help of the new attorney, on April 18th, I managed to purchase 12 more lots in the subdivision from a man who had bought the lots at a tax sale. Three of the lots would allow Kathy, Martin, and me to have land adjoining our existing property. This increased the size of our parcels to more than one acre each. After my expenditure, we applied to Mohave County on April 20th for permission to drill wells on our newly acquired property.

After waiting for approval for over six months, our well permit requests were ignored. I applied directly to the ADWR (State of Arizona Department of Water Resources) and the ADEQ (Arizona Department of Environmental Quality) for well approvals. The ADWR inspected and explained to the Mohave County Health Department that my applications were within the law. The ADEQ declared the water company at Lake Juniper defunct. Lake Juniper could no longer be declared, by Mohave County, as a wet subdivision.

Some of the Mohave County Good 'ol Boys objected to the state ADWR's intervention. The corruption in Mohave County had left us no choice. With the State ADWR, ACC (Arizona Corporation Commission) and ADEQ against them, they had to consider letting go of their reins, but the wells were still not permitted for several months to come.

I knew the County could not blacktop the roads because I owned the tax certificate of purchase on the private roads. In their greed, the County sold the tax certificate to me for back taxes, but the deeds to the roads remained in the name of Toup and his straw companies. There were boulders across the roads and spikes hidden under the roads that the County could not legally touch. Even though the situation was extremely dangerous to our well-being, Mohave County stated they had no authority to move them. The roads were private.

I could not move the boulders because I did not have a finalized tax deed on the roads and would not have for another year. Those boulders and the locked gates blocked access to most of the subdivision. In spite of all these factors that made all the properties worthless, the County was still taxing those lots at an assessed value of over $30,000 each. I owned some of those lots and checked the pertinent statutes.

I read that according to the tax laws of Arizona, such taxation was not legal. In brief, the law states that each property in a subdivision must have ingress and egress. I felt Mohave County was operating illegally in this regard, so in March, I filed a claim in tax court to have the assessed values reduced. Mohave County agreed to settle without a hearing. They reduced the assessed value of all the lots in the subdivision to $2,000 each.

If I had not decided to take that paralegal course, I would have been lawyer poor in short order. My late husband would have been upset if he knew of all the legal battles I had undertaken, but I believed he would have been proud of me. I was not going to show indifference to such corruption.

By the year 2000, Toup had refused to pay his taxes, and he was losing everything. His life was becoming a self-made pit of misery. His incoherent court filings included issues concerning his lack of knowledge of maritime law and admiralty law, which had nothing to do with the issues at hand. He begged the courts forgiveness for his lack of knowledge of those laws. Maybe in Toup's own fantasy world, the dry hole he dug near our subdivision was a "lake." Toup's fantasy world might well have contained his own private ocean.

Because I was fighting so hard for completion of the subdivision, many people in my community were concerned that I might pack up and move away. It really wasn't an option. I had too much invested to just walk away from everything. The attorney's and doctors had my cash. Where was I to go? How could I afford a move when I owned a house that had broken pipes and flooded all the time?

CHAPTER 21

Toup had finally tried the patience of the Mohave County power structure. His activities were beginning to draw too much public attention. The residents of Lake Juniper were acting in full rebellion. Our opposition to unfair legal protection was beginning to pay off.

Toup made one of his terrorizing trips to the subdivision on July 3. Martin Coole's son and a playmate, both nine years old, were riding their ATVs on the roads within the subdivision. Toup hated that activity. In December 1992, he had beaten a child for riding an ATV on "his" roads. The child spent two weeks in the hospital. I have met that child. He grew into a fine man, but I am sure he has never forgotten what Toup did to him.

Toup saw the two children, and he went crazy. He gunned his Porsche and headed for the children. The boys moved to the side of the road and stopped their ATVs. Toup steered his car right at the children and then he stepped on his brakes, skidding sideways just missing the first child's vehicle. He jumped out of his car, slapped the boy's hand, and grabbed the keys out of the ATV. He then pulled the boy off his vehicle, scratching the boy's arm and bruising his legs. He went after the second child. He turned off his vehicle, took out the key, and pulled him off his ATV. Once he got the boys cornered at a rock wall, he told them they would stand there while he called the sheriff. He called Susie Que, his favorite form of civil protection, on his cell phone.

In the meantime, Martin Coole had gone to find the boys and see what was going on. When he found the boys in a very bad situation, he yelled at Toup, "What the hell do you think you are doing?"

"Those boys will stay right there. I've called the sheriff and I am going to have them arrested. They are trespassing on my private property. They have no right to be riding those ATV's on these roads."

The boys were scared to death, and Martin told both children to go to the house. He informed Toup the deputy could come to his house and talk with the children. Martin had a gun strapped on his hip when he met Toup, and he did not want that fact to interfere with any investigation they might choose to make. He followed the children to his home and put his gun away. Then he returned to meet the sheriff. Martin later described to me what happened next.

"When Deputy Susie Que arrived, Toup told her that a few days earlier the boys stole his motor from the lake area. He claimed they were trespassing on his roads and that they should be arrested.

"The deputy, Susie Que, walked down to the landing of the lake where the motor had been stored. There were no signs of a motor having been dragged away. The motor Toup was talking about weighed more than both of the kids.

"Susie Que went up to the house to talk with the kids. She told me they were trespassing on Toup's roads. I told her they were no more his roads than they were mine, and I wanted him arrested for assaulting the kids. She told me there was nothing she could do to him because the kids were trespassing. I got mad and called her boss."

"Did the sheriff come out?" I asked.

"Nah," Martin said. "He sent the sergeant. The two got together and wrote a report that I signed. We won't know what is going to happen for a few days."

The report was taken to Deputy Attorney Nogut. Three misdemeanor charges were filed against Toup. The case against Toup was postponed twice and didn't get to court until November 27th—four months later.

On September 17th, the lot owners in the subdivision were called to a second meeting with the county fathers. I took my attorney with me. I was sure the County was going to suggest an improvement district again. I wanted to know how they were going to explain that I had to pay assessments imposed by an improvement district. As I interpreted the law, the County was to complete the subdivision using the assurance money from their contract with Toup. If they hadn't required enough money to protect the taxpayers, the taxpayers would pay.

As I expected, the County said they were ready to help the owners if we would sign up for an improvement district. My attorney asked Attorney Whiner three times, "Who is legally responsible for the completion of the improvements in the Lake Juniper Subdivision?" Three times, he was ignored. After the third attempt to get an answer, I spoke up and told everyone in the room that I could not recommend an improvement district. If we started that mess, we would all be forced to pay for the mistakes

Mohave County made. For many of us who now had bought land from the treasurer of Mohave County, the costs would be a very great hardship. I told the lot owners that if they would just wait before signing, I would file suit in either federal or superior court and let the judicial system tell us who was responsible for the completion of the improvements in the Lake Juniper Subdivision.

The County said that ten of the lot owners had signed to approve the new district, but none of the owners who owned more than one lot signed. There was to be no legally required majority approval. The County began to change the rules about how many signatures they needed. They said each owner, no matter how many lots they owned, had only one vote. That was not and is not to this date how the Covenants Conditions and Restrictions of the subdivision read.

I told my attorney, "I've heard enough. Let's go file a law suit." I got up from the meeting and walked out. Most of the lot owners left when I did, but my attorney stayed to see what else the County would say. He later told me they did not say much. They just did not understand why I felt Mohave County should be responsible for the completion of Toup's subdivision.

By the time my attorney arrived at his office, he had decided it was too early to file a lawsuit against Mohave County. I disagreed. I knew the process would take a long time, and there was no better time to get started than right then. He said I would have to file myself, so I did. I was getting used to being the only one stating facts and opinions, and there was no reason for me to stop until the issue was settled by the court.

I filed a lawsuit with the Mohave County Superior Court on October 2nd. I filed "Pro Se." I cited the law covering my lawsuit, and I explained that the County was trying to make all the property owners pay for the improvements. I described the assurances given by Mohave County and that the mandate of the legislature required Mohave County to complete the off-site improvements within the subdivision. Mohave County had sold the assurance land in 1998, but they had not begun improvements in the subdivision for over two years. I explained to the court what was going on, how the County had said that if we signed for an improvement district, the district could assess our homes for the improvements, and only then would they allow our private wells. I asked the court to order Mohave County to perform in accordance with the law and complete the subdivision as they assured me they would when I bought my property. I also asked the court to order Mohave County to stop blackmailing me with my water supply.

Knowing that the Mohave County Board of Supervisors held the purse strings of the judicial system, and in an effort to test that system and see if the laws of the state were more powerful than the almighty dollar, I could not be persuaded to back off.

Upon receipt of my lawsuit, every judge in Mohave County recused himself. The Mohave County courts were busy suing Mohave County for more funding. My case was moved to La Paz County.

The County responded to the lawsuit on October 17th, stating that they had immunity. They wrote that I had not filed a claim for damages with them and that the case must be dismissed. They explained to the court, that the only claim I had ever filed was a claim made over a year before and that no new, timely claim had been filed. They attached my claim to their response as an exhibit. The judge read my complaint, and he read the response from Mohave County including my previous claim. He didn't rule on the case until January 2001.

On November 27th, Kathy and her friend, Charlie Towns, my son, and I went to Toup's trial for assaulting the boys to see what was going to happen to him. The children were in the courtroom sitting with their fathers. Deputy Attorney Nogut entered the courtroom, and he kept looking over at us. Susie Que came in and took her seat. When Toup entered the courtroom, he strolled over to the defense table and sat down. It looked like Toup was feeling cocky.

He had beat on kids before and nothing happened. I wondered if he would again receive the full protection of the clique. The only problem I saw for him was that he had no family in that courtroom.

When the judge entered the courtroom and we were all re-seated, he noticed almost every seat in his tiny courtroom had an occupant. He leaned over and asked Deputy Attorney Nogut, "Why all the people?"

"They are all neighbors and relatives of the children, Your Honor," he replied.

The judge was the same judge whose injunction against harassment ordered against Toup was ignored by the sheriff and the county attorney. He was the same judge who wrote to me and explained he was not indifferent to my problems, but that he could not force the sheriff to act on his order after it left his courtroom. I wondered what he was going to do for these two little victims.

Toup moved from his seat and took a stack of papers to the court clerk. The judge called for the prosecution's case, and Toup jumped up out of his chair and went back to the clerk's desk.

"Toup, what are you doing?" the judge questioned.

"I have motions to file with the clerk," Toup replied.

"Well, please get it over with and sit down," the judge said.

Toup responded with, "I call for the rule." He wanted all the witnesses held outside the courtroom while testimony was being given to the court.

"Well, I'll allow it for now," the judge replied. "Would everyone who will be testifying today please go out in the lobby until you are called?"

The prosecutor, Deputy Attorney Nogut, called Martin Coole's son. The boy did not want to go alone into that room with Toup. Deputy Attorney Nogut asked the judge to allow Martin to testify before his son so he could be in the courtroom when his son testified. The judge agreed, and Martin told the court what he had seen. During Martin's testimony, Toup made seven objections. He claimed Deputy Attorney Nogut had not told him what he was being tried for. Deputy Attorney Nogut got out all the papers he had served on Toup and presented them to the court. Toup then said Deputy Attorney Nogut was not qualified to be an attorney for the state. He repeated the same objections over and over. When Deputy Attorney Nogut was through asking Martin questions, Toup stated he had no questions for Martin at that time. He reserved his right to question him later in the trial. Martin came and sat down in front of me, and his son was called to the stand. Toup objected to Martin's presence in the courtroom. The judge overruled the objection. He said exceptions had to be made concerning the rule because the witness was only nine years old.

Toup objected again.

During the testimony of both children, Toup objected over and over in an effort to confuse their young minds. Both nine-year-old boys were very capable of telling their side of the story. When he questioned the boys about the missing motor, the judge interrupted and asked Toup how big the motor was. Toup explained it was a big motor, probably weighing 400 pounds or more.

The judge asked the little witness laughing, "Did you pick up that big motor and take it away?"

"No. I never saw it," the child replied in earnest.

Kathy leaned over to Charlie and me, and she said, "He's really pissing that judge off!"

Charlie, being rather hard of hearing, answered aloud, "Yep. I hope he gets hung."

Deputy Attorney Nogut gave us an ugly look and he called the last witness for the prosecution. It was Deputy Susie Que. Her testimony really surprised me. Since she had been the officer who protected Toup while he destroyed the waterlines to my home, I did not expect anything constructive to come from her lips. She had originally stated the young boys were trespassing on Toup's roads. The hearing had proceeded so well until then; I was convinced she would blow the whole case. That did not happen. Susie Que's presentation to the court was very truthful, convincing, and official. The prosecution rested their case, and the judge asked Toup if he was ready to call his witnesses.

Toup asked the judge, "Are you going to find me guilty?"

"I never make a decision until I have heard both sides," the judge replied. "Please call your witness, present your side, or rest your case."

"I will not arrest my case," Toup blurted.

"I said call your witness, present your side, or rest, r-e-s-t (spelling it out) your case."

"I will not *rest* my case until you tell me if you are going to find me guilty."

The judge answered impatiently, "I will rest your case for you if you refuse to proceed with your portion of this trial and if you have nothing more to add."

Toup again refused to rest his case or supply new evidence, so the judge rested his case for him. That action ended Toup's foolishness.

The judge found Toup guilty of three class one misdemeanors, one assault (for the assault against both boys), and one endangerment. Without hesitation, he sentenced Toup to 60 days in jail on each count. The sentences were to run consecutively. Toup complained that he would appeal.

"You have the right to appeal," the judge answered dryly. "But right now you are going to jail." The judge wasn't going to allow Toup to leave his courtroom and then wait to see if the sheriff would follow his order this time. He ordered Susie Que to "secure the defendant and take him directly to jail." She placed handcuffs on him, then they left the courthouse.

"How long will he have to stay in the pokey?" Kathy asked.

"Six months," I explained.

"Is that all?" she asked. "Oh well, it's better than having him out there scaring the shit out of everyone. We'll all get some peace for six months."

After the trial, everyone gathered in the court's lobby. Deputy Attorney Nogut approached us. I automatically turned and took a step back. He proceeded to explain to the group the judge's decision and that the sentence Toup received was the toughest sentence the judge could have imposed. Did he really expect us to believe what he was saying? We did not believe Toup was even tried in the right court. We believed that assaulting another man's child the way Toup had deserved more punishment.

I reported to my attorney all the happenings I observed in that courtroom. He explained Toup had the right to be told if the evidence the prosecution brought before the court was enough to convict him before giving up his Fifth Amendment Rights and testifying on his own behalf. My attorney believed there would be an appeal.

The day after Toup was sent to jail for assault charges—November 28th—the neighbors and I got busy, and I applied again for permission to drill our own wells. With Toup in the pokey, it would be much safer for the drilling company, and by the time he was released, we hoped we would no longer be at his mercy.

On the same day, Toup appeared for an omnibus hearing before the superior court, because he had been accused by the State of forging the signatures of one of the superior court judges and one member of the Mohave County Board of Supervisors. The forgeries stemmed from the foreclosure trial the County had to pursue in 1998 in an effort to acquire clear title to the land given to the County as assurances for completion the Lake Juniper Subdivision. During that foreclosure hearing, Toup had warned both parties—the judge and the chairman of the Mohave County Board of Supervisors—that he would file liens against their assets On August 11, he had done just that; he filed UCC (Universal Creditor Claim) liens against their properties. He had hand-printed their names as accepting the liens. He was accused of doctoring two other documents, so there were four felony counts filed against him. At the hearing, he was to receive the evidence the State would use against him and supply the State with the evidence he would use in his defense.

Kathy had to go to work, so I went to the courthouse to see what was going on and report back. When the jailer brought Toup into the courtroom, he had one of those carrot-colored outfits that looked like summer pajamas. His hands were cuffed in front of him; he was shackled. His toupee looked as if it needed a little more attention. His face and eyes were swollen, and he looked pathetic. He told the judge he did not have the motions he had prepared for the hearing. He explained the jail had orders that prisoners could not receive papers unless an attorney gave them to the officers.

Deputy Attorney Nogut agreed to arrange for Toup to receive his papers. He gave Toup some blank forms he could fill out for the court. Toup asked the judge for his computer. The judge said he would supply Toup with paper and a pencil, but he would not order a computer brought into the jail for his use. The judge set another hearing for the next week.

Believing Toup was a mentally unstable man, I began to feel sorry for him. I told Kathy how upset I got seeing him in that courtroom in shackles. She had a fit.

"Get real. That man tried to kill you."

"I know, but he is a sick man," I said.

"Shit happens. If his family doesn't care and won't or can't help, he is better off in prison. If he goes there, you'll have a longer break from his crap."

"Sick people belong in a hospital," I said.

"Those hospitals were all shut down as being inhumane, and now all those mentally disturbed patients are out on the street causing havoc with society, and we are just victims of that court's decision. What the hell are we supposed to do?" she asked.

After Toup's omnibus hearing, a local daily newspaper ran an article about Toup and his legal problems. The article stated Toup had complained to the judge that the jail was forcing him to do labor. He also needed telephone privileges and access to the library. The judge said he would not address Toup's issue on forced labor, but he did order telephone privileges and access to the law library.

In the third hearing, Toup submitted papers to the judge, excusing the judge for cause. In his papers, he had requested Judge Blinders, but that judge was not next on the rotation schedule, and Toup pulled Judge Wise. Judge Wise denied the case, and it was sent back to the judge Toup didn't want in the first place.

Meanwhile, more was happening with the well-drilling issue. In a letter dated December 2nd, Director Mallard, director of the Planning and Zoning Department, informed me that it was the ADEQ (Arizona Department of Environmental Quality) and ADWR (Arizona Department of Water Resources) who had ruled against our well applications. I wrote ADEQ and ADWR and included Director Mallard's letter that blamed them for our inability to have a well. I explained to them why our homes needed a secure water supply.

A very nice man at ADWR quickly looked into the situation and called me.

"Mrs. Lewis, this is John Duran, from the Arizona Department of Water Resources. I just received your letter. I want you to know that Ms. Mallard's letter is simply not correct. My office has no objection to you folks getting your wells. I have reviewed your letter and would issue your permits today if I had the applications. You said in your letter that you sent them. Where are they?" he asked.

"I sent them to the Mohave County Health Department as required," I replied.

"I'll just have them faxed over here. When I receive them, if your distances from the septic systems meet state law, I will issue the permits. The wells must be 100 feet from the septic systems. Are they?" he asked.

"Yes sir. We had to buy more land, but we have more than 100 feet," I said. "I really appreciate your help. When you contact Mohave County, don't let them know you are being so nice to us. If you are nice to the people who live in the Lake Juniper Subdivision, you might get fired." I laughed.

"How's that?" he asked.

I explained, "The last two ADEQ representatives who had tried to help us didn't last long. One was early-retired a week later; the other was transferred. The Arizona Corporation Commission boss quieted both of the ACC lawyers who tried to help us. Neither of them works for ACC anymore."

"Hmm. Well, you don't need to worry about that, I am the boss," he explained. He faxed the necessary letters to Mohave County, and he was able to get the new Health Director to send our applications for wells to the ADWR.

Apparently, after the judge accepted my case for review—the county attorney was starting to get a little nervous. The county attorney seemed to have used his political influence to see that our wells were denied. Now that it looked like the winds were blowing in a different direction. He started changing his strategy. It became beneficial to his interests to allow our wells. He asked me if we got water to our wells, would I dismiss the case. Getting the case dismissed was his main goal because it took the heat off him for making such a legal and political mess out of the Lake Juniper Subdivision. I explained to him that if the County paid for the wells, I might consider it. According to Title II § 806.0I(G), water utilities were part of the assurances taken by Mohave County.

CHAPTER 22

In January 2001, the La Paz County judge filed a ruling in my lawsuit against Mohave County. This ruling was in response to the County's claim that they held immunity. The judge ruled that in a Writ of Mandamus (a court's order to do a job), the County cannot claim immunity. He explained that my initial claim against the County stated my problems with the County were ongoing and that many of the issues I had stated in my claim were the same issues I filed in my formal complaint. He stated that my lawsuit did not seek damages. He ruled that the claim was valid and the case could continue.

The County set up a meeting with my attorney and me (unofficially) for March 17th. There were several employees there, and they were still trying to convince me that I should drop the lawsuit and form an improvement district. The engineer that seemed to be the boss told me he resented my thinking that the County should bear the cost of completing the subdivision. He said that he had no intention of going into that subdivision and completing it as long as Toup owned anything in it. He did not intend to allow the county to complete Toup's subdivision for him. I knew he expected me to pay for all the costs for possession and completion of the subdivision. He obviously felt it was not the county's fault that Toup had failed to complete the subdivision. I agreed with him. It was not the County's fault, but the County signed the original agreement with Toup, and the County was the bonding agent.

I explained I did not have the money to finish the subdivision for Mohave County. I was not the one who bonded Toup's performance—the County did. I said I would do everything I could do to see that Toup did not own anything in the subdivision, so things could move forward.

Within a few days, my attorney prepared execution papers against Toup, ordering the sheriff to seize all Toup's property. We listed every property we could find that had his name, or his name in addition to Cowboy Joe and The Brats on the title.

Because Martin Coole and Kathy Mazur had chosen not to join me in obtaining a judgment against Cowboy Joe and The Brats in phase three of the lawsuit, they could not join me in this execution sale because all three names—Toup, Cowboy Joe and the Brats—were on all the land titles. My sole judgment against the three was for over $1.5 million, and I would be able to pay for the vacant lands at the sheriff's execution sale with my judgment or any portion of it. If I needed more, I also had my portion of the first judgment we received against the Lake Juniper Water Company, and Kathy Mazur sold me her judgment so I wouldn't run out of power.

I really did not want all that land. I didn't have enough funds to pay the nine years of past due taxes, penalties, and interest on everything. Many people owned Certificates of Purchase (CPs) issued by the county treasurer, and they had been paying Mohave County the exorbitant, inflated taxes for the land for over nine years. They couldn't appeal the tax amounts assessed because the land belonged to Toup LaPrix and he never paid his taxes. Only the landowner can appeal the taxes. Prior to filing a tax appeal, the landowner must pay the taxes. If the appeal is won, the landowner then gets a refund of the overage he paid.

My attorney and I contacted all those people holding CPs. We told them a levy was being filed, and if they intended to obtain treasurer's deeds or quiet titles on the lots they were paying taxes on, they should do it right away. They had only 90 days to get their business finished. Many of them applied for and received treasurer's deeds, and a few of them sold their CPs to me. I paid those few the taxes they had paid, 16 percent interest on their investment, and I added a little more profit to my offer for their time. I had to get Toup's name off every piece of land in the subdivision so the county would do their job.

I filed for a Levy of Execution through the sheriff's office. A levy is filed when a court judgment has been given and the creditor (me) has exhausted all means to collect from the debtor. A list of the debtor's property is prepared by the creditor and given to the sheriff. The sheriff immediately seizes all of the debtor's property. (Well, he's supposed to.) At that point, no property can be traded, sold, or disposed of until the creditor is paid the amount of the judgment or the property is sold at a sheriff's auction.

The tax department ignored or was not informed of the sheriff's levy, and they allowed anyone who was trying to purchase lots listed on the levy to receive a treasurer's deed. I could have sued the County for the lots sold after the levy was dropped, but I chose not to. The tax funds I would have been obligated to produce and pay to Mohave County for the land included in the levy amounted to over $250,000. My cash on hand did not come close to that.

During our collection efforts in April, the sheriff's deputy tried to explain to my attorney that the personal property (heavy equipment) could not be levied upon until ownership was established. By law, personal property is to be taken first, then real property can be secured. The excuse they used for not securing the personal property first was the lack of an ownership history on the heavy equipment. They said they did not know where it came from or who really owned it. Even though the laws state that personal property must be levied first, previous cases have allowed real property to be foreclosed on if the debtor does not expose personal property ownership. They would have to foreclose the real property that was still owned by Toup and his alter egos and then see if they could find out who owned all of the heavy equipment that was sitting on the land.

After a levy has been filed and the debtor has been given plenty of opportunity to respond and pay the debt, the sheriff holds a sale on the courthouse steps. This sale is posted in the legal advertisements in the local newspaper for two months. During that time, the debtor has the right to redeem his property rights by paying the creditor the judgment owed.

The day prior to and during the day of the sheriff's sale on April 4th, the family of Toup moved over $200,000 worth of Toup's heavy equipment off the lands in Lake Juniper. After a levy is posted, nothing can legally be removed from the property levied. Even though there was testimony to prove that the equipment was Toup's, his young nephew who had recently resigned as deputy from the Sheriff's Department, proclaimed to the county sheriff, his family's lawyer, my lawyer, and me that everything he moved off of the property belonged to Toup's dead father's trust.

When I called the sheriff's deputy on April 4th and complained that there were several men removing equipment from the property I had just bought, the woman deputy told me that the equipment belonged to Toup's brother, he had produced ownership papers, and if I did not let him take the equipment, she would have to put me in jail. My attorney was with me when I made the call and when I explained to him what she had said to me, he grunted.

"Just remember, you own a third of that stuff," I said.

"Well, we won't worry about that today. Let's go out and see what we bought today," he replied. As we got into his truck he said, "Where do you suppose they are taking that equipment? Shall we go see?"

We drove all over the neighborhood. Toup's nephew had dozers hidden in the bushes and screening plants hidden in the washes, and loaders were chugging down the streets.

"If that stuff is his, why is he hiding it everywhere?" I asked.

"I don't know, but that is a good question."

"You don't suppose he lied, do you?"

"Oh, surely not. But just in case, we will file for an immediate injunction on the whole lot of them." We went to the court and received the injunction right away.

I traced the ownership of every piece of equipment. It took 15 months to do all the research and track people down. According to the sellers of the equipment, either Toup's nephew lied about the ownership of the equipment or Toup's father's trust was in partnership with Toup. I saw many more years in the courtroom facing me. With Toup in prison, I would have to expose myself to more lying thieves. I did not want to spend the rest of my life fighting Toup and his family.

April 17, 2001 was a very special day for the subdivision. That was the day I received the deed to the roads in the subdivision. My first order of business was to remove the chains and locks from the gates. Jerry took our tractor and moved the boulders out of the road. After ruining 11 sets of tires, we managed to locate most of the spikes Toup had hidden in the roads.

Norv Elkins came to visit. He was proud of me for opening the gates. He entered the subdivision from the back alley, but when he realized I had opened the gates he left through them. Before he reached the city limits of Kingman, he had four flat tires. Thankfully, he had a set of new tires and they were insured against road hazard.

Lot owners came to see their property. It was the first time in many months they could travel the roads in the subdivision. They left the subdivision on flat tires.

A well driller ran over a set of spikes and lost two commercial tires. Two real estate agents lost four tires. I lost two tires on my car, one on my tractor and two on my bobcat. The list went on and on until I uncovered all of the spikes implanted in the roads.

The spikes were welded on very heavy metal bases. I managed to get the sheriff's office to take one set of spikes out of the road, but after that one call, they refused to return to the subdivision again.

I searched the roads for the spikes. Because Toup LaPrix was still in the area, I wore a gun and took my shovel. I uncovered many spikes, and I took one set of them to my attorney. I told him I was so angry, I felt like throwing the spikes through the front window of Toup's Porsche.

Well, that would be a criminal act. My attorney related my feelings to the Good 'ol Boys. He took the spikes to the Board Supervisor who was in charge of our district and explained to him that lives were being threatened and that the sheriff had refused to help locate the spikes and remove them. He explained my anger. He was then informed by the sheriff of Mohave County, that there was room in his jail for me. The supervisor did nothing.

By the year 2002, Mohave County had made no move to begin completion of the subdivision. I had no choice but to continue with my lawsuit. My attorney began to prepare an expensive application for summary judgment (issued only when there are no material facts in dispute). He had given me a court case to research. The appealed portion of that case was on the Internet, but the actual superior court case was not. He needed to see the whole case. I went to Flagstaff, found the files, and reviewed the entire case. It was perfect. In that case, dated 1981, the City of Flagstaff had assured the completion of a subdivision that failed, just like mine. The judge in that case had ruled that the assurance funds should not go to the individual lot owners because the city required just enough assurances from the developer to complete his project. The city would be using the assurance money to complete the subdivision. He went on to rule that if the City did not have enough assurance money, the City would have to complete the subdivision with city funds. If he ordered money given to the landowners for their personal losses, there would not be enough money to complete the subdivision. I got certified copies of the judgment in that case, and I took it back to my attorney.

My lawsuit did not ask for money for me, it asked that the judge order the County to complete the subdivision. My attorney was pleased with the case I brought back. He had agreed with the suggestion made by the county attorney, Billy Willy, Jr. that he would file for summary judgment, and the case would be over in no time. We submitted the paperwork to the court and waited for the judge.

CHAPTER 23

On April 19th, the first day of Toup's two-day trial for forgery was held. He was allowed to pick his jury, and he disqualified any prospective juror who knew anyone who lived in Lake Juniper. During the trial, Deputy Attorney Nogut presented his case, and then he sat back and watched Toup hang himself. Objections from the state's attorney to his ramblings were rare.

Kathy and I were not sure, but we both think there were several times during Toup's presentation to the jury that the judge and county prosecuting attorney found it convenient to take a nap. The next day, the jury found Toup guilty on all four counts—two counts for forgery and two counts for filing fake documents. The judge ordered him to jail without bond to await sentencing that would take place on May 16th. It appeared that the maximum sentence the court could order would be ten years. That much prison time for miswriting and misfiling documents! Nothing Toup had done to the judge or to the Board Supervisors could hold a candle to what he had done to my neighbors and me. Nothing he had done could ever have the negative affects on the lives of the judge or the board supervisor compared to the affect he had on the lives of those two nine-year-old boys he assaulted with his automobile.

I picked up the Mohave County newspaper. The front page of that paper had headlines that read:

ACCUSED ARSONIST TAKES PLEA; MAY GET UP TO 10 YEARS.

STABBING AT APARTMENT COMPLEX SENDS TWO TO JAIL.

JACKSON PLEADS GUILTY TO SECOND DEGREE MURDER.

MILITARY CHOPPERS SET DOWN BY MOUNTAINVIEW CEMETERY.

KHS TIGHTENS SECURITY (The high school)
SHOCK GRADUATES LAST OF PARTICIPANTS
KINGMAN SURVIVES MCVEIGH SAGA.

QUARREL ENDS IN MURDER, SUICIDE.
DEVELOPER CONVICTED OF FORGERY.

None of the headlines were about people helping people, as I had seen in the 1987 newspapers. The town that I thought would be a good place to retire in was proving to be a very different town. The Good 'ol Boys seemed to be destroying my American Dream and the lives of many people.

Tomorrow, the judge and the supervisor will laugh the whole event off and forget it. The two children will remember their horrible experience for the rest of their lives. That was our new justice system in the United States. The prison time ordered and served by the criminal no longer fits the crime they committed. I wondered, "Could I ever learn to live with that? 'Do we still have the best judicial system in the world?' as my late husband used to say."

On May 16th, Toup entered the courtroom for sentencing. He sat at a table before the court in the carrot-colored set of pajamas. His body was shackled. A younger man received permission from the court to approach Toup. He gave him a set of notes to read to the court.

The courtroom became silent. The judge was shuffling every paper in front of him. "Just one moment, please," he said. He began moving papers around again. After a few moments, he looked at the prosecutor and said, "There has got to be something missing here. This pre-sentencing report reflects a man who has a lily-white background. If I remember correctly, he was in custody during his trial, and it appears he is in custody now. I don't see a report."

Deputy Attorney Nogut, the same prosecuting attorney who had sent the defendant to jail six months before for abusing two nine-year-old boys—got up from his seat and handed the judge a single sheet of paper. He said, "My office just received this report by fax this morning. Sorry, Your Honor."

The whole past of the County's cover-up of Toup's activities ran through my mind. I knew, as did every spectator in the room, that the same prosecutor, Deputy Attorney Nogut, was the prosecuting counsel in the missing case, and the man who was possibly chosen to protect him all along. I wondered if the judge was putting the same two and two together that I was. Did the prosecutor really plan to withhold that report from the court and get away with it?

The judge asked the prosecutor, "Does your office have anything to add before I pronounce sentence?"

"All the State wants is for the defendant to quit filing all the papers he has been filing. He has swamped our office with frivolous, many times unreadable, paperwork," he feebly explained. His eyes kept falling to the floor.

The judge asked, "Mr. LaPrix, have you seen the report the prosecutor just handed me?"

"No, but I'm sure I don't need to," he said. "It is all lies, and I intend to prove it."

"Yes, well do you have statements to make before sentencing?" the judge asked.

"Yes, I do," Toup said. He then proceeded to read from the set of notes the younger man had given him. The notes told the judge that Toup would not consent to or accept punishment of any kind. Toup read that the court had failed to establish jurisdiction and had no power over him. Toup's voice stumbled as he read. Whether Toup understood what the notes were saying remained questionable. I knew then that while he knew what written words are, I wondered if he knew what they meant. When Toup finished reading the notes to the court, the judge was not amused.

The judge told Toup he still believed that Toup was listening and taking instruction from people who had their own agendas and interests to express. He said he believed they were using Toup as a pawn. He explained it was unfortunate that Toup would be the one to suffer rather than those controlling his actions. The judge had made similar comments throughout Toup's trial, and after hearing Toup read the notes, the court needed no more convincing. He told Toup that he agreed with the statements made before him that day. He also did not believe that Toup would allow the Probation Department to run his life, and that he was not a viable candidate for probation. The judge read his decision. For all four felony charges, he would spend three years in the slammer—one and a half years for forging the judge's signature to run consecutively with one and a half years for forging Supervisor Negate's signature. He explained that he was running the sentences consecutively so that people would not believe they could file as many false recordings against as many people as they wanted and still receive the same time. He then added six months on each of the other two counts, but that time was to be served concurrently with the other sentences.

The judge then explained to Toup that the clerk would come to his table, and he should place his thumbprint on the sentencing report.

Toup told the judge he was not going to do that.

The judge then called for the bailiff, and before the bailiff could reach the table, Toup had changed his mind and submitted to the thumb printing. All of Toup's royalty left the room at that time.

I was one of Toup's victims, but in my mind the drama unfolded a bit differently. Toup had caused a lot of physical, emotional, and financial damage to many people. County employees had proven by their actions that they were afraid of him. No one knew what he would do next, and no one with authority had the guts to go up against him. Even though the charges against him were for non-dangerous and non-repetitive offenses, he would spend his time in the penitentiary while I made an effort to improve his subdivision. With Toup in the slammer, the County should have begun their work on the project immediately. I was ready to get the work started and take advantage of Toup's confinement period.

I took the judge's ruling to my attorney in June, and I asked him if he was ready to help me yet. He admitted he was, and we got busy. He notified the court that he would be the attorney of record for the plaintiff, and all hell broke loose.

My attorney began receiving many calls from the county power. For the most part, the County wanted my attorney to stop the lawsuit. The County was again trying to make my legal costs higher so I would give up, just like they had done when I hired Attorney Law. My new attorney's secretary had resigned, so I went to work for him to fill in until he could find a replacement. When the County called, I took the messages. That eliminated about $2600 a month on my attorney's bill.

June was also the month that we got the wells up and running. I took my bills to the county attorney, Billy Willy, Jr. The County refused to pay them.

After working at it for about a year, the owners of the CPs (bought at tax sale) and I acquired the deeds to everything in the subdivision, including the roads and the utility sites. The utility sites included about three acres of land that held the wells that were supposed to supply water to all the lots in the subdivision.

Three months later, in July, the judge ruled by summary judgment that the County of Mohave was no different from the City of Flagstaff. If the County did not have enough money to complete the subdivision from the assurances they required of the developer, they would have to complete the subdivision with County funds.

July was also the month that marked the end of a lengthy battle—tracing the ownership of Toup's equipment. My attorney had Toup transferred to the courtroom in Mohave County from the prison in Safford, Arizona. Toup looked frail and worn. He still had that toupee that did not fit, and it was not combed very well. He was wearing slippers, orange pajamas, and he was dragging shackles and chains.

The judge overseeing the collection portion of my case against Toup and his straw companies traveled from Phoenix to hear this portion of the case. Under oath, Toup explained that the equipment belonged to a man in Dallas. He, of course, did not know the man's name and would be unable to give that name to anyone until he was set free from prison and could review his records. His testimony was that he had sold the equipment to the man with a name he could not recall and that the man was allowing him to use it to complete the subdivision, but it was not his equipment. Toup's brother testified that contrary to the statements previously made by Toup's nephew, the equipment did not belong to the family trust and he did not know who owned it, but it had been taken from my land at Toup's insistence.

The judge did not buy what Toup had to say. He told my attorney to write the order and he would sign it. Because there is a question as to the ownership of the seized property, the sheriff required me to post a bond in an amount equal to my judgment against Toup. Bonds protect the sheriff if he gets sued for selling property that is not owned by the debtor by providing enough bond money to pay the real owner for the property. In my case, bonding fees would have exceeded $150,000 cash. The creditor must post a bond in the amount of the judgment when.

The judge said I did not need to post such a large bond. My attorney suggested a $10,000 bond could be placed, just in case any of the equipment turned out to belong to someone other than Toup. The judge again told my attorney to write the order and that he would sign it. I did not intend to take Toup's toys. All I wanted was the power, in case I needed it in the future.

By the time the judge left the courtroom, he was so angry that he forgot to order Toup's return to the big slammer. Toup sat in the nasty, overcrowded Mohave County jail for several weeks before the newly appointed Mohave County Presiding Judge Blinders released him to be sent back to the minimum-security prison.

I felt my attorney had covered everything needed to prove my point to the Good 'ol Boys. From the time we filed the writ of execution to the seizure of Toup's property, the sheriff's deputy had lied about the ownership of that heavy equipment. She had stated that the equipment belonged to the Good 'ol Boys trust and that she had received the documents necessary to prove ownership. If I didn't let them take the equipment off my land, she would have to put me in jail. I had proved in this court that she lied to protect the Good 'ol Boys.

It might have been fun watching her bring the equipment back to my property, but I did not want Toup's equipment bad enough to post any kind of a bond with the sheriff. I was sure the sheriff's officers would have come up with a million reasons why I could not seize that equipment. I thought that Martin or Kathy could foreclose on the equipment if they wanted it. Martin owns an excavating business and he might be able to make use of the equipment. The equipment did not have the alter egos names on it, so Martin would not have to return to court to secure a levy. In court, I had proved Toup's nephew a liar. His reputation with the family attorney, the judicial system, and his father was blackened. My notice to him had been given. I had done all I needed to do.

Also in July 2002, Mohave County began sending laborers into the subdivision to begin construction on the water company's distribution system. Without showing some sort of construction activity, they would be admitting to the court that they did not really intend to follow the court's ruling. They worked at their job about three hours every Thursday.

The County refused to acknowledge the fact that I still owned the roads they were tearing up and the utility sites they were trespassing upon. The County failed to negotiate the transfer of ownership of the property to the County and pay me just compensation. By not condemning and taking the roads and utility sites, the County could avoid any and all liability risks from either road maintenance problems or liabilities for injuries occurring on the roads. It seemed to me that their plan was to move in, do what they wanted to do, and place all the liabilities on my neck. I was beginning to panic. What would I do if a laborer got hurt, or some stranger fell into the 4 ft. hole the county had placed across my road? I would spend the rest of my life in court and the Good 'ol Boys would have a field day. The constitution of the State of Arizona and the United States forbids the taking or altering of a person's property by a municipality without first paying the owner a just compensation. Even though the County was completing the roads as required by the court order, they still should have followed proper procedures. I believed they were getting themselves and me in deep trouble.

The county workers were working on the wells, but they had not paid my friend John for those wells and the equipment he had bought at personal tax sale. They were busy for three hours every Thursday at their work altering his property. It seemed the County felt that the water system was going to be their biggest problem, so they began that work earlier than any other work. Again, the County paid no attention to the proper procedures. My friend John is a retired judge from Oregon, but he knew how to communicate with the County. He told them to pay him $7,000 for his wells, and they could continue working, or they could face the music. They paid him in August.

County Attorney Billy Willy, Jr. suggested to the court that we enter into non-binding arbitration. The arbitration was to establish what the County would have to do to make me shut up. My attorney and I agreed to meet with the County and an arbitrator. Knowing that the arbitrator was a friend of Billy Willy, Jr. and was a retired judge of the county, I was glad to know that the arbitration would be non-binding. The County did not want to do anything, and I wanted them to do everything. Knowing the arbitrator was also a taxpayer of the county, I did not look forward to the next event. I knew I would feel a whole lot of pressure.

When my attorney, his clerk, and I walked into the conference room in September, I swear I felt the heat. The engineer boss who resented me because I expected the County to complete the subdivision was there along with Billy Willy, Jr. We discussed the needs of the subdivision, and the County said what they wanted to do. I said, "No." They ran into another room and came back with another offer. I said, "No." They ran into the other room repeatedly until I believed they were getting close to meeting my demands. We thought we had reached a fair deal, so I asked that they write it up and sign it. The agreement was better than nothing, but I was not sure I could accomplish the things that Mohave County expected me to do. I did not see why I had to do anything for them. I did not feel I owed them anything, but I was willing to try to help them get their job done. The county attorney said they could write it up and make me a copy, but the Board of Supervisors would have to approve it before it was signed. That would take several days. I agreed and left.

The next day, I was sent a written copy of what had been said on an audiotape of the meeting. But seeing the text in writing I realized it included something I was supposed to do that bothered me. The paper said that the County would prepare the water system, and I would take ownership of it and operate it. I could not do that. I do not know anything about running a public utility. I called the Arizona Corporation Commission and faxed them the proposed settlement agreement. I was told by the chief attorney not to sign the settlement. I would not be able to perform the tasks the County was expecting of me because I was not qualified. They said if I tried to fulfill my commitments, I would end up in jail. I would be breaking all the state's laws. The fines for even trying to accomplish the required work would be $1,000 per day. I got angry. That was the fourth time I had been threatened with jail.

I wondered, "Why was I paying an attorney?"

I called my attorney screaming. I told him I would not sign that damn thing. Why would he expect me to sign an agreement that would have me doing things that are against the law? He is supposed to know the law; he is supposed to be looking after my interests.

He said that if I did not sign, he would have to withdraw from my case. He reminded me that he had given up about $17,000 of his fees in order to reach an agreement with the County. It appeared that he didn't truly understand the legal ramifications of the agreement. I am sure he was upset at me for backing out of the agreement. It does not look good for an attorney when a client won't take his advice.

The next day, I took him a motion to withdraw from my case. I asked him to sign it. I took it and filed it with the court. I had him call Billy Willy, Jr. and explain that he had withdrawn, and that it was okay to negotiate with me.

I made an appointment with Billy Willy, Jr. for the next day, Oct 2, I went into his office at about 10:00 a.m., and I told him what he and all the legal beagles from the arbitration meeting had written, and the legal implications. I told him that if he didn't stop messing around and trying to get out of his responsibilities and come to an agreement with me that day, I would go back and hire the same attorney again, pay him a $17,000 retainer, and the war would be on. He knew I was serious. We worked all day long, with me explaining why I could not do what he was demanding, rewriting many of my demands and his. By late in the afternoon, we had reached a settlement agreement that I could live with. The names in this agreement have been changed but the contents of the contract have not been altered.

Billy Willy, Jr.
Mohave County Attorney
Arizona Bar #
Kingman, Arizona 86402-7000

IN THE SUPERIOR COURT OF THE STATE OF ARIZONA

IN AND FOR THE COUNTY OF MOHAVE

PATTI LEWIS, a single female,   Case No.: SA-2000-26

Plaintiff,

VS.

MOHAVE COUNTY, et al.   SETTLEMENT AGREEMENT

Defendants.

The Parties have agreed to the following:

A. What Mohave County will do:

1. *Roadways.* Mohave County will pave the roads in the Lake Juniper Subdivision. The roads will be constructed in substantial conformance to the approved Lake Juniper Estates Approved Plan. During construction of these roads, Mohave County will make every effort to preserve the existing trees where possible and as allowed by regulations. Mohave County will make alterations of the elevation of Coral Bay adjacent to Plaintiff's property to prevent the recurrence of flooding.

2. *Underground utilities.* The County will arrange for providing electric and telephone service to all lot lines at no cost to property owners. Mohave County will obtain a written commitment from the telephone company to install telephone service to each lot as needed, at no cost to the property owners.

3. *Water delivery system.* Mohave County will complete the installation of a functional water delivery system to service all lots in the Lake Juniper Subdivision, utilizing the existing wells as practicable. The system will be inspected and approved by the Arizona Department of Environmental Quality. Homeowners will assume responsibility for use, operation, and maintenance of this system. Cooperative or private

wells meeting all State Laws will not be prohibited or opposed by Mohave County in the permitting process.

4. *Fire protection.* Mohave County will obtain opinions from the Hualapai Fire District, the State and County fire and zoning authorities indicating that neither fire hydrants, nor any special fire infrastructure is required for this Subdivision. The County will make its best efforts to allow the Hualapai Fire District to obtain emergency access to a large water tank in the area owned by Toup's brother for the purpose of fire protection. Mohave County will utilize every effort to see that there will be a tank suitable for fire protection no further distance from the Subdivision than Toup's brother's tank. In the event that fire hydrants are required by competent authority as a condition of construction of a residence at any time during the next ten (10) years period, Mohave County agrees to bear the cost of installation of any such hydrants. This requirement will not apply to changes in CC & R's or other - requirements initiated by the homeowners or their representatives.

5. *Improvements.* All improvements constructed will comply with Federal, State, and local laws, regulations and ordinances as applicable to the Subdivision.

6. *Completion.* All improvements will be completed or conditions of this agreement will be met by Mohave County on or before March 1, 2003. If required actions or improvements are not completed by that date, appropriate relief or sanctions may be obtained by either party through the Superior Court in Cause No. SA-2000-26.

7. *Approval for lots sales.* Mohave County will assist in facilitating approval for sale of lots with the Arizona Department of Real Estate.

8. *Federal liens.* Mohave County will pay or discharge a federal tax lien that exists on all holdings of Toup LaPrix including the roads and water system. This lien is represented to be less than $4,000.

9. *Payment*. Mohave County will pay to Ms. Lewis an amount of $19,606.73 representing full and complete payment for any claims which Mrs. Lewis may have or should reasonably know she has against Mohave County, its employees, officials, agents, special districts, or other County public entities, including but not limited to claims for attorney's fees, costs, damages, or inverse condemnation. This section shall not release claims arising from the assessment of property by the County Assessor's Office.

10. *Illegal Parcels*. Mohave County will work with Lewis at no expense to her, to combine and/or split all remaining parcels allowed in the general area of the Subdivision. This includes but is not limited to parcels 330-14-046, 330- I4-045, 330-14-043, and 330-14-044 (otherwise known as the "Lake").

B. What Patti Lewis will do:

1. *Donate Materials*. Allow the County to use materials located at the lake site so long as the County does not remove any trees or cause any permanent aesthetic damage to property.

2. *Donate Roads and Well Sites*. Transfer all interest she has in well sites and roads as a donation to Mohave County. The County will provide written fair appraised value and all information necessary to assist her in receiving a tax benefit from the donation.

3. *State report*: Prepare a new format for an up to date state report for use by the property owners in acquiring the approval of new state reports allowing for the sale of their properties. The new state report will advise all consumers that upon purchase of a lot, should they fail to order the service of utilities by March, 2008, all lots that are not connected to electric and telephone will be responsible for a pro rata contribution to Mohave County for reimbursement of the County's expenses. All lots not sold or having utilities utilized by 2008 will pay the pro rata share of this provision. This provision will

not apply to lots 155, 158 and 161 as they have already been designated as well sites and no septic permits can be obtained for those lots.

Homeowner's Association. Establish a new Homeowner's Association to replace the now defunct association and incorporate the entity as a non-profit organization to assume ownership of the roads and the water utility systems upon completion.

Clouded Titles. Will attempt to satisfy the two liens remaining against Toup LaPrix that were filed prior to her judgment lien against LaPrix, to obtain clear title to the roads and utility sites. These liens being those held by The Mortgage Companies and the lot owner.

Water Cooperatives. Will work with the assistance of the Arizona Small Utility Owners Association, the ADEQ, Mohave County Health Department and all lot owners in establishing cooperative well systems to service a large portion of the lots in the Subdivision. Cooperative wells will be encouraged but private wells will not be forbidden if all state laws are met in the permitting process.

7. *Covenants, Conditions and Restrictions.* Will work with the property owners in amended covenants, conditions and restrictions created October 22, 1990 to comply with maintenance and support of the Subdivision improvements and will issue the same to every property owner in the Subdivision as well as the ADRE and Mohave County. Included in the amendments will be the lot owner's guarantee of reimbursement of County expenses for electric and telephone advances in the event there are insufficient connections to pay for those improvements. Should the lot owner fail to pay for a lot that has not been initiated service, the homeowner's association will be responsible for assessing that lot, collecting and paying the necessary funds to Mohave.

RESPECTFULLY SUBMITTED this 2nd day of October, 2002.

MOHAVE COUNTY ATTORNEY

PATTI LEWIS, Pro Se

I felt the settlement agreement was workable, and I left the county attorney's office feeling much better. The agreement received the approval of the Board of Supervisors on October 7.

Then the next phase of my work began. I paid the necessary personal judgments placed against Toup and obtained the lien releases I needed to clear title to the lands. Those things had to be done so I could transfer clear title of the properties to the County. When that was accomplished, I immediately deeded the necessary lands to the County. That stopped my exposure to the liabilities the County was placing on my shoulders. They accepted the deeds. Even though it was costing me a lot of money, I wasn't going to be liable for any damages that the County might cause.

By November 1st, I had assembled a majority of the lot owners and they approved amended CCRs (Covenants, Conditions, and Restrictions) to accommodate the settlement agreement. If I could actually get all the items in the agreement accomplished, they agreed they would not sue the County separately.

CHAPTER 24

After the settlement agreement was signed in October, the laborers who had been working on the plumbing for the water system since July continued their schedule of working three hours a day, mostly on Thursday, but sometimes the day changed to Wednesday. When they started their work in July, they decided they needed a place to store their materials and equipment. They found lot 29 at the far end of the subdivision. It had a pad prepared for a 2,000 square foot home, so some excavation of the lot had already taken place. They stripped the lot of 90 percent of its trees and vegetation, stored their materials, and parked their equipment on the lot. Upon seeing the destruction of my trees, I cried, and then got angry. I was careful to include, in the settlement agreement, that the County would protect the trees. Knowing that the County had cut down many of my trees, I believed that the employees did not know the value of those trees. The workers had broken all the rules of the subdivision's drainage report by strip-grading lot 29. In the subdivision, the trees help prevent flooding. All landowners are required to replace every tree removed from their property during lot preparation with a like tree.

It seemed quiet in the subdivision, but I noticed surveyors and other people working. By November the utility company had come to install electricity to every lot and the roadwork began in January 2003. The trees started falling. Piles and piles of felled trees were laying all over the subdivision. Jerry made a video of the fallen trees, and Ruth and her husband took pictures. They were far from professional, but they filled the need for proof. I complained to the county engineer about the trespass and destruction. He said he would look into it.

As the County's work progressed, the felled trees began to turn brown, and I could picture in my mind a great fire. There was no water in the subdivision to put out a fire yet, so I called the county engineer in February and inquired as to when the trees would be removed from the subdivision. The answer I got caused the hair to rise on the back of my neck. The man with the foreign accent said, "Well, they are your roads."

After hearing that comment, I knew that my original thoughts were correct. It was the county's plan to enter the subdivision, do as little as possible to get past the judge's order, and leave the subdivision with a hell of a mess to clean up.

I explained that the roads had been deeded to the County several months before, and I asked him if he had read the settlement agreement. He said, "I've never seen it. I don't have any idea what is going on or what the agreement says." His accent threw me off, and I did not think I understood him correctly, so I asked again if he had a copy of the settlement agreement. He said quite slowly, "No, I have never seen it."

I faxed the agreement to him. His work had to be completed by March 1, 2003; it was already February, and he didn't know what the Board of Supervisors had agreed he would do. He sent men out to gather the trees and remove them from the subdivision. They took some and left some.

Giving just consideration to the attitudes of the county engineers, I began to take more pictures. I knew I had not given the County enough AB to complete the base of the roads. Unless the County took the AB that Toup had stored on the roadbeds and placed it where it really belonged, they would have to purchase more. There was plenty of AB to complete the job; it just had to be cut and then filled in where it was needed. There were large areas where the AB was 6 ft. deep.

When the dump trucks came with more AB, I began to get concerned. After the workmen went home, I snooped around. The newly acquired AB had been spread so thin that there were areas on that road that had no base cover.

I knew the new AB did not meet the required specifications. I could tell by its color where it came from, and in the past, that product had never been able to meet road specifications. I took pictures.

On February 15th, Billy Willy, Jr. advised me I could go to the assessor's office and explain how I wanted the parcels joined or split so that they made a workable situation. I asked my attorney if he wanted to go to the meeting. He filed a notice of appearance with the court, became my counsel again, and went to the meeting with me. The employee chosen to speak with us was working in the mapping department. He told us to get the land surveyed, get the divisions approved by zoning, get everything recorded and paid for, and then his department would issue parcel numbers. He explained we were to get it all done by March 1st, or the deal was off.

"Impossible. It will take two months just to get the survey," I said.

"Oh well," he replied.

I knew then that the county had no intentions of legalizing the parcels they promised to legalize in the settlement agreement. It was not their intention to spend any county money on surveyors. The problems with this noncompliance came up and caused much harm later.

Because of rain, the roads were not paved until mid-March, and the water system was still being worked on in July. The roadwork concerned me. To my astonishment, the pavers came in on March 22nd and laid paving on top of the roads. In areas, there was no base product and other areas still had 6 ft. of base product. I decided then that the homeowners needed to hire their own engineer to inspect and approve the road construction. The homeowner's association would be expected to take that mess the County called roads and maintain them. All I could see was big dollar signs.

The road work was certified as complete on March 27, 2003 by the county engineer. Four days later, I was having coffee with my realtor, Ruth Dotson. She said, "When are they going to get the roads finished?"

"Ruth, they are finished. The paving crew said they were finished. The county engineer certified them, and the engineer they have inspecting the water system has come to the house to tell me they will be finished in five days," I explained.

"You're kidding, right?" she said.

"No. The county attorney said they have done everything they agreed to do and that the work is substantially complete. He has received papers from the ADEQ that gives the homeowners the ADEQ's approval to operate the water system. The approval states it covers all 73 lots. He said the engineer hired by the County has certified the systems' completion, and even though they have never been out here, the ADEQ is satisfied with the work. I don't know how Billy Willy, Jr. knows the work is inspected by the ADEQ, but that is what he says," I said.

"What do you think?" she asked.

"I think people are going to die."

"What? Why do you think that?" she asked.

"Well, I guess the best way to explain my beliefs would be to show you the problems I see. Are you game? We can take a short ride in your car or mine, and I will show you what I see," I said.

As my realtor, she was anxious to get everything finished and get the water system going. There is no market for lots in a subdivision without water facilities. She was receiving three to five calls a day from prospective buyers asking when the County would be finished with their work. She needed some answers.

As we left my front drive, Ruth asked, "Are they going to clean up the mess they made on the fronts of these four lots? I mean look! They bladed out the fronts of these lots, and they left all the dead trees and rubbish laying right there. How are they gonna stop the water coming off Coral Bay from flooding these four lots? Whew! What a mess! And lot 29, are they gonna replace all those trees that they stripped off that lot?" She was talking so fast, I could hardly get a word in edgewise.

"I don't know, Ruth. Everything's certified. Let's drive over to lot 184. I have a few things to show you."

Written on the paved road at the corner of lot 184 was an engineer's marking. Within three feet of that mark, there was a 4 ft. long crack in the pavement. Coming off the main crack, were many small cracks that looked like spider webs. The new pavement on the entire corner of the road looked rough and appeared to be separating.

"I asked the engineer with the accent when the paving crew would be back out to complete their work," I explained. "He informed me they were finished and their work had been certified."

"You are kidding, aren't you?" she inquired again. "What engineer in his right mind would approve the completion of his work, knowing the clean up and repairs had not been done and the roads are falling apart? He can't certify a mess like this as being complete, can he?"

"He did," I said. "Come on and I'll show you the rest of the mess. Get your camera out. Do you have film?"

"I brought my digital camera. Bobby will be here soon, and we can take all the pictures you need."

"Great. Go over to that water system that they say the state approved. I want to show you a real professional installation. The electrical connections for the east well are installed under the main water lines for the well, and the two connections are rubbing together. They stuck that old board in between the two lines to separate them from each other."

"Oh my God! What's gonna happen when that old rotted board gives up and falls apart?" she asked.

"Well, I guess everyone connected to the system will have hot water in their toilets if the electric hits the water lines," I replied. "When the homeowners association refused to accept the deed to this system, until its problems were corrected, the County stopped allowing private wells out here again. People are desperate for water. They will turn on that "approved" system and people will die."

We reached the well site and Ruth started laughing. "Hey look, Patti. That pipe needed support and they tied an old rotten board to it with bailing wire. Do you think that will hold? I wish Bobby were here. We have to take a picture of that. Do you think those small boulders, old wood, and bailing wire will keep that distribution line from falling over? I don't believe an engineer certified this work. My grandson could have done a better job."

"Kinda depressing, isn't it," I asked.

After a short time, Bobby (Ruth's husband) drove up. He had on his cowboy hat, he had his lap top computer, and he was ready to work. He took pictures of the well sites, the garbage, the dead trees, and the cracked paving. He said, "These roads look as if a five-year-old child could have done a better job with his Tonka™ toys. I can't believe they are certified by a licensed engineer."

"That's what they told me. I think the thing that scares me the most is that the County has proved by constructing this mess and calling it certified, that they don't give a damn about the lives and safety of the taxpayers. Someone up there in control is a vindictive sadist. These roads are already falling apart. The water system is a hazardous joke. There are no street signs, no fire protection, and I know that these lots are going to flood. Just get as many pictures of the bad things as you can. I'm gonna need them," I said. There could be no guarantee on the work performed because none of the work was done by licensed contractors.

"What are you going to do?" Ruth asked.

"Get the judge out here if I can," I replied.

Bobby was having a field day. He loved to take pictures, and he loved to use his laptop. The need for pictures was unending.

When we got back to my home after our picture-taking trip, Bobby sat down at the table and did his work. He had seen many flaws in the road construction that I had never noticed. The cleanup of the mess made to the lots I owned and the replacement of the destroyed trees and vegetation was going to cost a lot of money. Bobby made me a computer disc that had all his pictures on it. He knew which pictures to take. As I looked at them, I cried.

After Bobby and Ruth left, I began to feel the stress. The County had destroyed the fronts of many lots and I didn't want to face the landowners. "Write it down," I thought.

I did not have an attorney on file with the court, so on March 28th, I immediately filed, pro se, a request to the court, seeking a motion to Compel Completion of the Settlement Agreement and for sanctions and relief. I knew how many years it had taken me to get this far, and one day wasted would be one day too many. I also asked the court to come to the subdivision and view the completed project.

Billy Willy, Jr., responded to my Motion to Compel on April 8, 2003, arguing that the work was certified as complete and that an on-site inspection by the court was not necessary. He submitted certified statements from the engineers working for the County that were intended to be used to influence the court's decision that stated the work was "substantially" complete.

The first thing I did was to report to the board of the homeowners association all the troubles I was seeing with the roads, the water company, the land separations, and the refusal of the County to compensate me adequately for my property. They had used over $9,000 of my materials and nine acres of my property. In the very least, they could have given me the proper documents proving the donations. About a week earlier, on April 2nd, the homeowner's board had voted to spend homeowner's dues to hire independent engineers to advise them as to the adequacy and safety of the water company and the construction of the roads.

The chairman of the association and I went seeking an engineer. We were turned away at most of the offices because no one wanted to be in the position of having to disagree with the Mohave County engineers. One engineer in Lake Havasu City agreed to inspect the project. We did not need to get him a set of plans because he believed he had a set the County had given him to bid the project several months before. We were to meet with him next Friday.

When we went to Lake Havasu City, we learned that the engineer had been asking questions of the County. The county deputy engineer in charge of the project, the one with the accent, had informed him, that if he worked for us, he would not be able to work for the County in the future.

Any work for the County would be a conflict of interest. The threat was ignored. The engineer chose to inspect the project for us. We paid him his required retainer, and we left knowing our mission would be accomplished.

The Lake Havasu City engineer contacted the Arizona State Board of Engineers and was given the name of an engineer who was considered an expert in asphalt construction. He called the asphalt expert, and they met at the subdivision April 17, 2003. After an hour or two of inspecting, both engineers came to my home.

"Well Patti," the Lake Havasu City Engineer said. "You people have some real problems out here. All either of us can tell you right now is the road construction we inspected will not last a year. What we viewed is extremely hard to believe. Any engineer who certified this work should lose his license. He is a disgrace to the profession. The homeowners should not accept either the roads for maintenance or the water system for operation. We will issue preliminary reports of our findings, but both construction projects appear to be a joke. It would be impossible to maintain these roads."

Listening to my argument for and the county attorney's argument against the need for an on-site inspection by the court, in May, the court denied my request for an on-site review. I needed my mouthpiece if my concerns were to be heard by this judge.

My attorney had collected several lots in the subdivision through attorney fees he earned from me, and his family's trust had purchased three lots, for the price of taxes owed. He did not really want me facing the court alone and screwing things up, if he could justify financially helping me out. He explained his financial position to me and let me know, in no uncertain terms, that his future work would be billed by the hour and that I would have to pay all the costs involved in the new litigation as they came in. He prepared a conflict of interest waiver. I took it to another attorney for approval. The second attorney said, "Go on and sign it. You can fire him anytime you want to."

I agreed to pay him his hourly rate as I sold property, and I suggested he could file an attorney's charging lien on all my property. I paid him a large portion of the sales I accomplished. Without an adequate water supply, the lots in the subdivision were not selling. The surrounding acreage that I managed to sell was picking up some of the slack.

The judge ordered a status conference be held in May so he could review my complaints and the county attorney's explanations to those complaints. My attorney explained my concerns once again. He informed the court that I had hired engineers to review the work and that nothing the County did was acceptable. Billy Willy, Jr. argued again that county engineers certified the work and that their certifications could not be questioned. After that conference, the judge decided that perhaps I was correct and a site review by the court was in order. A date of August 22nd was set for an on-site review. It was agreed that the only people present during the review would be one engineer from each side, the plaintiff and her attorney, the defendant and his attorney, the judge, and a clerk of the judge.

On August 22nd, we went to the courthouse to escort the judge to the site. In one car, my attorney, our Lake Havasu City engineer, and I headed the procession. We were followed to the subdivision by the judge riding in a pick-up truck with his clerk, Attorney Whiner, acting as attorney for the County in his car, and a deputy county engineer in his own vehicle.

Billy Willy, Jr. explained he could not attend the review. He had to meet in Colorado City to discuss the polygamist problems that had recently surfaced there. He had ignored the polygamy problems for the entire thirty years he sat as county attorney. He had entered into this contract with me and now he was too busy looking into a thirty-year-old problem to review the mess the County made of the subdivision. Something didn't compute.

As we approached the subdivision, we found a long line of white pick-up trucks and men standing around waiting. It appeared each truck could only carry one man, and I said to my attorney, "Looks like a lynching."

The County had sent everyone involved in the construction from the smallest laborer to the asphalt supplier to speak his or her piece. The judge was not impressed, and he said so. He reminded the crowd that this was not his plan, but since all the extra people were sent by the County, and being paid taxpayer's dollars for their time, he swore everyone in.

About two days before the court's visit to the site, it had rained. The rains had been steady for a couple of days, but they were not harsh. Harsh rains, known to the area, arrive within an hour and exceed one inch. These rains totaled less than one-third inch accumulated over two full days. The roads were covered with runoff of dirt and debris, and the cracks in the roads had doubled in size. I knew we had a mess to clean up, but the judge would have a good look at the problems first.

The sight was filthy and unsightly. I could imagine Toup standing in the background laughing at all the incompetence. My mind recalled the day when he stood before the Board of Supervisors and said the County was not capable of completing his project, and if the homeowners persisted in their actions against him, they would be shooting themselves in the foot.

As we began our review of the problems, the Lake Havasu City engineer explained to the judge the drainage problems, the shoulder problems, the apron problems, and the roadbed height problems. The County got out a tape measure, and they were busy explaining why things were the way they appeared, including an excuse for each item. The clouds moved in quickly, and it began to rain. It was a quiet rain and tolerable, but it caused concern that we might not get through the inspection as we had planned.

The deputy county engineer, the one with the accent, had an excuse for everything. He talked so much that no one else had much of a chance to speak. He explained to the court that he had changed the design of the original engineer, and his design was much better. All the while, the judge was looking at mud running down the street, water flowing into electric transformers, flooded lots, and piles of debris stacked everywhere. He could see one lot had been strip bladed, two partially bladed with piles of dirt and sand stored on them, and a construction mess. I had placed small white flags in the locations of every fallen tree that had stood ten feet or more past my property lines.

The judge asked about my concerns. I began to explain that the piles of rock and debris left lying on the living trees would cause the death of the trees if the mess wasn't removed. I told the judge that the flags I had placed would show him how far onto my private property the County had gone to remove my trees.

At that point, the man who had installed the water system, working every Thursday for three hours, stated that the mess was there when he got to the job. He was lying. I had before and after pictures. He was under oath. He blamed the utility company for the mess. I responded, "The contract the County has with the utility company says the County will be responsible for the landscaping, grading, and cleanup."

The judge told me with much authority, "Mrs. Lewis, I will take your testimony in court." I knew to keep my mouth shut.

The Lake Havasu City engineer pointed out all the flooding and drainage problems created by the County's failure to follow the approved plans.

When we reached the cul-de-sac where my home is and where the road (Coral Bay) was constructed in a "V" design, the judge looked down to the bottom of the hill below the road. He asked who owned the lots at the bottom of the hill. I explained that I did, and the deputy county attorney immediately told the judge, "Mrs. Lewis re-designed this road to prevent flooding of her home." The judge gave no sign of response.

I said, "I didn't design anything, nor was I consulted."

After giving me a shut-up-unless-I-ask look, the judge asked me what the lot numbers of the lots at the bottom of the hill were, and I gave them to him. He wrote them down. The small rains we were standing in were passing water from the road onto those lots. While ducking his head to avoid being hit in the face with raindrops, the judge asked, "Mrs. Lewis is there anything else I need to see?"

"I have just one more thing, Your Honor. If you would like to come in your truck, I'll just point it out to you," I replied.

"That will be fine."

I took off walking down the road to the intruded lots. The judge and his clerk came in the black pickup truck, and I stood next to my property marker with my hand on the survey stick. The destruction and trespass to those four lots exceeded 30 feet. The truck turned around, and the judge left the subdivision.

Five days later, August 27th, it rained again. The weather department said it rained one-half inch in four hours. I printed out the weather reports as they showed up on the Internet. The flowing water scattered mud and rocks all over the paved roads. The water moved all over the subdivision trying to find an exit. The dedicated wash areas were all blocked by the high pavement, and 22 of the lots suffered devastating flood damage.

The president of the homeowner's association asked me if I would get the roads cleared of the debris as quickly as I could. I agreed to clean them up, but before doing that, Ruth, Bobby, and I took pictures. We made a video of the mess, and Bobby made digital pictures. The land was so badly washed away that many of the lots had a 4 ft. drop-off before the land began to level out. My garage was full of water. All those things I had planned to give away or throw away someday were finally thrown away.

The roads were dangerous, but they were still owned by the County. I wondered if we should be messing with them, but the County had made no move to clean them up to prevent a tragedy, so on the weekend, Jerry took my heavy equipment, and he and his helper cleaned the streets.

The engineer we had hired explained that the roads had been built three to 6 ft. higher than the approved plans, the drainage plans had been ignored, and no new plans were made. If we could convince the court of the needed alterations, I might survive the financial loss that was apparent before me. Nine of my lots received damaging floodwaters. The road crossing the main wash collapsed.

The history of the monsoon seasons in the area showed rainfall much more severe than any rain that had fallen since the roads were paved. Way back in September 1997, when Toup got angry, raised the roads, and caused the flooding of my house, the rainstorm had dropped 1.3 inches of rain in one hour.

In January 2004 Billy Willy, Jr. resigned his position, and we went to the judge's courtroom in Parker, Arizona. Billy Willy, Jr. wanted to introduce a new attorney who would be handling the rest of the case. The judge said hello to the new man and laid the groundwork for the trial. The little social trip cost me another $1500 in attorney fees. The status conference could have been handled by telephone, but Billy Willy, Jr. insisted we go to the court in person.

Much to my surprise, at that hearing the judge informed us that he would be handling the remainder of the case as a breach of contract. He suggested that the attorneys get together and settle the matter, as it should not be tried. He asked my attorney for a brief review of the damages I was claiming, added up all the items he was given, and suggested that the County might start negotiations at a figure of about $890,000.

I almost choked. I did not want the taxpayer's money. I wanted my subdivision completed. I wanted everyone to have a potable water supply, paved roads, fire protection, and no flooding. To accomplish this, the County was going to have to spend a lot of money. The Good 'ol Boys were not willing to admit there were problems. In their view, no more work would be done without a court order. The trial was set for May 11th.

Trial preparation began that next day. The period before the trial—the discovery period—allows both sides to ask for evidence and information they need from each other. The asphalt engineer that was hired by the homeowners was given all the road construction data from the County as required by my attorney, along with the contract between the asphalt company and the County.

The Lake Havasu City Engineer made an inspection of the water system. The County had not turned over to him any keys to the system, so his investigation was very limited, but his report was as thorough as he could make it. Making sure the water system was safe and that it was able to produce clean potable water was more important to me than any other complaint I had made. I could tell by the reports that the ADEQ had not inspected that water system, and the county was in no hurry to turn over the system keys to our engineer.

I put my paralegal training into gear and made a list of the rest of the public information I felt we needed for our case. I requested all employment (work) logs made by the County. I contacted the ADEQ and asked for the entire file on the water system, and I sent them a check for the copies requested. I asked for all records of communications between the County and the State concerning private wells in the subdivision made since the date of the settlement agreement. I asked for all as-built plans prepared of the completed projects.

The County asked me to supply them with every communication I had with anyone concerning the subdivision. They wanted to know how many lots I owned, how much money I had spent, and where I got it.

The information the County was supplying as evidence was information obtained from public records that went back as far as 1989. The designs for the roads were approved in 1990, and the water system designs had been voided and destroyed by the ADEQ in 1992 because by that time, they did not meet the construction regulations required by the State.

We scanned the documents into the attorney's computer, and he added a search engine to his programs so we could find things quickly. I bought him a laptop computer and a projector, in exchange for some legal fees, so we could show everything we were exhibiting to the court and the witnesses at the same time.

One of our engineers was so angry; he suggested I file an inquiry (request for review of job performance) with the Arizona Board of Technical Review (BTR). He thought they might tell us what needed to be done to repair the mess, but in any case the board had the right to know the type of work being certified by their engineers. Their investigation report could save me more engineering costs. I filed the inquiry in September.

The attorney for the County filed for an emergency injunction with the court, seeking an order to have my inquiry withdrawn. The judge gave them an immediate hearing. My attorney called me and said I had 30 minutes to get to his office. When I got there and listened to the County's complaint, I laughed. Here are all these Good 'ol Boys asking the judge for an order of protection from me.

The judge refused their plea. He said it was my right to seek assistance from any federal, state, county, or local agency at my disposal, and that there was no way he was going to violate my rights.

The investigative committee for the BTR talked to me and looked at all the pictures. I swear some were laughing when they looked at the picture of the collapsing road. They sent me a letter stating their recommendation to the board that a letter of concern should be filed. Their recommendation was ignored, and the board dismissed the inquiry. When I got the news that the engineer's board accepted the work as certifiable, I decided never to care about the importance of an engineer having an Arizona license. The license and certification stamps indicate only that the engineer has paid his dues to the State. It does nothing to guarantee the quality of the work.

If I proved breach of contract in court, the laws not only allow damages but also punitive damages. To me, the breach of contract was obvious. There was no way they would admit to me that they had screwed up and were willing to fix the problems. Instead of admitting there were problems and suggesting fixes for them that I could accept, the County paved the way for a court trial.

The judge allowed only four days for the hearing. People were rushed through like hogs in a slaughterhouse. Most of the evidence and professional testimony came from the prosecution, but the County made a deal with my attorney and many witnesses were swapped around, supposedly to expedite the trial proceedings. At times, the public listening to the trial couldn't tell if the witness was for the plaintiff or for the defendant. Many of the County's witnesses were hesitant to respond to either attorney's questions. The County's retired engineering boss was walking back and forth in the back of the courtroom. Criminal prosecutor Deputy Attorney Nogut appeared in the courtroom and sat in the back row. The engineer who spoke with an accent finally told the truth. His instructions were to provide low budget construction—no cuts, no fills. (Meaning, if the road was too high, leave it there, if too low, leave it there. Don't worry about flooding; we are not following the approved drainage plans anyway.)

The water engineer testified the system could not provide water to all 73 lots. He explained that there was enough pressure for each lot to receive water and every lot had a water connection, but another well, perhaps two with a holding tank, would be necessary to service all the lots in the subdivision.

My attorney asked the engineer, "Do you know the term "Super Bowl Flush"?"

"Yes Sir. That is when everyone on the system is trying to use the water at the same time."

"If the system should receive a Super Bowl Flush, would all lots receive the water they need?"

"No Sir," he replied.

After the trial, my attorney learned that the as-built plans for the water system—submitted to the ADEQ—and the plans submitted to us by the County for use in the trial were different. The final as-built plans were given to us by the engineer that Mohave County had hired to oversee the systems' construction after the trial. Those plans showed the ownership of the water system as being the Lake Juniper Homeowner's Association, when, in fact, Mohave County owns the system.

I felt that in the future those falsified plans could jump up and bite the homeowners in the butt, so I asked my attorney to submit the plans to the court for review. I felt that because the plans were forged, the judge would look at them. I was wrong.

The judge submitted his order, showing only findings of facts, in September 2004:

IN THE SUPERIOR COURT OF THE STATE OF ARIZONA IN AND FOR THE

COUNTY OF MOHAVE

HONORABLE (Judge's name)　　　La Paz County Case　　　No. SA-2000026

JUDGE OF THE SUPERIOR COURT

DATE: SEPTEMBER 23,2004

PATRICIA L. LEWIS, a single female　　　I CASE NO. SA-20000026

Plaintiff,　　　ORDER

vs.

MOHAVE COUNTY, a body politic and corporate of the State of Arizona, John Does
I-X; Jane Does I-X; ABC corporations; and XYZ partnerships,

Defendants.

On October 7, 2002, the parties entered into a settlement agreement. According to the
agreement, Mohave County was to do the following:

1. Pave the roads in the Lake Juniper Subdivision. The roads were to be constructed
in substantial conformance to the approved Lake Juniper Estates Approved Plan. During
construction of the roads, Mohave County was to make every effort to preserve the
existing trees. Mohave County was also to make alterations to the elevations of Coral
Bay Drive adjacent to the plaintiff's property to prevent the recurrence of flooding.

2. Arrange for providing electric and telephone service to all lot lines at no cost to the
property owners.

3. Complete the installation of a functional water delivery system to service all lots in
the subdivision, utilizing the existing wells as practicable. The system will be inspected
by the Arizona Department of Environmental Quality.

4. Obtain opinions from the Hualapai Fire District and the State and County fire
zoning authorities indicating that neither fire hydrants nor any special fire infrastructure is

required for the subdivision. The County was to utilize every effort to see that there will be a tank suitable for fire protection no further distance from the Subdivision than Marc Neal's tank.

5. Provide the plaintiff with written fair appraised value and all information necessary to assist her in receiving tax benefits from her donations.

A hearing was held on the matter during which both sides presented evidence and testimony. Based on the evidence and testimony presented at the hearing, the Court makes the following findings:

A. ROADS

Mohave County has breached, to some extent, the settlement agreement concerning its obligation regarding the roads. Based on the testimony, the Court finds as follows:

There was much testimony concerning the elevation, which was the correct benchmark, and whether or not the original survey was correct. Whatever the correct benchmark was, the roads were put in by the original developer. It was he who made the road changes from the approved plans which included raising them significantly from the original plans. The roads were almost 100 percent complete and the aggregate base was almost 75 percent complete when Mohave County began work on the roads. The cracking and erosion of the roads was caused by the lack of aggregate base and compaction in some places, improper drainage, and lack of a fog or chip seal. The major problem area was on Anchor Drive, and specifically on the edges of the road. In addition to the lack of aggregate base and compaction on the edges of the roads, a greater thickness of asphalt on the edges was also needed.

In order to rectify the road situation, one of two things could be done. The first would be to reconstruct the roads at the original plan elevation. That option, however, is not the best one. The better plan would be to redo the road edges where needed with more aggregate base, better compaction, better drainage, thicker asphalt on the edges, and put on a fog or chip seal.

The alterations and re-paving of Coral Bay by Mohave County did not alleviate the flooding of the plaintiff's property. Plaintiff's lots 146-149 are still subjected to flooding after the new design of Coral Bay.

Additionally, Mohave County has not put in the required monuments and street signs.

B. TREES AND VEGETATION

Mohave County did not breach the settlement agreement by removing and not replacing trees and vegetation. The trees were already down when Mohave County began work on the subdivision. Whatever vegetation was removed by Mohave County was minimal and necessary for the completion of its work.

C. UNDERGROUND UTILITIES

Mohave County has breached the settlement agreement by not adequately cleaning up the areas around the utility installations. Proper clean up is implied in the settlement agreement regarding the installation of utilities and water meters.

D. FIRE PROTECTION

Mohave County has breached the settlement agreement concerning fire protection. The agreement required Mohave County to "Utilize every effort to see that there will be a [water] tank suitable for fire protection no further distance from the Subdivision than Marc Neal's tank." Mohave County has not provided the required water tank suitable for fire protection.

E. WATER DELIVERY SYSTEM

As a preliminary matter, the Court denies the plaintiff's Motion To Supplement the Record, and the Court will only consider evidence and testimony presented at the hearing that was subject to cross-examination. Mohave County has not breached the settlement agreement concerning the water delivery system. The settlement agreement calls for Mohave County to complete the installation of a functional water delivery system to service all lots. There is a water delivery system in operation that services all lots. Although the water delivery system may not adequately respond to a simultaneous extreme multi-use by all seventy-three lots, it is functional in accordance with the settlement agreement.

F. DONATIONS

Mohave County has breached the settlement agreement by not providing the plaintiff with written fair appraised value of her donations and all information necessary to assist her in receiving tax benefits from her donations.

G. RELIEF

The Court makes no rulings at this time concerning the proper relief to be granted to the plaintiff. The Court proposes an informal settlement conference to discuss all the options with the hope of reaching an agreement.

IT IS ORDERED setting this matter for a telephonic status hearing on Tuesday, September 28th, at 10:00 a.m. to discuss the conference and select a date.

DATED this 23rd day of September 2004.

After reading the court's order, I realized that if I appealed on the water system issue, the judge had it in his power to deny me any relief other than my attorney's fees. The way the judge wrote his order left me in a bad situation.

I knew we had proved at trial that the water system did not meet the any laws or regulations mandated by the state. According to the settlement agreement, "all improvements constructed will comply with federal, state and local laws, regulations and ordinances as applicable to the subdivision." The construction of the system was so poor that it had become the joke in the community. Just to look at the set up caused one to laugh. No one would be stupid enough to try to operate such a mess. The engineer in charge of the construction of the system admitted at trial that the system did not comply with the laws and regulations of the state.

If I appealed before the relief was granted, the judge could get angry and award me one dollar as a form of relief. I would still be looking at more legal expenses, and there was a good chance I would not recover any of the costs I had incurred. By allowing the judge's findings regarding the water system to go unchallenged, my community would suffer. There would be no water system capable of servicing the lots, and my conscience would be hard to live with.

I had sued "the body politic", and because there was ongoing litigation, I had no civil rights. Anything I needed to do that involved permits, licenses, or information to be obtained from the county had to go through the county attorney's office. The paperwork was not to be forthcoming. According to previous case law, the judge could drag the case out another ten years. No matter what avenue I took, the judge's order left my community and me to be victims condemned.

When we appeared at the conference the judge ordered on September 28th, he allowed us 30 minutes. The attorney for the County talked and jumped around in his chair for 25 of those minutes. He explained what the county could do to correct the breach. He explained that no plans had been made, and that the county felt no matter what they did, it would not be enough to satisfy me.

The judge was about to send us on our way when I spoke up and said I wanted to say something. What the hell. The judge said the conference was to be informal. Rather than wearing a dress, I wore a pantsuit. I wanted to stress "informal."

After getting permission from my attorney allowing me to speak, I asked the judge where the inspection report from the ADEQ was. Explaining that the evidence showed there had been no inspection by ADEQ, I wanted to know if the judge had seen one.

He asked my attorney if what I had said about the evidence was correct. My attorney assured him it was and explained the name of the exhibit. The exhibit was an Approval to Operate document written by the ADEQ. Included in the document was the statement made by the ADEQ that said in no way was it to be construed that the water system had been inspected by the ADEQ. It also included a state disclaimer on the system's entire distribution system.

The judge said he would review the evidence and if the ADEQ had not inspected the water system, he might need to order that inspection. I was still convinced that if the water system was put into operation as it was built, people were going to die. The utility sites are unsafe, the construction is unsafe, and the entire system is rusted and filthy.

In October 2004, I donated to the Fire Department $38,500 worth of land adjoining the subdivision. I was hoping that the County would work with them to provide proper fire protection to my community. I received the appraisal and the tax papers from the Fire Department, and the fire chief began plans for a new station. As written earlier, the County breached their contract by not legalizing my parcels. They failed to do the proper survey in a timely manner, which cost the community. The fire chief applied for a Community Development Block Grant, issued through the county, to help in the construction of a new fire station planned for the land I donated. An initial grant of $90,000 was approved by the county employees. That figure was later reduced to $58,588. The County sent the chief a letter dated May 24, 2004, stating that they were withdrawing the grant because the property I donated did not "meet all legal requirements, a split or rezone of the property had not been made, a written appraisal had not been submitted and they had to wait for the Court to issue the final decision relative to the legal pending case." The date of the letter was 13 months after the completion date of the settlement agreement.

It is frustrating to devote my time, money, and labors to a County that stabs me in the back every time I try to help my community.

A status conference was called by the judge in January 2005. When my attorney asked the judge about the ADEQ inspection, the County's attorney explained to the judge that the judge had already written his order and that the order could not be changed. There was no way that attorney wanted the ADEQ inspecting the water system.

I read in case law that if a judge has not made a decision (including relief for the prevailing party), he has the power to change his views and orders if the interest in justice would be served. The judge withheld that relief.

My attorney cited the court rule that stated a decision includes relief for the prevailing party and attorney fees. He explained that since the judge's findings did not order relief for the plaintiff, my attorney failed to understand that the findings were the completed order.

The County's attorney said the judge's order was signed and it was the only order we were going to get.

The judge told my attorney that what we received was his order, but he intended to get things settled before he considered relief. The judge also said there needed to be an inspection of the water system by the ADEQ.

On May 28, 2005, the county attorney assigned to this case filed a Notice of Compliance. That motion stated that the County had complied with the court's order. My attorney quickly filed a Motion to Strike the County's Notice of Compliance. The County had not laid a shovel in our subdivision to repair the damages they caused or finish the job as the court ordered. No fire protection had been provided. No roadwork had even started. I had not been compensated for my roads and utility sites. My properties were still flooding and the roads were full of rocks, sand, and debris.

Another status conference was scheduled for August 2, to review the lawyer's communications to the judge.

On July 28th, lightening struck the mountain near my home and started a fire, which came within a half-block of my property. Helicopters and airplanes managed to contain the fire and no structures were damaged. Seeing that fire so close to my house and knowing there could have been water to help extinguish the fire if the Good 'ol Boys had done what the court ordered, left me wondering if the battle I was waging for my safety would ever end. I was kept away from my house and my animals were still inside the house. My neighbor was home and she promised to collect my animals if the fire got any closer. That was a relief, but I was still scared. In my mind, the County had shown me how willing they were to abandon my community's and my legal rights to basic safety. It is time for a change. We don't need government workers who "could not care less."

In July, my attorney relocated to Safford, Arizona, and he and the county attorney attended the status conference held on August 2nd via telephone. I decided to attend in person. I took along my pictures of the fire, two friends, and my grandson. I had decided that from now on, whenever the judge speaks, I will be looking him in the eye. Before the conference started, the judge suggested that I move up closer to the telephone, so I could hear everything. I moved to the plaintiff's table.

The County's attorney explained to the judge that the Notice of Compliance was submitted to let the court know that the Board of Supervisors had approved the expenditure and intended to complete the required work. This attorney talks a lot but says little. After listening to him repeat his tale and explaining to the court that all I wanted was a new trial because I was unhappy with the judge's previous order, the judge moved to my attorney for comment.

My attorney said he would accept the filing of the Notice of Compliance, if the records showed that the notice was only a status notice and that the record showed not one shovel had gone down. He told the judge that I was losing sale opportunities of my land because all of the buyers want to know when the subdivision will be completed properly. The water system is a major problem because it has not been inspected by the ADEQ. He described the fire and explained that I was in the courtroom with pictures in hand. He told the judge he did not know if he had covered all my concerns and asked the judge to allow me to speak if I had anything to add.

The County's attorney told the court they would be able to tell the judge when that first shovel was coming down within four weeks. He said that the notice for bids for the project would be posted August 3rd (the next day). It seemed quite a coincidence that everything was being posted one day after this conference. Why hadn't they been posted and an acceptable contractor hired months before? The engineer's report had been submitted to the County in March and had even been revised once.

The judge explained that he didn't think I was as worried about when the first shovel went down, as I was when the last shovel went down. He asked if I had anything to add, and I explained the need for a decision and a timeframe for completion. I explained that my attorney and I had inquired of the ADEQ and that the ADEQ had not been asked to inspect the water system. I explained to him that people didn't want to purchase my land until they knew when the work would be finished. I asked him if he wanted the pictures I was holding.

The judge reminded the county attorney that he had ordered the ADEQ inspection. He said he wanted the pictures and that I should approach the bench and give them to him.

I did, and the hearing was adjourned.

On August 11, a monsoon storm hit the subdivision. The roads in the subdivision again suffered extensive damage and many lots were flooded. My home and garage were flooded. My grandchildren and I were mopping up the mess and one child said to me, "Granny, how much more of all this crap can you take?"

"As long as I have you kids to help me clean up these messes, I'll be fine," I answered.

In reading the case laws, I found court situations such as these could take ten years or more. The Constitution of Arizona has a provision that says a decision shall be received in no more than 60 days after a trial. Well…

I promised Mike Mazur I would see the land fraud through to the end, and I will keep that promise. If it takes the rest of my life, I will seek justice. I wonder how long my sentence will be, waiting while this judge "sits on it."

I have suffered at the hands of drug addicts and thieves. I have lost my husband who was my best friend and lover, and I lost two good friends. I have lost my foreman. I have lost my neighbor and watched his wife suffer. My home and lands have been flooded. My body has been put through hell. I will wait for justice.

If there is ever to be justice for all, it cannot be born in a society that is run by vultures without conscience. All around us, in all communities large and small, we are observing a process of the gradual degradation of humanity. Everything is measured in dollars, including the price of crime. Criminals are plea-bargained back onto the streets where nothing will change for the better. The biggest thieves of all may be those who bargain with elected officials in an effort to use public service for their own design. Seldom are these criminals ever brought to the courts to face the justice system, yet it is this same group of people who have left the longest trail of human carnage behind them.

APPENDIX

One of the candidates running for supervisor in the 2000 election was a representative of MCEDA. When I announced, in March 2000, that I was running against him, no other candidate had surfaced. A "Good 'ol Boy" decided he would enter the race about a month later. Many people had had their fill of the Good 'ol Boy system and many were learning to hate MCEDA. I was completely unknown, but I hoped that if I kept my name in the hat, with three people running, my candidacy would stop the election of MCEDA. To me, the people involved with MCEDA appeared to be self-serving and corrupt. They didn't seem to care anything about the future of Mohave County. My children would suffer the consequences of their acts. My children and their children would become victims of this corrupt group.

My motto: "Help me Clean up Mohave County," was popular with many people, but I cannot say any of those people were running the politics of the county at that time. When the voting machine counters broke down and the votes were hand counted by the Good 'ol Boys, it was nice to learn that the MCEDA candidate would not be sitting in an executive chair. The election was won by the "Good 'ol Boys." The MCEDA representative left town, and I had a lot to add to my book.

While on the campaign trail for six months, I met many wonderful people. I began to see that there were a few bad apples in the barrel, and they were spoiling the whole bunch. Many of the eligible voters did not bother to register to vote. They said the elections were so corrupt that voting was a waste of time. Considering the state of the political structure, who was I to say they were wrong? To me it was obvious that the Good 'ol Boys resented my appearance as a candidate. During my campaign, I listened to the true investors of Mohave County: the common citizens. I learned that many of the people had suffered at the hands of Mohave County's power structure. Many were being hurt financially. Many were concerned for their safety. None of the people I visited knew what I was going through myself.

When questioning the staff of the County, they referred me to the same handful of people every time. Some worked for the County, some did not, but the staff placed all the blame of the mismanagement of the County on the same small handful of people.

The problems I had experienced with Toup paled to some of problems people in the community were facing. I realized that one person alone could not combat the corruption.

In addition, without much effort, I uncovered excessive amounts expended on contracts that were breached, unfulfilled, or poorly executed totaling over $11,150,000. In some instances, it could be called de-facto embezzlement.

My God Box was full of lists. My computer was full of information I had received, and I began to feel better about my determination to expose the corruption and lies in my county.

In the six months of my campaign in 2000, I learned too much. I quickly learned that I had bitten off more than I wanted to chew. Trying to work daily in the midst of such corruption was not what I wanted to do with my life.

The old adage "power corrupts and absolute power corrupts absolutely" should become the motto for Mohave County.

Here are some of the tales I was told:

Who will move my garbage at a reasonable price?

In 1993 the *Mohave Daily Miner* reported a man missing. A local man bought a neat garbage collection truck. He entered into contracts with many people in the county to pick up their garbage. He took advance service deposits from potential customers that totaled some $10,000, giving the promise that the people's garbage bill would be much less expensive. No one had an exclusive contract for trash collection in the area he solicited. The man and his truck disappeared with the people's money. Waste Management then acquired a long-term contract with the County, and no one ever found out what happened to the man.

My questions to the county attorney regarding that event were, "Where would a man go with just $10,000? Was he the criminal in this case or was he a victim condemned? If the sheriff refuses to search for the man who is supposedly a criminal, how will the victims get their money back?" I got no response. "Did you issue a warrant for him?" I asked.

I don't recall," he answered. "It has been a long time."

Do we have to have MCEDA?

From April 3, 1995 to October 10, 1996, Mohave County paid out $1,299,804 to the MCEDA and their bogus ventures.

In reviewing the individual accounts, I found checks written for infrastructure, Yucca road improvement, and the Yucca Truck Stop. I don't know how many taxpayers were made aware of what was going on, but there is no truck stop in Yucca, Arizona! In reviewing the cancelled checks, I happened to see for the year 1995, that a check for $91,846.08 was written to a convicted counterfeiter for heavy equipment use, corporation fees, reimbursement, and equipment rental. I wonder what the other checks looked like.

In 1995—or earlier—MCEDA invited a steel plant to come to Mohave County. The plant would eventually employ hundreds of residents of the community.

The plant began operations, over the protests of every environmentalist in the area. In reports made by the owners, the plant could not pay the high prices for electricity or purchase the equipment the State was requiring to prevent the environmental hazards their plant was emitting.

Untrue statements regarding the pollution emissions of the steel company were submitted to the ADEQ and the Mohave County Board of Supervisors when the plant was in the planning stages and when it was constructed. The company's need for the special major pollution permitting and inspections, required by the State of all companies with excessive pollution problems, was avoided for a few years. The ADEQ had accepted, without question, the company's original report qualifying its own emissions. That activity seemed strange because the corporation was known for its high pollution activities in other states.

"Hey. It is a good deal for the hospital," Kathy explained, "Every respirator the hospital owns is in use. They have to get more. Every bed is full and they are sleepin' in the halls."

After two years of operation with high pollution ratings, the ADEQ declared the company did not qualify as a minimum polluter, as stated in the company's reports. The major polluter was allowed to continue operation without a valid environmental permit for a few more years, and then the State gave them a whopping big fine that exceeded $8 million. About one quarter of that fine money was designated for the construction of new roads in Golden Valley. That area of the county had few paved roads, and the designation was meant to help the pollution problem in the area.

The people living in Golden Valley probably received the most exposure to the pollution, but they were not the only citizens who suffered. Where the rest of the $8 million was used remains a mystery to the plant's victims.

In providing justification for the large fine imposed by the State on the polluter, the Arizona Attorney General's officer explained that when this manufacturer applied for their "minor source" pollution permit in 1996, they "did not tell the truth."

When ADEQ discovered the problem in May and June of 1998, they declared the plant a "major pollution" source. The problem that really concerned me was the fact that the state agency in charge of protecting the public had done nothing adequate to investigate this firm before they were allowed to operate within the state boundaries. ADEQ tried to get the problem corrected by belatedly qualifying the company for a major source pollution permit. That action would bring big bucks generated for the State but not for the victims in Mohave County. While permit negotiations dragged on and failure to comply continued, carbon monoxide, nitrogen oxide, and volatile organ compounds the plant was emitting were classified as "non-deadly" to the community.

All those people who required respirators could consider the source as a civil issue and file a suit against the steel plant, but none of the fine money would be given to any one individual. Wouldn't it be nice if the taxpayers could fine the governmental employees who lied to them? Nitrogen oxide, carbon dioxide, and volatile organ compounds will always be dangerous to any community. Now we get back to the question, "How many people have to die before the ADEQ can get involved?"

When the pollution problems were exposed in 1999, the Mohave County Health Department was quoted as saying, "That is not our responsibility. ADEQ takes care of that." The ADEQ's main offices were in Phoenix. It was a long drive to Mohave County at 3:00 a.m. when the pollutants could easily be emitted. Why should anyone have to get out of bed at 11:00 p.m. to check on a rural community? The governor bestowed special awards on the counterfeiter for his efforts in economic development. I guess she had a real good reason. After all, look at the $6 million fine money the State received when one of his efforts polluted our air!

When the governor persisted in shoving what she interpreted as the meritorious economical efforts of the felon down the throats of the Mohave County taxpayers, the people became even angrier. The daily newspaper found the governor's award announcements important enough to publish the article on the back pages of their paper next to the *Dear Abby* column.

In July 1995, the Mohave County Board of Supervisors agreed to help fund MCEDA. Between April 3, 1995 and July 18th, 2000, $2,124,097 in County checks were distributed to MCEDA for special projects. This group devised a way to spend millions and millions more taxpayer's dollars than the County had previously claimed they did not have to spend. They placed roads and infrastructure, including wells, along deserted desert property owned by a select few of the members. The roads were built in 1999 to provide access to a new energy plant designed to use 3500 gallons of water a minute.

MCEDA declared that, in the end, the energy plant would provide more tax dollars for the County. The contract guaranteed that if a water shortage should occur, the plant would receive the water first, and if there was water left, the others using that aquifer would then be able to receive water. In the contract, I could not find a price the County was to receive from the plant for the water usage. If they produced energy, they would place it on the grid and it would be auctioned to the highest bidders.

All industrial improvement votes placed before the board, passed two to one. The hold out was Supervisor Negate. Being a rancher, she showed great concern for the environment. To her credit, she voted against the power plant. She said she was not satisfied with the research. I had reviewed the studies and I agreed with her. All the water availability testing or research reporting supplied for the energy plant seemed to be based on research reports that were 15 to 20 years old.

In addition, the residential population growth that had taken place near the energy plant was being ignored. She voted against the corporate welfare package designed to fulfill the needs of that plant, as well as the needs of the private landowner who owned the bulk of the property in the area of the energy plant. Again, I agreed with her.

After her opposition, the two male supervisors tried to strip her of all her committee representations, including posts she was appointed to by the Arizona governor and the federal government. The men accused her of being senile. (They accused me of that, too.) That activity did not set too well with the governor or her friends in the federal government. Another problem the County seemed to ignore was the environmental problems taxpayers and their children could face if unusually large quantities of water are drained from the aquifers that feed the dry desert lands. No one can blame the water-guzzling plant for what has happened to date, but someone should show more than indifference to the problem.

In 1999, within miles of the new water-guzzling plant site, a mother nursed her newborn baby for about five months, after which she started the child on a powdered formula that required mixing it with water. The community water well servicing her home started to run dry. Not being informed by the well owner, the ADEQ, or the Mohave County Health Department of the existing problems related to dropping water levels, the mother continued to feed her baby formula mixed with water from the tap on her kitchen sink. With the well water levels dropping due to the drought and heavy usage in the community, the nitrate that floats near the top of the water in the well came closer to the pump and became more and more concentrated. The water received by the baby contained a high nitrate count, and the baby received brain damage from nitrite poisoning.

In an adult, nitrate will cause few, if any, medical problems. In a child, nitrate can be lethal for children up to age five, but it is most damaging to babies under one year. Their little bodies contain natural bacteria in their digestive tract that converts nitrate to nitrite, which is toxic. The ADEQ attributed such poisonings to septic systems located on lots of one acre or less. They suggested the State require a special system, with costs to the homeowner of several thousand dollars more than a conventional system, be installed in all the new building projects that had the smaller lots. This baby's parents owned a house located on a ten-acre parcel. The ADEQ will probably find more cases of nitrite poisoning when the water-guzzling power plant lowers the water table. Only when more statistics are produced involving tiny human victims will we know for sure.

Mohave County has a lot of nitrate in the soils. I am a licensed landscaper and have been for over 12 years. All one has to do is dig a hole, stick a tree in the hole, cover the root, and put a lot of water on it. If I added a half-gallon of silica sand and some ten-penny nails in the hole, it would help retain water and iron for the roots of the tree. The tree would grow like crazy. A little fertilizer goes a long way in the desert.

In the interest of economic development, the Mohave County taxpayers were forced to pay $400,000 per employee in corporate welfare to encourage a plant to move into the area bringing along only 25 to 30 employees. The County even mortgaged the jail to get the deal completed! The County spent over $2 million in Highway User Road Funds, granted by the federal government, on roads leading to the electric plant. Few citizens use that road because it is out in the middle of nowhere! The County "borrowed" $1.5 million from the Mohave County Landfill Fund and promised to pay that money back when they get all the rest of the debt paid.

With the contractual demand of Mohave County that stated the employees of this plant are guaranteed $10 per hour (and would most likely not get more), these employees would make only $20,800 per year. Creating jobs at income levels below the national poverty line as not exactly what I would call economic development.

If everything went as MCEDA proposed, the energy plant was to completely repay Mohave County the expended funds through property taxes over a period of 14 years and Mohave County would have paid back all debt incurred.

After five years passed, the new plant still looked deserted most of the time. In 2004, the county manager stated that if the tax obligations of the plant continue as they were billed and paid in 2004, the taxpayer's debt would not be clear for 39.5 years.

Why does the county reward men who can't keep their zippers up?

In 1996, Mohave County hired a nice looking man named Ray for a comfortable administrative position. He was about 5 ft. 8 in. tall and always immaculately dressed. He wore well cared for shoes, professionally laundered shirts, and new suits. He knew he was good looking. Two women who worked in his department filed a joint sexual harassment suit against the County and Ray in 1997. The settlement between the women and the County included $25,000 in hush money for the women. Ray received one full-year severance pay, about $90,000 according to the charts, to tide him over until he could find employment elsewhere.

Regardless of Snide's claims that the fault of the county's financial woes lay in the benefits given to the county employees, he did not say he meant the money spent in payoffs to settle all the legal disputes between employees. Whether the man was guilty or not, the payoff appeared to be tantamount to rewarding a corrupt act within a corrupt system.

During Snide's second term in office, two women employed on his staff charged him with sexual harassment. Risk management found some validity to their claims and moved them to new jobs. Snide was re-elected for the third time. As of the last newspaper review in 2005, the women have stated they will not give up their fight.

How could the county fail to notice that a public fiduciary was stealing so much money from the disabled and elderly?

In 1998 a Public Fiduciary named Daws, hired by Mohave County, managed to steal over $900,000 from his department's trust. After years of embezzling public funds, he was caught, tried, and sent to prison. The County was responsible for their employee's action and was expected to pay back the money he stole from supplemental income funds he managed for disabled and aging victims. Whether the people ever got their funds back is unknown.

Does the county ever do honest research before they hire a contractor?

Public officials and contractors were hired with little or no background review by the elected and hired leaders of the community. Many people were hired in positions of trust because they were friends of a board supervisor.

Another example of Mohave County expertise in character analysis was a contractor who was hired by the supervisors to build a juvenile detention center. No one with authority bothered to check the validity of his credentials. The contractor received a hefty down payment on the project (about $465,000).

This same contractor convinced the Hualapai Fire District of Mohave County that it would be cheaper for them to hire him to build a substation if he could build the juvenile detention center and the substation at the same time. He convinced the fire district board that the materials would be cheaper if all the materials for both projects were purchased at the same time. Believing the supervisors had already checked the contractor's credentials, the fire district board advanced the fake contractor $80,000.

The Fire Department asked for and received a large tax increase in an effort to cover the loss. The taxpayers are still paying the district the high tax rate.

The fake contractor disappeared to New Mexico and proceeded to rip off the taxpayers of New Mexico. Unlike Mohave County, California and New Mexico found him and quickly prosecuted him.

The construction performance bonding for the company was a forgery and the taxpayers of Mohave County were the victims who had to foot the bill. The amount embezzled by this contractor would not bankrupt the county. Yes, it would cause a hardship for the taxpayer, but so would housing this criminal in the Arizona correctional system. The county attorney does not like to send non-violent criminals to prison. Remember, "In fraud and theft cases, the victims must pay for their losses. Those are civil issues."

When the paper published the information that the contractor had done his dirty deed in New Mexico, the Mohave County authorities had to do something. They did. Only it was a day late and a few hundred thousand dollars short. The moral question of "Do we stop this guy before he hits another state?" did not seem to be a priority of the Mohave County authorities.

Did the juvenile center really need plate glass walls?

Mohave County next decided to change the location of the Juvenile Center and move it to land owned by a favored Mohave County contractor. The Board of Supervisors immediately accepted the favored contractor's bid to construct the new juvenile center. They then hired a consultant at $1,750 per day to help this contractor do the job correctly. The juvenile center, with its ceiling-to-floor-plate glass windows, ran $400,000 over the amount budgeted for the project. The Board of Supervisors could not find enough money in the treasury to operate the entire facility, so two-thirds of the building remained vacant. The Mohave County Good 'ol Boys were rapidly getting wealthier at the taxpayer's expense.

Do you think the expense of the new justice court was warranted at this time?

In 1998 the county supervisors decided the county needed another justice for the magistrate court and then a new courthouse. Taxpayers complained that the plans the Board prepared would destroy some very mature cypress trees that line the grounds of the main courthouse. To correct that problem, the original building budget for this project was overrun by $600,000.

When will Stockton Hill Road be completed? We need the access to the Kingman Hospital and that road has been under construction for 15 years.

During the campaign, the candidates were invited to visit a small town located about 30 miles north of my house. The people had many valid complaints. A short stretch of road that provided access to all their emergency facilities was a county-owned dirt road. The county road grader had been sitting idle at the end of that emergency road for two years. This essential road had become almost impassable. Valuable response time was being lost. The road department had not responded to the people's complaints. The citizens explained that many years ago the County started a paved road that was to connect their community to the larger city of Kingman. It was never completed and no one knew why, but they wanted a supervisor who would get the road finished. Medical facilities in the area are non-existent. Transporting a person by ambulance to proper medical facilities would take half the time on the new paved road. The County paved the road a distance of about 15 miles and then the paving abruptly stopped. The road was not even passable. They were willing to vote for the person that promised completion of that road. I did not know why the construction had stopped so I was in no position to make that promise. My opponents, however, did. When I left the meeting, I drove home on the road that was the topic of the citizens' complaint. Though the distance I traveled was about half as far, my trip home took much longer than my trip to the community. The concerns of the people were quite valid. The County had built a paved road that just stopped in the middle of nowhere.

The stretch of dirt road that led to the pavement was so poorly maintained that even in my four-wheel drive vehicle, I could not travel any faster than five miles per hour on the unpaved portion. It has been five years since that election, and the road is still not completed.

I went snooping. The county engineer claimed they ran out of funds to finish the construction. I found that excuse hard to digest. I knew the county fathers had just spent over $10 million to provide infrastructure for one energy plant.

When I began to talk with citizens who had lived in the area for many years, I received a different story. From them I learned that one of Toup's relatives owned a ranch that crossed the area needing to be paved. He didn't want a paved road through his open range; he had cattle to protect. The County did not feel they could afford the fencing and wells he demanded they place on his private property if they paved the road. Finishing that road would not improve the county's tax base. For many years to come, the needs of the cattle would supersede the medical needs of the people.

I never see a sheriff or a deputy. Where is the sheriff spending all of the money he gets?

The records showed that the Mohave County sheriff had overrun his 1996-1997 budgets by $1.6 million. The people voted to pay for the sheriff's needs through bonding until the year 1997. Speaking for the Good 'ol Boys who had paid highly for the election of the sheriff, the Board of Supervisors voted two-to-one to allow the override amount to be included in all future budgets for their four-year term. The sheriff's excessive spending drained $6.4 million extra from the general fund of the county during Snide's 12-year reign. The taxpayers had not witnessed an end to the sheriff's overspending.

In 1999, a .025 percent tax was added to the county's sales tax to build new county offices and one of the first recipients of those funds was the sheriff. After he got his nice new building, he stated that because of the low wages paid to his deputies, Mohave County was a training ground for new officers, and the cost of the training was exorbitant and he needed more money. When I was reading the sheriff's comments in the paper, I wondered, "Where were all these underpaid officers when we needed them in Lake Juniper? What is the real reason the sheriff cannot keep his employees? Where is all the taxpayer's money going?" Other taxpayers were asking the same question. The people's comments were, "How does one get the sheriff to come out of his office? Where are the officers when we need them? I have never seen a sheriff in our community."

Are you planning to raise my taxes again?

The Mohave County supervisors continue to state there has been no property tax increases during their term in office. They officially approved increases imposed by the fire district, the school district, the library district, and other districts that appeared on the property tax bills. The assessor then increased the values of the properties some 38 percent for the 2004 and 2006 tax years. Consequently, the average property tax bill in Mohave County had increased from $800 per year to $1600 per year over a two-year period. The assessed values of the properties continue to rise so drastically that thousands of taxpayers are filing for reviews. The tax assessor tried to explain, through the newspaper, why the increases were necessary. The taxpayers are not convinced, but few changes in assessment values were accomplished at the reviews.

Will you have a county credit card?

When the taxpayers began to complain, the *Mohave Daily Miner* and the *Mohave Standard* newspapers would print articles about the county's overspending.

When the public chastised Snide for his credit card spending, he bragged about his efforts in economic development. In actuality, he and Supervisor Golf managed to position Mohave County on the edge of bankruptcy. At the end of his first four-year term, the county was in the worst financial condition it had been in since it was declared insolvent in 1900.

Snide, whom I refer to as "the self-serving supervisor/puppet controlled by Good 'ol Boy interests," stated the county deficit had resulted from wage increases, merit raises, and additional costs paid for employee medical benefits. The funds he complained of totaled $1.3 million. Hogwash! The legal fees for his vindictiveness and his corporate welfare expenditures were much more damaging to the county than the county employees' pay scales. Many of the county employees were receiving poverty wages. Mohave County was requiring new corporations coming into the community to guarantee pay minimums of $10 or more, but according to the county employees' public statements, the County was not meeting their own goals in the pay scale department.

Do I have to have a prison two blocks from my house?

Earlier in this writing, I explained that a supervisor had taken a trip to Hawaii. No one knew why he took that trip. In 1998, a private prison was invited to locate on the I-40 industrial corridor. It did not matter how loudly the taxpayers protested; the Board of Supervisors ignored all opposing voices. Many people were concerned because the location of the new prison was within view of their homes. Some believed that once the prison was established, their homes would lose value. Others were concerned about their family's safety and the amount of water the prison would drain from the already overtaxed aquifer.

In a feeble effort to quell the taxpayers concerns, the Board of Supervisors explained to the public that the prison was being designed to house inmates from Hawaii who had committed only minor offences, such as DUI.

At the public meeting, when the concerned citizens of the county questioned the expense and danger of moving criminals from Hawaii to Mohave County, the two supervisors in favor of the construction of the prison, laughed at them, taunted their remarks, and most generally made the questioning citizen feel like trash under their feet. This supposedly comic activity was always used when these men were asked questions they couldn't or wouldn't answer. They didn't try.

After construction began, many changes in the original inmate population plans changed. Hawaii backed out after a couple of years, and the State of Arizona came to the builder's rescue. In 2004 the new governor stated that the prison's status would change to a state-run prison. When the ownership of the prison changes to the state, the state prison will house convicts regardless of the offenses they have committed.

When the property owners in the area bought their land and built their homes, the zoning in their area was agricultural / residential. Sitting in open meeting and watching the Board of Supervisors openly laugh at citizens for voicing their oppositions to zoning changes to allow for the prison and the other life threatening industry made me angry.

The Board of Supervisors stated they changed the zoning classifica-tions in the I-40 highway area to fit the needs of the entire county rather than the needs of a select few. If the people living in the area that was re-zoned did not agree with the board's actions, they could move. Some did, but most still get up in the morning looking out the kitchen window at a prison.

Can we get new voting machines?

The voting procedures were antiquated with a potential to be easily corrupted. As in many areas in the United States, voters were still required to punch holes in a little card and hand-carry that card back to an election judge sitting at a table waiting for it. When I went to vote in September 2000, I got my voting card and its envelope. I went into a little open booth area, punched my holes in the card, and then handed the card to an atten-dant. She sat there staring at me with my ballot envelope in her hands. I asked, "Is that all?" She held my ballot in one hand, reached over with the other hand, and gave me a little lapel sticker that stated, "I voted today." I kept looking over my shoulder as I left the building, and the attendant never put my ballot in a box, she just held it in front of her until I left the building. The computer often failed and some of the Good 'ol Boys hand-counted the votes. This was the state of the democratic process in a county in which I had been poisoned, cheated out of thousands of dollars, and left to die. I could only conclude that I punched the holes in the wrong spots, so the ballot was tossed.

EPILOGUE

After eleven years of living in Mohave County, Arizona, I earned the right to be extremely concerned about my town, my state, and my country. I know that publishing this exposé might only add fuel to the fires already present in my community, but perhaps it will also encourage honest citizens throughout the country to take back control of their lives, their rights, and the just application of our laws.

One must never lose their sense of humor, especially if they plan to relocate to Arizona. To be sure, I haven't lost mine. I assembled the following list of things to do for potential immigrants.

Pack a gun. You are allowed to wear them openly in the community. There are rattlesnakes, mountain lions, and coyote packs in Arizona. Being armed is appropriate, since some of the most dangerous animals walk on two legs.

Before moving to Arizona, get your heart checked by a really good cardiologist. A weak heart can't survive in Arizona unless you are deaf, mute, and blind, and able to turn your back on current events.

Make sure your lungs are in the best of condition. If you have a respiratory problem, you might not survive the County's economic development projects.

Pack a snakebite kit and a lot of law books. You will surely need both.

Pack your own safe drinking water. A water hauling truck, in good condition, is a real plus.

To avoid confusion, register as a Republican before leaving your present residence. It helps when you get to Arizona and want to register to vote in Mohave County. Oddly, those Republican voter transfers don't get lost.

Try to hide your assets so you can receive the Arizona aide known as A.H.C.C.S.S. Your children will receive much better healthcare than you could afford through an independent insurance company. There are a lot of freebies for people who can qualify for that program.

Pack a cellular phone. Sometimes the phone company will deny you a phone if the guy you bought your land from has failed to negotiate his bill.

If you plan to purchase land, be sure the road to the land is paved and all the utilities are installed and working. The assessments made by improvement districts are so high that 10% of the landowners lose their property because they can't pay the unusually high assessments.

Pack a Tap Zapper for your phone. If the tap detector proves to be useless in detecting snoops, at least you won't have busy circuit signals for weeks on end. Your phone will be the only one working.

Plan to rent. You might decide to move out right away. If you rent a house and decide you don't like it, you can hock or sell all of the landlord's appliances and fixtures and still avoid criminal prosecution. The policeman told me it's only a civil issue in Mohave County.

If you buy, buy a small cheap place. Plan to buy a couple of pigs and plant a bean sprout. The tax assessor has a hard time fudging on the values of agricultural property. Remember, livestock is more important to Arizona than humans are. If she does over-assess your land, you can appeal. "Your property is agricultural."

Remember, the Mohave County Attorney stated on the front page of the Kingman Daily Miner that you take a risk when you purchase land in a secured subdivision in Mohave County. Don't purchase in an approved subdivision.

If you buy, be sure to purchase flood insurance. If you know how to build an ark, keep one in your yard.

If you develop fantasies of false security in Mohave County, good psychiatric help is available in Las Vegas.

Be sure there is a doctor or a good nurse next door. Often the emergency vehicles get lost on the way to rescue you.

Before you move to Arizona, be sure your children have completed their schooling and have a good position in another state. You may need their financial assistance unless you are in the business of buying and selling drugs.

If you are pregnant or have a new baby, for your baby's sake, wait until that child is at least six years old before moving to rural counties. Desert aquifer water levels are dropping, which may result in nitrite poisoning in your young children.

Pack gas masks for your whole family. Much of the air is not safe to breathe.

The most important thing you will need to survive in peace that I can think of is a criminal file that proves you are at least a felon. Now if you have been convicted three or four times, that's even better. If the convictions show "firearms enhanced," you have got it made.

If you are a convicted felon who has done your time and you have been released from parole or probation, you can vote in Arizona. Just register to vote and lie when you sign the application. Most likely, no one will question you. But if they do, holler discrimination.

This list was compiled in fun, but it could also be a serious list. If your county and state are following in the same footsteps as mine, or if you can relate to my adventures, then I ask you…Isn't it time you did something about it and returned your country to the laws and the constitution honest people try to abide by?

Get busy. Communicate with your neighbors. Meet together regularly. Get united and fight for your rights and equal treatment under the law. Our children and grandchildren need the knowledge we have gained through experience. Share your knowledge with them. Move closer to them if necessary. Teach them of the corruption in the political circles, and help them learn to protect our voting rights and our courts. Never allow yourself or your loved ones to become *Victims Condemned* by the neglect, greed, and ignorance of elected officials and their corrupt backers.

I was truly protected during my battle against evil, and you will be too.

May your God or Protector guide and keep you and yours. This book was written to share my love, concerns, experiences, and caring with you and your family, and to try to expose some truths….

Patti